Business Intelligence with Looker

Design, Develop, and Diagnose: The Comprehensive
Looker Guide for Admins, Developers, and Users

Shiva Krishna Neeli

Tanya Leung

bpb

www.bpbonline.com

First Edition 2025

Copyright © BPB Publications, India

ISBN: 978-93-65890-402

To View Complete
BPB Publications Catalogue
Scan the QR Code:

www.bpbonline.com

Dedicated to

My wife Vedasri and my daughters Saanvi and Yashvi

- Shiva Krishna Neeli

My parents Kevin and Shirley

- Tanya Leung

About the Authors

- **Shiva Krishna Neeli** is a manager of data engineering at SADA Systems Inc, specializing in business intelligence. He brings extensive experience from his varied roles as a developer, administrator, architect, and manager within business intelligence teams at prominent organizations, including Live Nation and Fidelity Investments. Shiva's academic background includes a master's in computer science from the University of South Carolina, Columbia, SC, earned in 2004. He completed his bachelor's at the Mahatma Gandhi Institute of Technology, Hyderabad, affiliated with Jawaharlal Nehru Technological University, Hyderabad, in 2002.

  With a keen interest in business intelligence, data engineering, and artificial intelligence, Shiva has hands-on experience with a wide array of BI tools such as OBIEE, Cognos, Tableau, Domo, and Looker. He has successfully led numerous projects for diverse corporations, from startups to large enterprises. Shiva is also passionate about mentoring developers and analysts across various business intelligence platforms.

- **Tanya Leung** is a data engineer at SADA Systems Inc, who has worked extensively with several Google Cloud Platform services, most notably Looker. Prior to SADA Systems, Tanya completed her bachelor of science in computer science from the University of Colorado Boulder in 2020.

  Tanya has worked extensively on both sides of data, from data processing and pipelining, to data analysis. She seeks to bridge the gap between data engineers and data scientists to maintain data quality from start to finish.

About the Reviewers

❖ **Pradeep Koppaka** is an accomplished business intelligence professional with over 15 years of experience designing and delivering end-to-end analytics solutions across banking, healthcare, life sciences, retail, and media sectors. He has partnered with global enterprises such as **Bank of America, Wells Fargo, UBS, Credit Suisse, PIMCO, Cardinal Health, Pfizer, Biogen, British American Tobacco, Dolby Laboratories, Warner Bros.,** and **KLA-Tencor**, driving impactful data transformation initiatives.

Pradeep brings deep expertise in **Looker, Tableau, Power BI, SAP BusinessObjects, Databricks, Snowflake**, and **PySpark**, with a strong focus on data modeling, semantic layer design, and performance optimization. He is known for implementing scalable BI architectures and introducing analytics-layer strategies that enhance agility and long-term maintainability.

Currently serving as a **senior Looker consultant at InfoServices**, Pradeep helps organizations modernize their BI ecosystems and unlock greater value from their data assets.

❖ **Chowdam Lakshmi** is a highly skilled BI and cloud analytics professional with over 4 years of experience at industry-leading organizations. She has been instrumental in developing scalable data solutions and optimizing BI workflows for Google through Infosys, leveraging her expertise in Looker, SQL, GCP, and BigQuery.

Lakshmi thrives on solving complex data challenges, designing efficient data models, and building impactful analytics solutions that drive business success. She has a proven track record of creating high-performance BI systems, enabling organizations to make data-driven decisions with speed and precision.

She will continue to innovate in the data analytics space, focusing on optimizing data pipelines, uncovering insights, and driving strategic initiatives. Her passion for cloud infrastructure and data modeling allows her to develop solutions that enhance efficiency and unlock new opportunities in the ever-evolving world of analytics.

Acknowledgements

We would like to express our sincere gratitude to all those who contributed to the completion of this book.

First and foremost, we extend our heartfelt appreciation to our family and friends for their unwavering support and encouragement throughout this journey. Their love and encouragement have been a constant source of motivation.

This book would not have been possible without the invaluable contributions of our many clients. Through shared experimentation and a commitment to learning, they offered the rich experiences that were instrumental in shaping the content and insights presented here.

We are immensely grateful to BPB Publications for their guidance and expertise in bringing this book to fruition. Their support and assistance were invaluable in navigating the complexities of the publishing process.

We would also like to acknowledge the technical reviewers and editors who provided valuable feedback and contributed to the refinement of this manuscript. Their insights and suggestions have significantly enhanced the quality of the book.

Last but not least, we want to express our gratitude to the readers who have shown interest in our book. Your support and encouragement have been deeply appreciated.

Thank you to everyone who has played a part in making this book a reality.

Preface

As business intelligence increasingly drives success in the modern era, this book empowers readers with the foundational concepts and hands-on examples necessary to create and manage powerful and insightful content within the Looker platform.

Comprising 10 chapters, this book provides a comprehensive guide to the essential development and administration concepts within Looker. We begin by covering Looker fundamentals, along with the creation of reports and dashboards. From there, we delve into LookML, exploring its creation and advanced applications for handling complex use cases and ensuring long-term maintenance. The Looker administration section will equip you with the skills to maintain, troubleshoot, and optimize the platform. We will also explore how Looker content can be embedded into other websites. Finally, the book concludes with a Looker project, detailing the elements required to create a real-world project with practical content.

This book is designed to be a comprehensive guide for those new to Looker, including analysts and developers eager to master the platform. It also serves as an invaluable reference for experienced developers seeking to deepen their expertise. Furthermore, seasoned administrators will find it an essential resource for advanced insights and best practices.

Chapter 1: Getting Started with Looker - This chapter provides a foundational introduction to the powerful business intelligence platform–Looker. It guides readers through the various essential ways to interact with Looker's capabilities from the outset. A key initial step involves detailing how to gain access to a dedicated practice environment, enabling hands-on learning from the very beginning. We then explore the intuitive Looker interface, familiarizing you with its layout and navigation elements. The chapter further covers vital actions such as efficiently finding existing content and effectively viewing and interpreting interactive dashboards. Understanding the organization of content through folders is also thoroughly explained, ensuring users can manage and access their data assets seamlessly. By the end of this unit, you will possess a clear understanding of Looker's core purpose, its key features, and its fundamental components. You will also gain valuable insight into how business users practically leverage Looker for their daily analytical needs.

Chapter 2: Creating Reports and Dashboards - This chapter delves into the heart of data analysis within Looker, beginning with an in-depth introduction to the Explore interface. We will guide you through the process of creating compelling visualizations, transforming raw data into insightful graphical representations. The discussion then extends to Table Calculations, demonstrating how to derive new metrics directly within your explores for deeper analysis. Furthermore, you will learn to leverage Merge Results to combine data from disparate sources, providing a unified view for comprehensive understanding. The chapter also covers the critical aspects of exploring dashboards, teaching you how to interact with and derive insights from pre-built data presentations. Crucially, we will also explore visualization best practices to ensure your data is not only accurate but also effectively communicated. By the end of this unit, you will be proficient in exploring data, creating and customizing various visualization types, developing custom fields for bespoke measures and dimensions.

Chapter 3: LookML Development - This chapter dives deep into the foundational elements of Looker, starting with an exploration of LookML files and the integrated development environment. We will differentiate between development and production modes, a crucial concept for managing your projects. You will learn the steps for creating a new project and understand the vital role of Git for version control in collaborative development. The core of the chapter focuses on LookML code, detailing how to define essential elements like dimensions, measures, and explores, and how LookML translates these into SQL queries. We will also cover caching and the powerful concept of derived tables, including how to create persistent derived tables to enhance performance. Finally, we will explore LookML dashboards, learning to create them and effectively organize them by moving them outside the default folder. By the end of this chapter, you will be adept at writing LookML code, leveraging derived tables for advanced SQL functions, and creating dynamic LookML dashboards.

Chapter 4: Advanced LookML - This chapter explores advanced LookML concepts, empowering you to write more efficient and flexible code. We begin by exploring extends and refinements, powerful features that facilitate code reuse and simplify long-term management of your LookML projects. Next, you will discover the Looker Marketplace and Looker Blocks, pre-written code snippets designed to accelerate development, especially for common data sources like Salesforce or Google Analytics. The chapter then shifts focus to creating dynamic content within Looker using parameters and templated filters, which allow for user-driven data exploration. A significant portion is dedicated to Liquid, an open-source templating language, where you will learn its basics and how to apply it with practical examples to build highly interactive experiences. We also cover aggregate awareness, a key optimization technique for performance. Upon completing this chapter, you will be proficient in leveraging code reuse, utilizing pre-built blocks, and creating dynamic, high-performing Looker content using advanced LookML techniques.

Chapter 5: Beyond Looker - This chapter expands on Looker's versatility, exploring its powerful integrations and extensibility features. We will begin by examining the Looker mobile application, demonstrating how to access your data insights on the go. The discussion then moves to Connected Sheets, showing how to seamlessly leverage Looker data within Google Sheets for familiar spreadsheet analysis. You will also learn about Looker Studio, understanding its role in the broader Google business intelligence ecosystem and how it complements Looker. Furthermore, we will dive into how to deliver data through Action Hub and implement data actions, enabling direct interactions with your data from within Looker. The chapter also covers the exciting possibilities of building custom visualizations to meet unique analytical needs. Finally, we will explore various third-party tools, such as LAMS and Gazer, that can significantly enhance Looker's usability and deliver superior customer experiences. By the end of this chapter, you will be able to integrate Looker with external tools, extend its native functionality, and optimize data delivery for diverse user scenarios.

Chapter 6: Looker Administration - This chapter covers the different ways administrators can manage their Looker instance. Each section underneath Looker's Admin tab is detailed. Here, admins can see the different ways they can control aspects of the Looker instance, from visualization color palettes, early access feature availability, to third-party integrations. The Admin tab also has several ways admins can monitor data usage, user activity, and database interactions. Additionally, the chapter also reviews the different platform editions and license types available. After this chapter, Looker admins should know what they can control from each Admin tab.

Chapter 7: Looker Security - This chapter goes over the different ways Admins can manage access control across the Looker instance. It goes over the three pillars of access: data, feature, and content, and provides common access scenarios and how to implement them. Also contained in the chapter are other ways admins can personalize the user experience, including custom homepages, authentication methods, and session durations. By the end of the chapter, admins should have a firm grasp on how they can make sure users have an experience tailored to who they are.

Chapter 8: Troubleshooting, Performance Tuning, and Best Practices - This chapter provides different ways Looker admins and developers can tune their Looker instance in order to improve performance. It also goes over common LookML errors developers are likely to encounter and their resolutions. Finally, it provides general best practices that admins and developers should keep in mind managing the instance. By the end of the chapter, admins and developers should be able to troubleshoot several different types of issues they may encounter when using Looker, and provide solutions to those issues.

Chapter 9: Application Programming Interface, Software Development Kit and Embed - This chapter goes over the several ways developers can surface content and tasks beyond Looker. It goes over the basic setup required for developers to connect to the Looker API, as well as the setup required to embed content outside of Looker. Developers can programmatically access Looker through the API and SDK, and the differences between the two methods are also explored here. Developers will also learn the different types of embedding that Looker provides and how to implement those different types. By the end of the chapter, developers will know how to code with Looker and utilize code to bring content outside of Looker onto external apps.

Chapter 10: Looker Project Walkthrough - This chapter is a basic overview of the whole Looker process–it provides steps that all admins and developers will likely have to take when they first set up the instance. It acts as a walkthrough and a checklist for what admins should expect when they first start their Looker instance. By the end of the chapter, admins should have one full functional project and dashboard.

Code Bundle and Coloured Images

Please follow the link to download the
Code Bundle and the *Coloured Images* of the book:

https://rebrand.ly/4dff34

The code bundle for the book is also hosted on GitHub at
https://github.com/bpbpublications/Business-Intelligence-with-Looker.
In case there's an update to the code, it will be updated on the existing GitHub repository.

We have code bundles from our rich catalogue of books and videos available at
https://github.com/bpbpublications. Check them out!

Errata

We take immense pride in our work at BPB Publications and follow best practices to ensure the accuracy of our content to provide with an indulging reading experience to our subscribers. Our readers are our mirrors, and we use their inputs to reflect and improve upon human errors, if any, that may have occurred during the publishing processes involved. To let us maintain the quality and help us reach out to any readers who might be having difficulties due to any unforeseen errors, please write to us at :

errata@bpbonline.com

Your support, suggestions and feedbacks are highly appreciated by the BPB Publications' Family.

Piracy

If you come across any illegal copies of our works in any form on the internet, we would be grateful if you would provide us with the location address or website name. Please contact us at business@bpbonline.com with a link to the material.

If you are interested in becoming an author

If there is a topic that you have expertise in, and you are interested in either writing or contributing to a book, please visit www.bpbonline.com. We have worked with thousands of developers and tech professionals, just like you, to help them share their insights with the global tech community. You can make a general application, apply for a specific hot topic that we are recruiting an author for, or submit your own idea.

Reviews

Please leave a review. Once you have read and used this book, why not leave a review on the site that you purchased it from? Potential readers can then see and use your unbiased opinion to make purchase decisions. We at BPB can understand what you think about our products, and our authors can see your feedback on their book. Thank you!

For more information about BPB, please visit www.bpbonline.com.

Join our book's Discord space

Join the book's Discord Workspace for Latest updates, Offers, Tech happenings around the world, New Release and Sessions with the Authors:

https://discord.bpbonline.com

Table of Contents

CHAPTER 1
Getting Started with Looker

Introduction

Since the early stages of digitization, organizations have been collecting data that can be useful to improve their business. Business Intelligence includes the process and tools to analyze the data, get insights, and take actions that will help in making informed decisions. Databases have been around for a long time and are helping to collect, organize, and process the data efficiently. Business Intelligence tools were created to query, show the data that is easy to understand for a wider audience, and present visually to tell a story. These tools have features and functionality to query the data from databases, analyze and present the data visually to help make better data-driven decisions. Looker is one such tool that was created by *Lloyd Tabb* and *Ben Porterfield* in 2012 and later acquired by Google in 2019. It was created mainly to process, and explore large volumes of data in the MPP databases like Redshift, Teradata, BigQuery and Vertica, etc.

Structure

In this chapter, we will go through the following topics:

- Ways to interact with Looker
- Getting access to practice environment
- Looker interface

- Finding content
- Viewing the dashboards
- Folders

Objectives

After studying this unit, you should be able to understand the purpose and key features and components of Looker and how business users use Looker.

Looker can connect to any SQL source including traditional databases like oracle, SQL server, DB2, etc., and the modern cloud-based databases, like Snowflake, and BigQuery. The database can host any data, including transactions from a home-grown application developed internally in your company or industry standard applications like Salesforce, NetSuite, SAP, or any other applications.

At the core, Looker has a modeling layer that is built using a proprietary language called LookML. This layer has all the business definitions, calculations and relationships between the tables in the database.

Ways to interact with Looker

We can interact with Looker in multiple ways:

- It has a built-in web interface using which we can build explores, visualizations called looks, and dashboards that will work with the model layer described previously and bring the results back from the database and present in a web interface.

- Explores, looks, and dashboards can be embedded in external applications.

- Looker content can also be delivered to emails or other external applications like slack or any other file storage applications like Google Cloud storage buckets at frequent intervals.

- Using REST API, we can manage Looker, and data can also be retrieved.

Here are some of the key features of Looker:

- **SQL based**: SQL is the most popular and widely used language for data analytics. Looker is built on SQL. LookML generates SQL which is sent to the underlying database that understands. So, if you understand SQL, learning LookML is very easy.

- **Built for Scale**: Looker is built for modern and cloud data warehouse platforms like BigQuery, Snowflake and MPP databases like Teradata. However, it also works with on-prem databases.

- **Multi-cloud**: Looker application can be installed in any cloud (AWS, GCP, Azure etc.) or on-prem environment.

- **No extracts/In-database architecture**: Unlike some other applications, data is not ingested onto the Looker platform. All the data exists in the database and will be retrieved on-demand only when requested through queries, explores and dashboards. This eliminates the stale data issues and also maintenance issues with data extracts.

- **Unified Modeling Layer**: Looker's model includes business logic that can be reused across multiple reports and dashboards. This acts as a single source of truth and will help remove confusion about definitions and calculations across the departments/users in an organization.

- **Agile development**: Multiple developers can work on the same project and supports modern principles of software development like version control, iterative, reusable code etc.

- **Browser based**: All the components of Looker, including model, connections to database, administration, etc. are browser based. There is no software or application that needs to be installed on a computer for Looker development.

- **User-friendly self-service interface**: Business users without much knowledge of SQL or other technical details can create reports using the explores created by LookML developers.

- **Security**: Looker can be secured at different levels, including dashboards, reports, and data within the reports. Looker also supports user authentication natively or using other mechanisms like LDAP, SAML, SSO, etc.

Getting access to practice environment

Let us see how the application (Looker) looks and get access to a Looker practice environment:

1. Go to **connect.looker.com**

2. Create an account or sign-in.

3. On the left-hand side, you will see a drop down to create a sandbox environment:

SANDBOX

Practice environment

Apply your knowledge

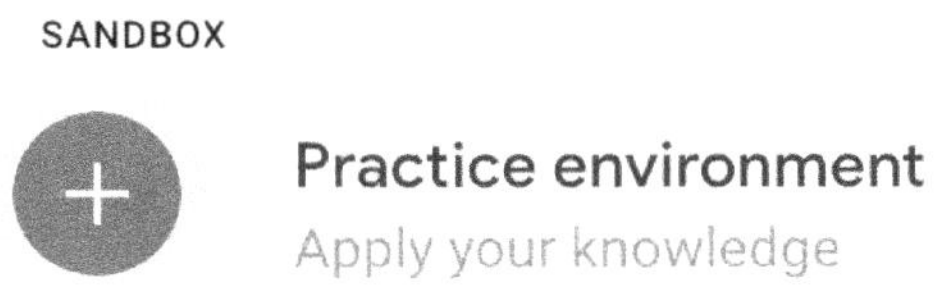

Figure 1.1: Sandbox creation

Click on the plus sign, create an account, and follow the instructions to create a sandbox environment. This environment stays up for a limited time. However, it should give enough time for the next exercise. We can create another environment if needed.

There are mainly four types of users that interact with Looker:

- **Administrators**: These users are responsible for managing users, configuring and managing authentication mechanisms, managing database connections, network configurations and other system-wide settings, monitoring and taking actions for Looker application needs.

- **Developers**: Developers are responsible for creating the LookML code, connect to the database, convert the business logic into LookML, create user friendly explores so that Looker can generate efficient SQL.

- **Explorers**: Explorers are responsible for creating visualizations using the explores created by developers.

- **Viewers/Dashboard users**: These are the end users/mostly business users who interact and use the dashboards to analyze the results and take actions.

Looker interface

In an actual Looker instance (setup by your company), you can login to Looker using a username (email) and password unless your organization has single sign on enabled.

When you first login to Looker, you will see the Looker navigation menu on the left, Looker content in the middle, curated content on the right and some icons on top right corner as shown in the next figure.

Let us get familiar with these:

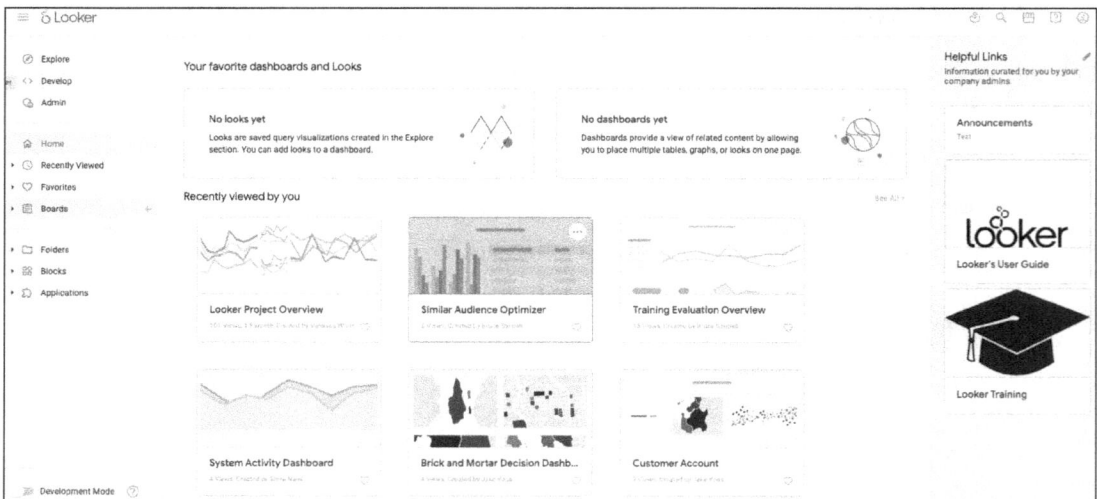

Figure 1.2: *Looker home page*

The following outlines the primary elements of the Looker interface:

- **Main navigation:** Main navigation (the three bars a.k.a. burger sign) can be turned on or off by clicking on it. Main navigation has three main links, one for each type of user.

- **Explore**: This is for report developers. If you click on it, you can see the Looker explores created by the LookML developers, which contain the data elements needed for building a report. Clicking on an explore will take you to another window that has a report building interface:

- **Develop**: This menu is mainly for LookML developers. It further has sub menu items:

   o **Content validator**: This is a tool that searches for various Looker objects and validates the code, and you can fix the errors.

   o **SQL Runner**: This will take you to the SQL Runner interface. This is a Looker native SQL writing interface/editor, which will be useful to look at the database objects, write SQL queries and build visualizations using those queries.

   o **Projects**: Projects are containers of Looker objects. Clicking on Projects will take you to the Projects interface, where you can create a new Project, configure new models, and existing models. Where you can configure the access to database connections for each project.

- **Admin**: This is for Looker administrators. It has pages for system wide settings, Database connections, Users, Groups, Alerts and Schedule monitoring pages and other system maintenance pages.

Other links Home, Recently Viewed, and favorites are self-explanatory. Boards are explained as follows:

- **Boards**: Boards are places where you can add Looker content like dashboards, looks along with other links (to external pages) and other descriptions which will help find the information people are looking for.

   Additionally, Looker will have blocks and applications, which we will learn in detail in the coming chapters.

In the end, you can see Folders. Under Folders, you can see two types of folders:

- **My Folder**: This folder is for users who logged in to Looker. The users can save their own content in this folder.

- **Shared Folders**: This is the main folder where the Looker content—dashboards and Looks are stored and shared among users.

It can have further subfolders to organize the content. Looker Content is of two types:

   o   **Looks**: These are single visualizations or reports.

   o   **Dashboards**: They contain more than one visualization or report.

The subfolders are as follows:

- **People**: This folder has a separate folder for each user and their content. So, this is MyFolder of each user in the company. (If your Looker environment is a closed system, you may not see this folder)

- **LookML dashboards**: This folder contains dashboards that developers created using LookML. These are written in YAML.

At the bottom of the navigation menu, you will find a Development mode toggle that is visible and useful to the LookML developers:

- **Development mode toggle**: This is for developers who have development access. When the toggle is on, you can see a blue bar on top. When this is on, it will make changes only for the developers without affecting other users on the platform. We will learn more about this in the coming chapters.

- **Curated content**: The right-side bar contains information specific to your company. Expect to see notifications, help resources and more curated from your data team

  On the top right corner you can see:

  - **Search**: This will let you search for content with keywords and shows all the content—Models, Looks, dashboards etc. to that matches with the search.

  - **Marketplace**: This has prebuilt Looker content that you can import into your Looker instance, which will give you ready-made models with dashboards, visualizations, and applications to manage your Looker instance.

  - **Help**: This will have links to—Support access, documentation, user guide, keyboard shortcuts, release version, and notes.

  - **User profile**: Account, profile details that includes users first name, last name and other Looker component's details etc.

  - **History**: This will show the objects that the account accessed recently.

  - **Schedules**: This will show all the schedules the account holder has created.

  - **Alerts**: This will show all the alerts the account holder has received.

  - **Sessions**: This will show current browsing session info including the browser version, location, login times etc.

In the examples that we use in this book, we will connect to the public dataset published by Google called the look ecommerce, a sample ecommerce database. To get access to this public dataset follow these steps:

1. Go to **console.cloud.google.com**.
2. Create an account or login with your Google account.
3. Click on the **BigQuery**.
4. Search for the public dataset: `thelook_ecommerce`.
5. This dataset will have the tables, data that we will use throughout this book.
6. Try the following sample query to see the data:

```
select * from
bigquery--public-data.thelook_ecommerce.users
```

Dashboard users/viewers form a large percentage of users in the company. Executives, business users who just want to view the dashboard to do their daily activities come under this category.

In this chapter, we will see how a dashboard user uses looks and dashboards and their activities including finding content, organizing content, sharing the dashboards and sending/receiving alerts.

Finding content

Developers create and save the dashboards and looks to be used by other Viewers in **Shared Folders**. To find the content, you can refer to the following steps:

1. Navigate to the shared folder from the main navigation bar. It can have subfolders or **Dashboards** and/or looks saved either directly in a folder or sub folder.

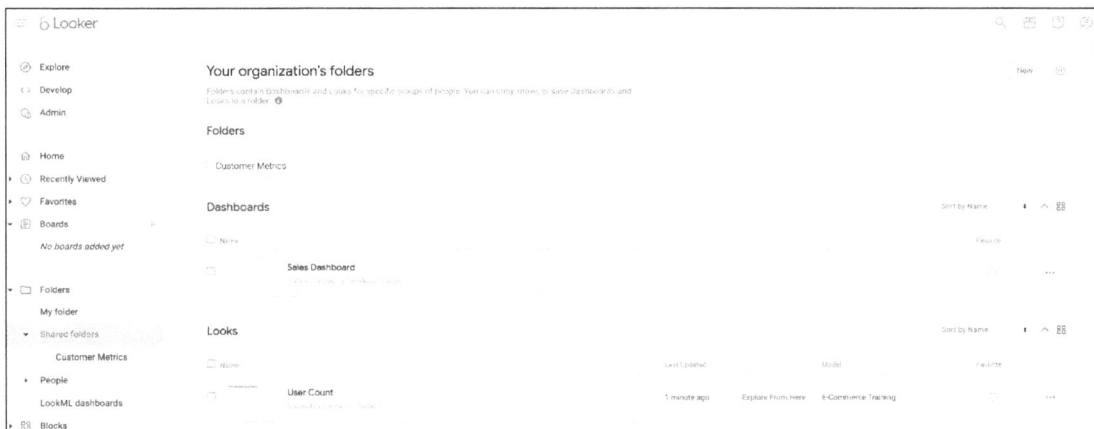

Figure 1.3: Shared Folders

2. Search with a keyword by clicking on the search icon on the top right-hand corner.

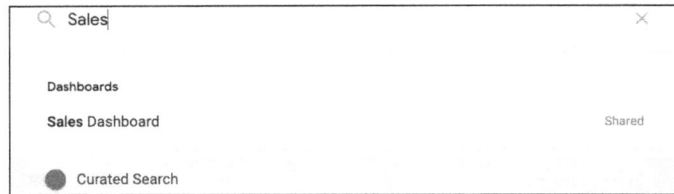

Figure 1.4: Search content

3. If the dashboards/looks were favorited, those can be found in favorites.

Viewing looks

Once you find a look that you want to view, you can click on it, and it will take you to the Look interface:

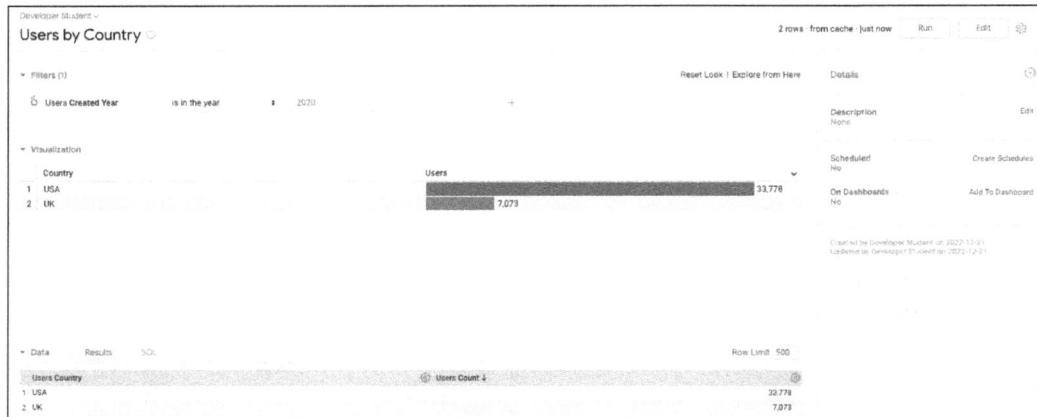

Figure 1.5: Sample Look

A look has a number of elements:

- **Navigation Breadcrumbs**: On the top left side, you can see the folder the dashboard is saved under. Clicking on the breadcrumb (for example: Customer Metrics) will take you to the folder.
- **Name/title of the Dashbaord**: It shows/ reflects the name/title of the dashboards, for example, **Users by Country**.
- **Favorite Icon**: If you select the heart symbol next to the name, the dashboard will be saved under favorites in the main menu and can be found easily.

On the right hand-side you will see:

1. Query result details like number of rows, whether the results came from cache, when was the last run, what is the timezone.

2. Run and Edit buttons to run the look and make changes respectively.

3. A gear icon showing different options:

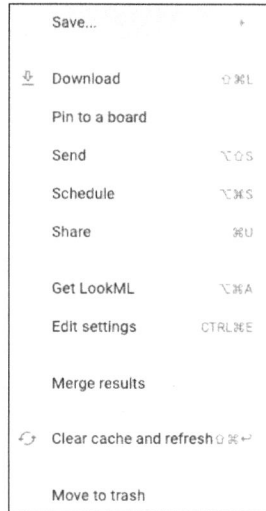

Figure 1.6: *Look Menu*

The following are the steps to download the Look:

1. Clicking on **Download** will let you download the visualization into different formats:

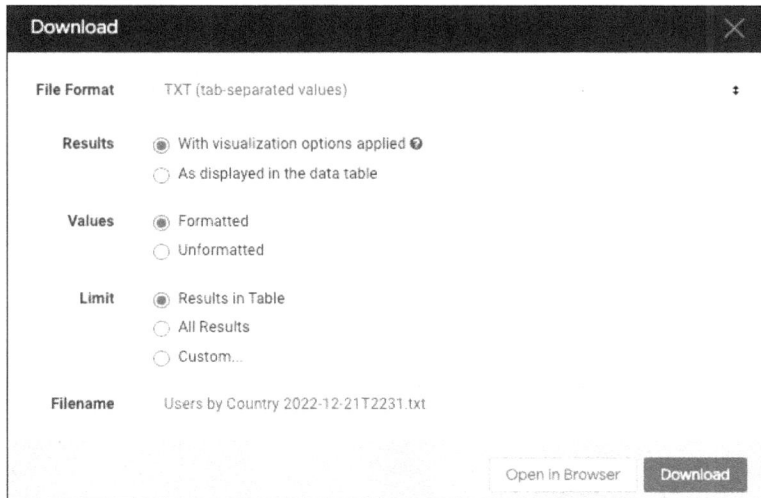

Figure 1.7: *Download options*

2. Send will open a window to send an email. We can add email IDs and select the format and other filter or advanced options:

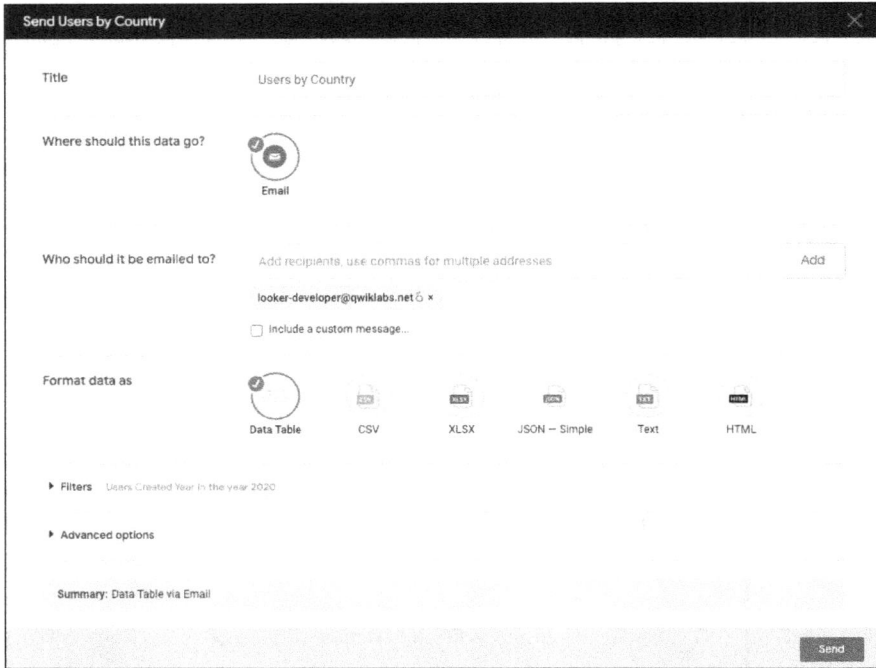

Figure 1.8: Send options

3. Schedules will open a similar window with additional **Deliver this Schedule and Trigger** options:

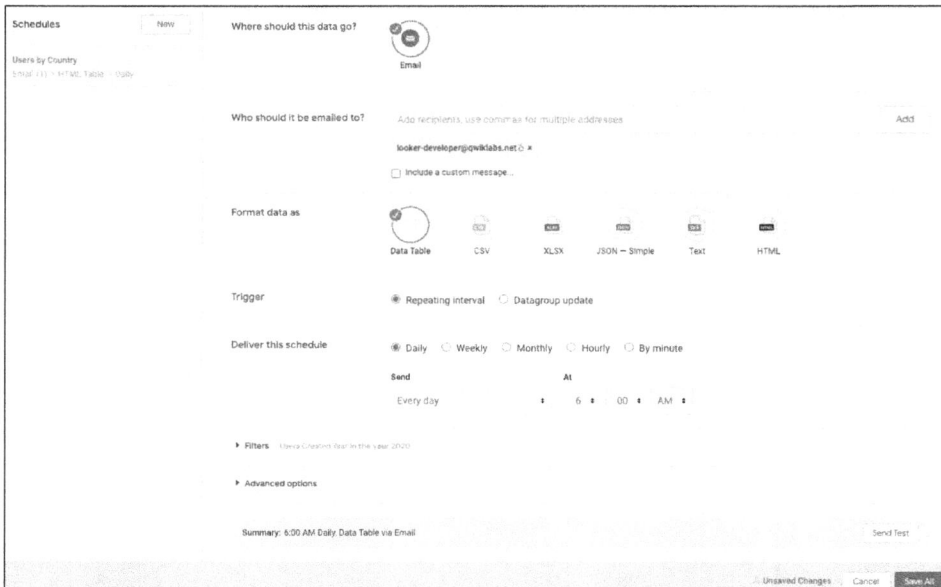

Figure 1.9: Schedule options

4. Share will give a URL/link to share with others.

Figure 1.10: *Look URL*

The main components of the look include the following:

- **Filters**: Filters that are controlling/restricting the data included in the results

- **Visualization**: Actual look/visualization that displays the data. The visualization may have additional functions including hovering over to see data, drill downs, links and so on.

- **Data**: The data that is powering the visualization with row limit and the SQL that Looker uses to bring the data from the database. Additionally, the data can be sorted and each column/field in the data section has a gear icon which has other operations (we will learn about these while creating a look).

Viewing the dashboards

When you click on a dashboard, the dashboard opens on the right-hand side of the navigation menu/main menu. The main menu can be hidden/shown by clicking on the burger sign on the left top:

Figure 1.11: *The Hamburger Menu*

A dashboard has a number of elements:

- **Navigation Breadcrumbs**: On the top left side, you can see the folder the dashboard is saved under. Clicking on the breadcrumb (for ex: Customer Metrics) will take you to the folder.

Customer Metrics
Business Pulse ♡

Figure 1.12: *Navigation Breadcrumbs*

- Name/title of the Dashboard.

- **Favorite icon**: If you select the heart symbol next to the name, the dashboard will be saved under favorites in the main menu and can be found easily.

- **Last updated time**: For example: 18m ago. That means the dashboard was last updated 18 mins ago.

18m ago C⁺ ⟲ ⋮

Figure 1.13: Last refreshed

- **Reload icon**: Clicking on this will rerun the dashboard.
- **Hide Filters**: Will show/hide filters on the dashboards.
- **Dashboard Actions menu**: The three dots will show options/actions available:

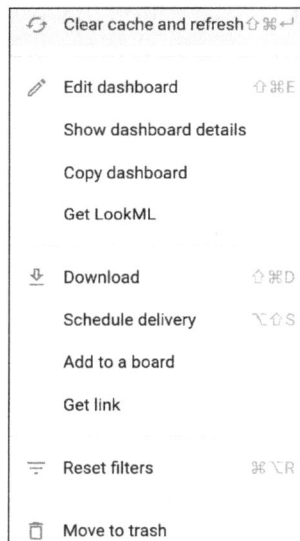

⟳ Clear cache and refresh	⇧⌘↵
✎ Edit dashboard	⇧⌘E
Show dashboard details	
Copy dashboard	
Get LookML	
⬇ Download	⇧⌘D
Schedule delivery	⌥⇧S
Add to a board	
Get link	
⟲ Reset filters	⌘⌥R
🗑 Move to trash	

Figure 1.14: Dashboard menu

- o Download, Schedule delivery, and Get link has the same functionality as we saw in Looks.
- o Reset filters will remove the selected filters and set it to default values (if any).

We will learn about some of these options in detail in the next chapters:

- **Dashboard Filters**: Filters will restrict the data displayed in the dashboard. There could be a variety of filters including radio buttons, check boxes, tag lists, calendars and sliders and so on.

- **Dashboard Tiles**: Each individual report/look is in a dashboard tile and each tile has further options, as shown in the following figure:

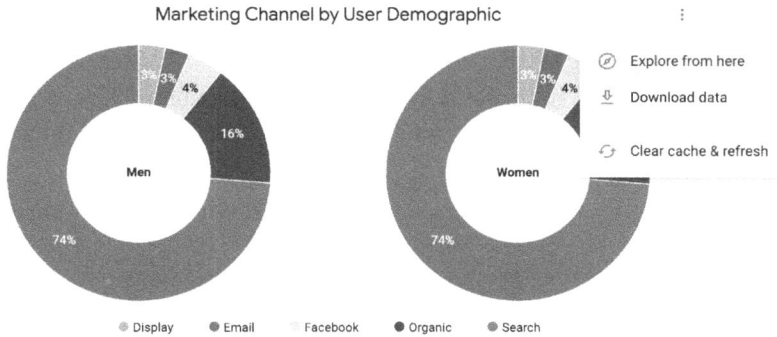

Figure 1.15: Dashboard Tile and options

- **Explore from here**: To explore the tile further.

  1. Download data to different formats:

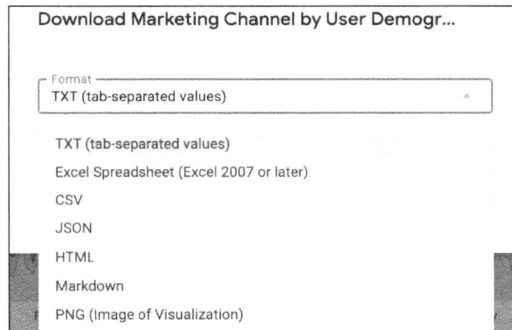

Figure 1.16: Download options

  2. Clear cache and refresh to update the data and show fresh results from the database.

Folders

Looker content (Dashboards and Looks) is stored in folders and sub folders. Access/ security to these folders can be managed using **Manage Access** option (available in the gear icon of the folder/sub folder). The following figure shows the menu options for a folder:

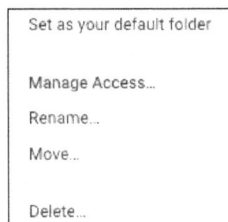

Figure 1.17: Folder menu

There are two types of access levels to a folder:

- **View**: The users or group can only view the contents of the folder.
- **Manage Access, Edit**: Like the name suggests the user or group can View, make changes to the folder including changing name, deleting and so on and also control who can access the folder.

   Users who have this access level can see the following options for the folder/sub folder:

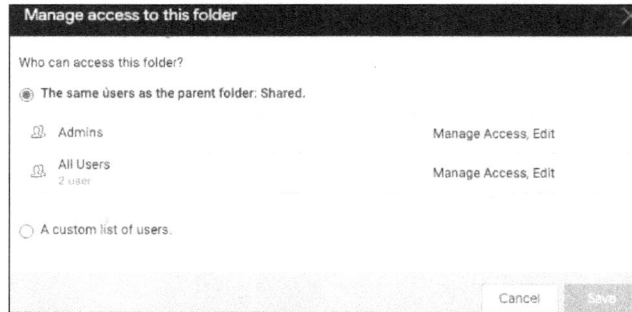

Figure 1.18: Manage access

Otherwise, the users will only see a read-only window showing who has what access.

Creating a new folder or subfolder

To create a new folder/subfolder, refer to the following steps:

1. Navigate to the parent folder and click on **New**, and select **Folder** option:

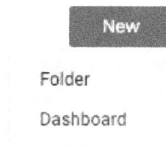

Figure 1.19: New folder/dashbaord

2. A window shows where you can enter the **Name** of the folder/subfolder.

3. Click on **Create folder**:

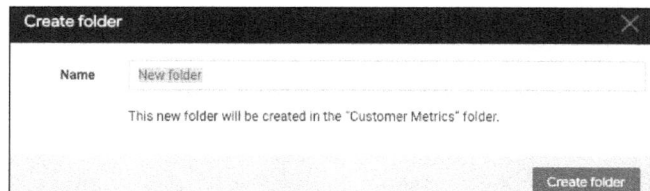

Figure 1.20: Folder name

a. To rename a folder, you can select the **Rename** option from the menu.

b. To move the folder to a different parent folder, click on move and select the folder where you want to move the folder.

c. To copy or move **Dashboards**, go to the folder and select the dashboards, you can see options on top. Similar options are available when you click on the 3 dots on the right side like shown in the following figure:

Dashboards Copy Move Upgrade Convert Looks to Tiles Move to Trash

Figure 1.21: Folder options

Boards

Boards are places where you can add Looker content and other information which will help find the information people are looking for. There are two types of things you can add to the boards:

- Looker content - Dashboards and Looks
- External links to documents, websites and descriptions

That means boards do not have any contents on its own, but they have links to other Looker pages or websites. Here are a couple of use cases for boards:

- A user/analyst is interested in multiple dashboards that are in different folders and sub folders for his daily tasks. Instead of navigating to those folders separately, the analyst can create a board and add links to the dashboards on the board.

- An e-commerce company is running a special promotion/seasonal sale. To track the marketing, sales and customer metrics, the user must look at multiple existing dashboards built for other purposes and gather reports and monitor some other applications. In this case, the user can create a board, add all the dashboards and external applications that are needed onto the board.

To view existing boards, there are two options:

- You can expand the **Boards** option in the left navigation menu. You can see the boards you created in your list.

- You can also browse existing boards by clicking on **Browse all boards**. Like it is shown in the following figure:

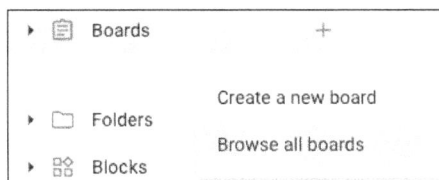

▸ ▤ Boards   +

▸ ▢ Folders   Create a new board

▸ ▨ Blocks   Browse all boards

Figure 1.22: Board creation/browse menu

Once you find the board that you are interested in, click on the board or click on go to board link. It will open the board on the right-hand side. The following figure shows how a board looks in the interface.

Sample board:

Test Board

Figure 1.23: Board navigation

Boards have the following components:

- **Title**: Name of the Board on the top left. Test Board is the title in the preceding example.
- **Share the board link**: This will open a window that has a link/URL to the board.

For example: **https://yourcompanyname.looker.com/boards/5**

It also has the access details showing who can access the board.

The Board Information shows **Description** and other details. You can add a description that is helpful:

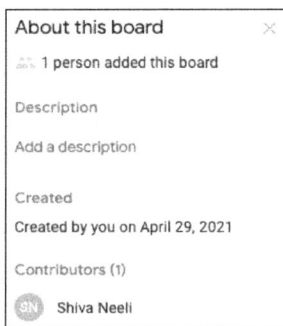

About this board   ×

1 person added this board

Description

Add a description

Created

Created by you on April 29, 2021

Contributors (1)

Shiva Neeli

Figure 1.24: Board info

The main part of the Board has the following:

- **Sections**: To organize the links in sections. Each section has a title.
- Links under sections. There are 2 types of links:
  - o   Saved Content, i.e., looks and dashboards
  - o   URL Link to add external URLs

Creating a board

To create a board, perform the following steps:

1. Click on the plus icon next to the **Boards** option in the left navigation menu and select **Create a New Board**.

2. Enter the name of the board and click on **Create Board**.

3. A new Board will be created. Here you can add a section title and write description:

Untitled section
Tell people about this section...

Figure 1.25: Board title

4. In each section, you can add either dashboard content or the external link to a webpage, google sheet or document and so on:

Saved content

URL Link

Figure 1.26: Add content to Board

5. Additionally, you can add description to the board in the Board information/ About this Board.

Adding content to existing Board

If you want to add a dashboard or Look, there are two options available.

*   From the place where you are viewing the dashboard or look, you can use the **Add to Board** option in **Dashboard** actions or look actions menu (three dots on the right).

*   On the dashboard, use the plus symbol next to the title and select the board from the pop-up window:

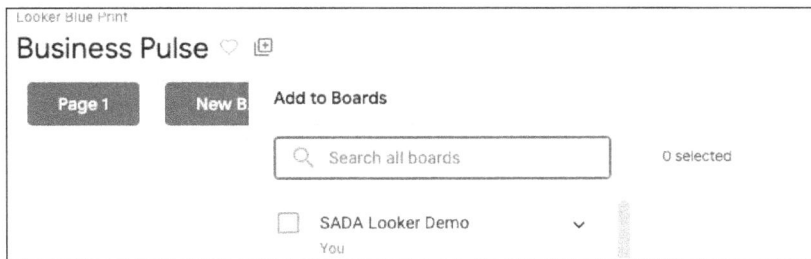

Looker Blue Print

Business Pulse

Page 1   New B   Add to Boards

Search all boards   0 selected

SADA Looker Demo
You

Figure 1.27: Add dashboard to Board

Adding or removing a Board to and from your list

List is displayed under the Boards menu item. This will reduce the number of clicks and make it easy to go to the board. To add a board to your list, there are two options:

1. In the **Browse all boards** window, you can click on the **Add** button next to the go to board link:

Go to board   Add

Figure 1.28: Add Board to list button

2. You can select the **Add to my list** option under the title of the board. This will be displayed only on the boards created by others as boards created by you are already in the list by default.

3. Removing a board from the list is also possible, option is available in both the navigation menu and the **Board Options** menu.

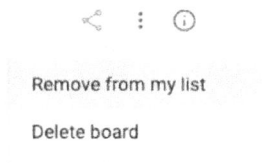

   Sidebar:

   ▸ Seasonal Sales   ⋮

   ▸ Test Board
                    Remove from sidebar

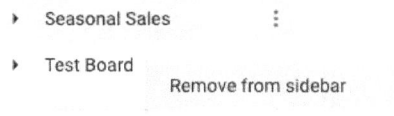

Figure 1.29: Remove Board from list:sidebar

Board Options menu:

≪ ⋮ ⓘ

Remove from my list

Delete board

Figure 1.30: Remove Board from list: Board Options

Alerts

We can alert/notify the users when a metric on a dashboard tile/ visualization met a specific condition. For example: we can notify when the total sale units are above or below a number so that the user can take action further.

To create alert, click on the bell icon of the tile and a window pops up that has different options including the following:

- **Condition**: Criteria for alert. For example: Total count > 1000 or total sales < 1,00,000 (1 Million)
- **Medium/application**: Email/Slack or other applications
- **Destination**: Email ID

- **Frequency**: How frequently you want to check the condition and send alerts. Lowest frequency is 15 minutes
- **Alert Permission**: whether to make the alert visible to everyone (Public) or just only to you (Private)

The following figure shows the preceding options:

Figure 1.31: *Creating Alert*

For example: The preceding alert checks the condition at the set frequency and sends an email only if the condition is met.

Alerts viewing: If admin enables the option to see the alerts, a bell icon indicating the alerts and the number of alerts:

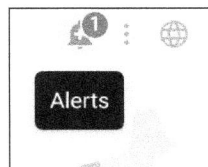

Figure 1.32: *Alert bell icon*

Following Alerts: Alerts created by other users can be followed by clicking on the bell icon and selecting the **Follow** button next to the Alert.

Figure 1.33: *Follow alert button*

Conclusion

So far, we learned about Looker origin, architecture, usage and and different components, how they will be used mostly by Viewer Users. Viewers are the majority of the users in an organization.

After this chapter, you should be able to understand Looker architecture, navigate the Looker application, use the content and consume it in different ways and also create some alerts to automatically notify the users based on the metrics.

While a read only user can consume the content as is, he/she cannot make changes. In an organization usually there will always be a need to change the existing content and/or create new content.

In the next chapter, we will learn how an advanced user or analyst can make some changes or create new content without knowing the technical details or SQL.

Join our book's Discord space

Join the book's Discord Workspace for Latest updates, Offers, Tech happenings around the world, New Release and Sessions with the Authors:

https://discord.bpbonline.com

CHAPTER 2
Creating Reports and Dashboards

Introduction

In the previous chapter, you learned how to use Looker, view, and organize Looker content, which is the functionality of business users. However, all the content was created by creator users. In this chapter, we will learn how the Standard (Creator) user creates the content—Dashboards and looks that can be used by others/viewers, what features are available in the Looker interface for creators, different visualization types, what options are available to customize those visualizations and options to create some on the fly metrics. We will conclude with best practices that prescribe the best fit visualization for different types of data.

Structure

In this chapter, we will be talking about the following topics:

- Introducing Explore interface
- Creating visualizations
- Discussing Table Calculations
- Exploring Merge Results
- Exploring dashboards
- Visualization best practices

Objectives

In this chapter, we will learn a few Looker terms, and components of the Looker Explore interface and analyze the data using that interface. After studying this unit, you should be able to explore data, create different types of visualizations, customize those visualizations, create custom fields to create additional measures and dimensions, and create dashboards that can effectively present the data to help the data analysis.

Introducing Explore interface

Data analysis is the process of exploring data to answer questions that help make business decisions. Some examples of the questions are Sales for a particular year/timeframe, User Count by region, and Orders for a category. Through the Explore interface, Looker provides the capabilities to explore data, build visualizations, and answer such questions. To access the Explore interface, log in to Looker. In the main navigation page on the left, click on **Explore**. An illustration of the same is shown in *Figure 2.1:*

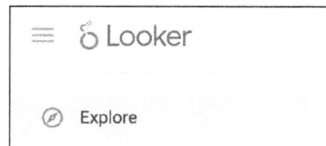

Figure 2.1: Explore option

It will open an Explore interface. An Explore interface has different components to create visualizations, as seen in *Figure 2.2:*

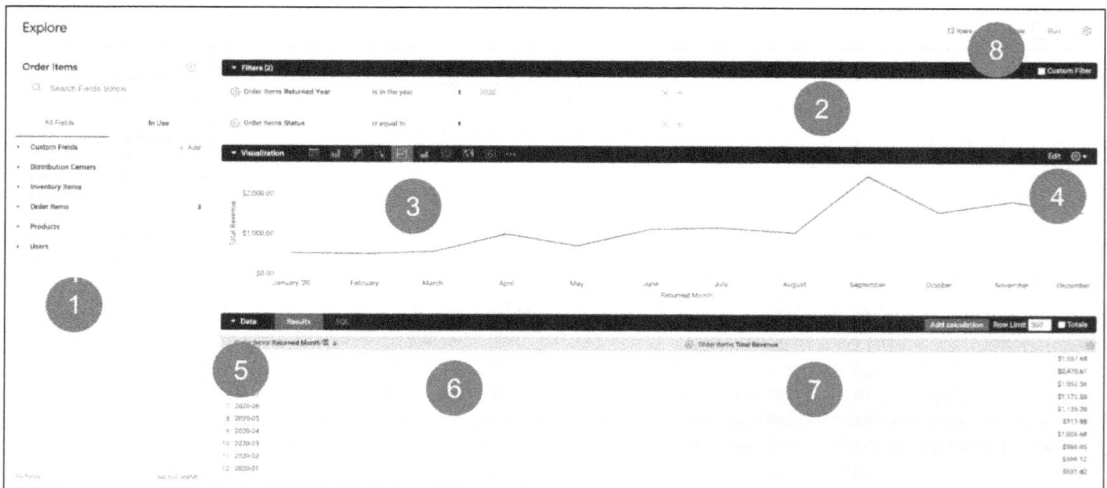

Figure 2.2: Explore interface

Various components of Explore interface are discussed as follows:

1. **Field picker**: It is the place where fields are available and can be selected to be included in the visualization. It has options to search for a field, a tab that shows the already included fields, and a place to create custom fields based on the existing fields.

2. **Filters**: Filters are the conditions on fields that can be added to restrict the data in the analysis. They can be added by selecting the filter icon next to the field or in the menu options (*gear icon*) of the fields.

3. **Visualization**: The visualization pane is where different visualizations are selected and displayed. Multiple visualizations are available out of the box. Each visualization has specific requirements, for example, at least one dimension and one measure for the bar chart.

4. **Edit visualization**: Options to customize the visualizations. Format, labels, fields, and other customization options are available.

5. **Data table**: Results in table format. It has further options to include totals, limit the results and pivot the results to convert rows into columns.

6. **Dimensions (in blue)**: Attributes of data like name, location, etc. A dimension has further options that can be viewed by clicking on the *gear icon.*

7. **Measures (in orange)**: Calculations of data like sum, count, etc. A measure has further options that can be viewed by clicking on the *gear icon.*

8. **Run**: A button to run the query and get results.

Once a visualization is created, it can be saved as a look, as a tile on a new dashboard, or added to an existing dashboard. There are other options to download and send to email or other destinations as shown in *Figure 2.3*:

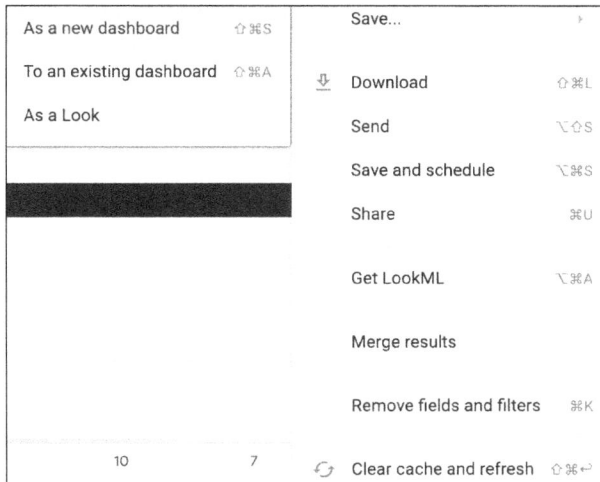

As a new dashboard	⇧⌘S		Save...	▸
To an existing dashboard	⇧⌘A	⬇ Download	⇧⌘L
As a Look			Send	⌥⇧S
			Save and schedule	⌥⌘S
▬▬▬▬▬▬			Share	⌘U
			Get LookML	⌥⌘A
			Merge results	
			Remove fields and filters	⌘K
10	7	↻	Clear cache and refresh	⇧⌘↵

Figure 2.3: Save options

Looker Explores are the objects created by the LookML developers that package the required fields for analysis. Explores have views/tables which are further divided into fields called dimensions and measures. Dimensions are attributes or qualitative values like name, category, city, and more. Dimensions are displayed in blue color in the field picker as well as the data table in the Explore interface. Measures are quantitative values that involve some calculations like count, total, average, and so on. Measures are displayed in orange color in both the field picker and Explore interface. Each Explore is designed to answer some business questions. Explores include the views/tables that are related. For example, there might be an explore to answer order-related questions like sales, number of orders, returns, and more, along with another explore to answer questions about the users.

Creating visualizations

Looker provides many visualizations out of the box that can be used to display the data effectively to help with the analysis. In the following examples, we will use the explore - Order items from the sample e-commerce model to answer a few sample questions using visualizations.

Single Value

This visualization shows a single **key performance indicator** (**KPI**). It is mainly used to display high-level or summary metrics on a dashboard.

Question: What is the Total Sales amount for the Year 2022?

Fields used: Dimension: Created Year; Measure: Total Sale Price

Steps:

1. From the Field Picker, select **Explore**, and from the list of Explores available, select **E-Commerce Training** and select **Order Items**:

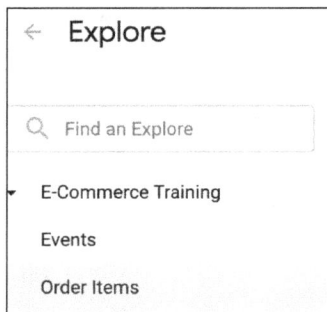

Figure 2.4: Explore navigation

2. From **Order Items** explore, expand **Order Items View** and select **Created Date |** **Year** and click on the **Filter by field**:

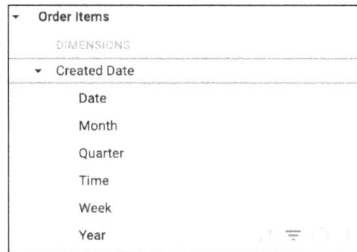

Figure 2.5: Date Selection

3. The field will be added to the **Filters** section. Change the option to `is in the year` and enter **2022** as we need to get sales for 2022:

Figure 2.6: Date Filter

4. From the list of available measures from the **Order Items View**, select the **Total Revenue From Completed Orders** (in orange color). The column will be added to the **Data** pane in the **Results** section.

5. In the **Visualization** part on the right, select the **Single Value** option. This can be further customized using **Edit Visualization** options:

Figure 2.7: Viz selection

6. Click on the **Run** button on top. It shows the Total Sales for the Year 2022. This run button, in fact, built the query, sent it to the database and got back the results, and displayed it in single-value visualization:

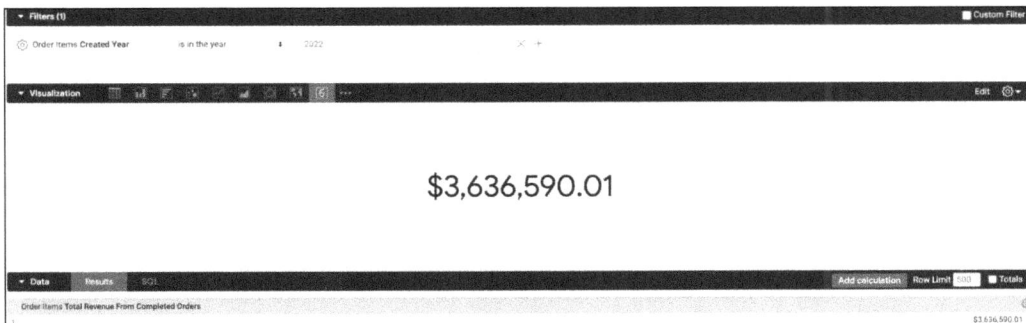

Figure 2.8: Getting results

7. The results can be saved on a dashboard by clicking on **Save as a new dashboard** and creating a new dashboard with the name `Training Dashboard` and click **Save**:

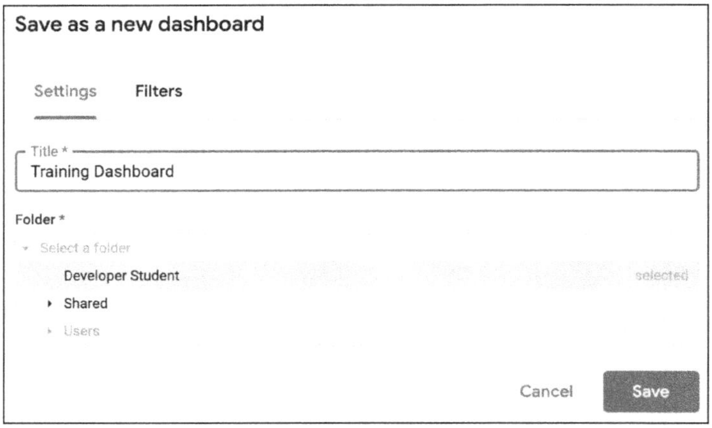

Figure 2.9: Save as dashboard

8. You will see a green bar appear on top that shows a link to view the Dashboard, as shown in *Figure 2.10*:

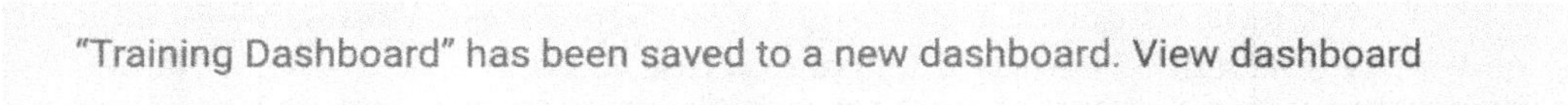

Figure 2.10: Saved Dashboard link

9. Click on the **View Dashboard**, it will show the dashboard we just created with a filter and the single value visualization as shown in *Figure 2.11*:

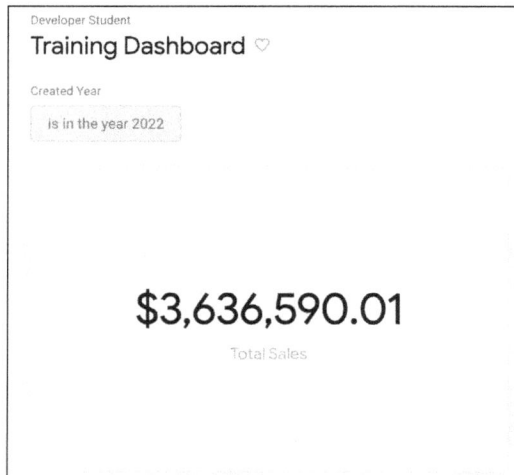

Figure 2.11: Dashboard View

Table

This is the most common visualization on dashboards. If there are multiple dimensions and/or measures or for list reports, table visualization is used.

Question: Total count of Orders, Item Count, and Revenue by Status for the year 2022.

Fields used: Dimensions: Created Year, Status Measures: Total order count, Total Item Count, Total Revenue

Steps:

1. From **Order Items** explore, expand **Order Items View** and select **Created Date | year** and click on the **Filter by field**:

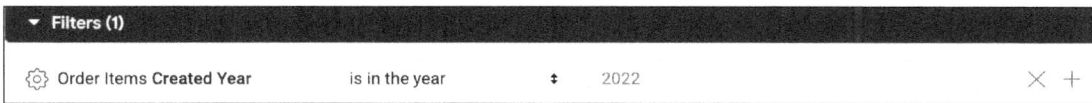

Figure 2.12: Date Filter

2. From **Order Items** explore, select **Status, Order Count, Order Item Count** and **Total Revenue**:

	Order Items Status	Order Items Created Month ↓	Order Items Order Count	Order Items Order Item Count	Order Items Total Revenue
1	Returned	2022-12	99	99	$4,487.55
2	Processing	2022-12	513	518	$22,899.29
3	Cancelled	2022-12	307	320	$16,381.47
4	Complete	2022-12	6,727	6,875	$315,848.34
5	Shipped	2022-12	1,285	1,310	$59,099.41
6	Cancelled	2022-11	275	289	$12,633.04
7	Complete	2022-11	8,051	8,277	$376,911.39
8	Returned	2022-11	89	89	$4,207.38
9	Cancelled	2022-10	288	296	$13,679.92

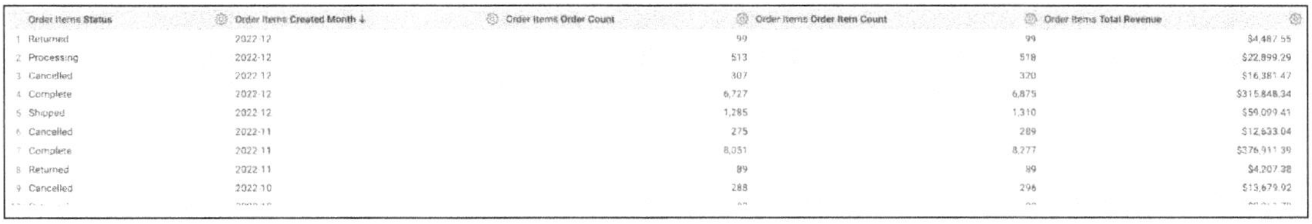

Figure 2.13: Data Pane in Explore

3. Select the **Table Visualization** from the list.
4. Edit **Visualization** and in the **Series** tab, for the column **Total Revenue**, enable **Table Visualization**. Final table visualization will show as in *Figure 2.13:*

	Status	Order Count	Order Item Count	Total Revenue
1	Complete	77,070	79,025	$3,636,590.01
2	Cancelled	2,852	2,934	$137,157.09
3	Shipped	1,285	1,310	$59,099.41
4	Returned	857	858	$38,493.76
5	Processing	513	518	$22,899.29

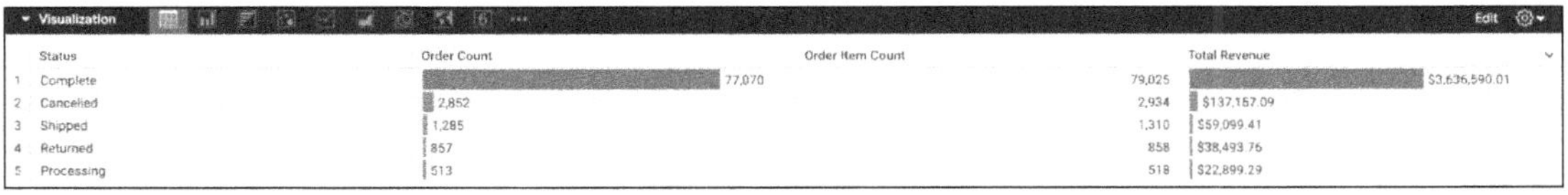

Figure 2.14: Table Viz

5. Click on **Save** to an existing dashboard. Select the **Training Dashboard** and give a name to the visualization - `Orders by Status`.

Pivot Table

It is a slight variation of Table; one dimension is shown as a row and another as a column.

Question: Total count of Orders, Item Count, and Revenue by Status and month for the year 2022.

Fields used: Dimensions: Created Year, Created Month, Status Measures: Total order count, Total Item Count, Total Revenue.

Steps:

1. Complete the steps for **Table visualization** up to *Step 3*. Another option is to click on **Explore from here** on the dashboard table visualization orders by Status.

2. The Explore interface opens with the table definition. Add another field **Created Month** from the same **Order Items View**.

3. The **Order Status** is shown as rows. To convert these values to columns, we need to pivot the column Status. There are two options to Pivot: firstly, from the **Field Picker** (In Use or All fields) section, hover over the **Status** column and select the **Pivot Data** option, or in the **Data** Section, click on the *gear icon*, and select **Pivot** from the menu:

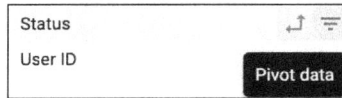

Figure 2.15 (a): Pivot option in explore

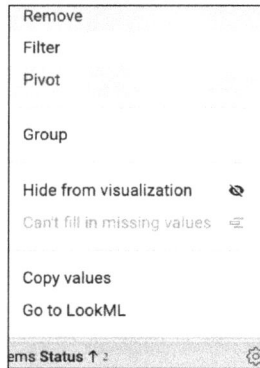

Figure 2.15 (b): Pivot option on the selected fields

4. In the **Visualization** edit option, under **Series** section, disable the cell visualization on **Total Revenue** by turning the blue toggle off:

		Cancelled			Complete			Processing			Returned			Shipped		
Status	>															
Created Month	˅	Order Count	Total Revenue	Order Item Count	Order Count	Total Revenue	Order Item Count	Order Count	Total Revenue	Order Item Count	Order Count	Total Revenue	Order Item Count	Order Count	Total Revenue	Order Item Count
1 2022-12		307	$16,381.47	320	6,727	$315,848.	6,875	513	$22,899.29	518	99	$4,487.55	99	1,285	$59,099.41	1,310
2 2022-11		275	$12,633.04	289	8,051	$376,911...	8,277				89	$4,207.38	89			
3 2022-10		288	$13,679.92	296	7,210	$338,100.	7,389				83	$3,961.73	83			
4 2022-09		270	$13,745.44	277	6,661	$316,055.	6,829				71	$3,606.90	71			
5 2022-08		230	$11,411.77	232	6,746	$312,360.	6,913				74	$3,800.96	75			
6 2022-07		225	$10,652.89	233	6,286	$291,085.	6,441				75	$3,233.41	75			

Figure 2.16: Results in Table Viz

5. Click on **Save to an existing Dashboard**. Select the **Training Dashboard** and give a name to the visualization -Monthly Orders by Status.

Bar chart

A bar chart shows the measures using bars or stripes. It is mainly used to compare and contrast data.

Question: How do the sales of one year compare to the other?

Fields used: Dimensions: Created Year Measures: Total Revenue

Steps:

1. From **Order Items** explore, expand **Order Items View,** and select **Created Date |
Year** and **Total Revenue** from **Completed Orders Measure**.

2. In the **Visualization** section, select the **Bar chart** option. This can be further customized using **Edit**. For example, the values can be shown on the bar by enabling **Value Labels**.

   Try other options here and see the changes on the chart:

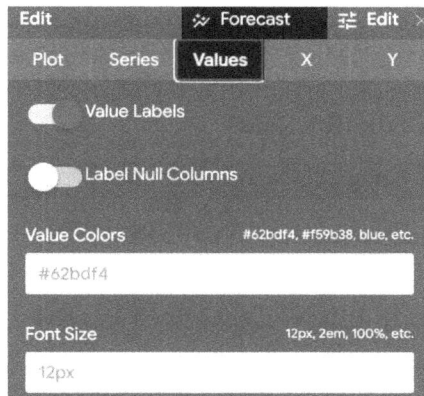

Figure 2.17: Visualization edit options

3. The bar chart will be shown as *Figure 2.17*. This can be saved on the **Training Dashboard**:

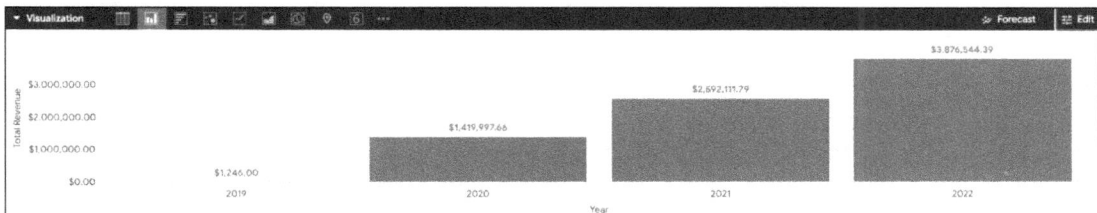

Figure 2.18: Bar Visualization

Line chart

A line chart shows the measures using a line. It is mainly used to show the values over a time period.

Question: Did the Sales increase or decrease during the year 2022?

Fields used: Dimensions: Created Year, Created Month Name Measures: Total Revenue

Steps:

1. From the field picker, select **Explore** and from the list of explores available, select **E-Commerce Training** and select **Order Items**:

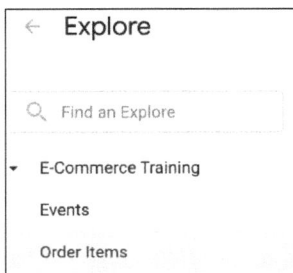

Figure 2.19: Explore Navigation

2. From **Order Items** explore, expand **Order Items View** and select **Created Date |
Year** and click on the **Filter by field**:

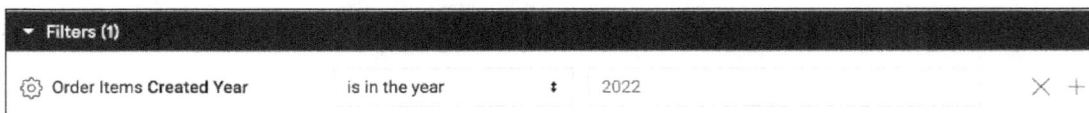

Figure 2.20: Date Filter

3. From **Order Items** explore, expand **Order Items View** and select **Created Date |
Month Name** and **Total Revenue** from **Completed Orders Measure**.

4. In the **Visualization** section, select the **Line Chart** option. This can be further customized using **Edit**. For example, the values can be shown on the bar by enabling **Value Labels**:

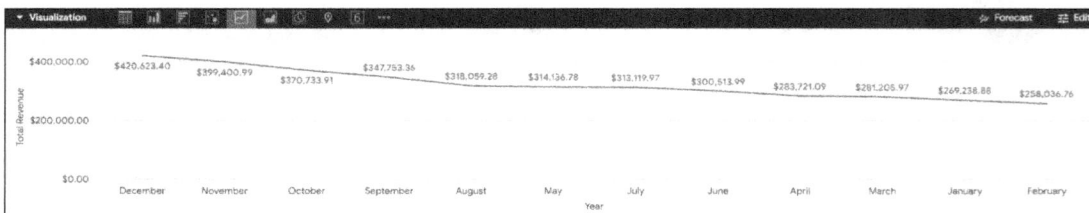

Figure 2.21: Line Visualization

5. The visualization shows the months and revenue in a line as shown in *Figure 2.20*. However, if you observe the x-axis, the months are not in ascending order. To keep the months in order, select/add the **Month Num** and sort:

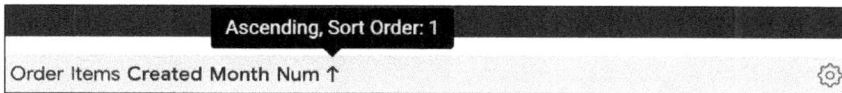

Figure 2.22: *Sorting column*

6. Also, hide the **Month Num** from **Visualization**:

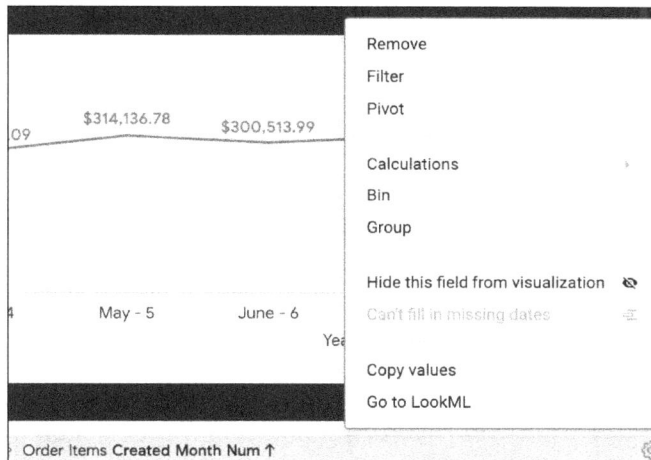

Figure 2.23: *Hiding a column*

7. The Chart shows the months in order now, as shown in *Figure 2.24*:

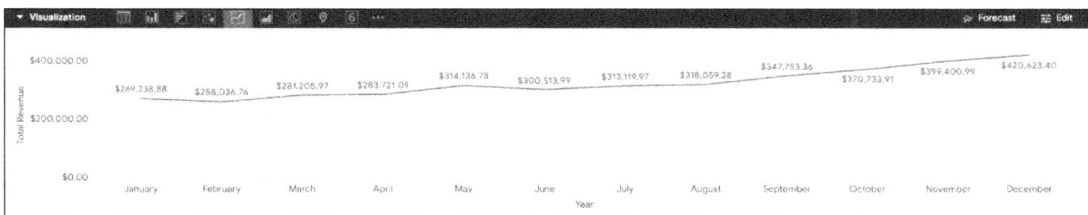

Figure 2.24: *Final Line chart*

Pie or Donut chart

A Pie or Donut chart is used to show the proportions of categorical data, with the size of each piece representing the proportion of each category.

Question: What are the top 5 categories of products sold in the year 2022?

Fields used: Dimensions: Created Year, Category Measures: Total Revenue

Steps:

1. From the field picker, select **Explore,** and from the list of explores available, select **E-Commerce Training,** and select **Order Items**:

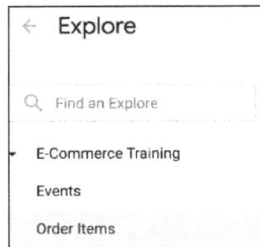

Figure 2.25: *Explore Navigation*

2. From **Order Items** explore, expand **Order Items View** and select **Created Date |Year** and click on the **Filter** by field:

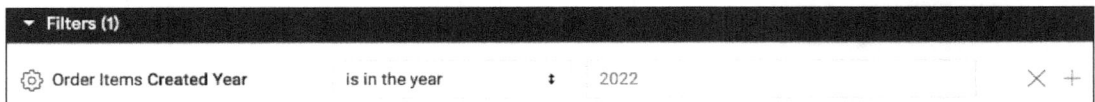

Figure 2.26: *Date Filter*

3. From **Order Items** explore, expand **Products View** and select **Category** and from the **Order Items View** select **Total Revenue** from **Completed Orders Measure**.

4. In the **Visualization** section, select the **Pie chart** option. This can be further customized using **Edit**.

5. The results show all categories and the revenue for each category. As we need to show only the top five categories by revenue, we can sort the **Revenue** column in the data section and also limit the rows to 5:

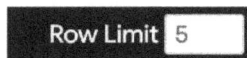

Figure 2.27: *Limiting rows*

6. Click **Run** and the result will be shown in the visualization section as a **Pie chart** with the top five categories:

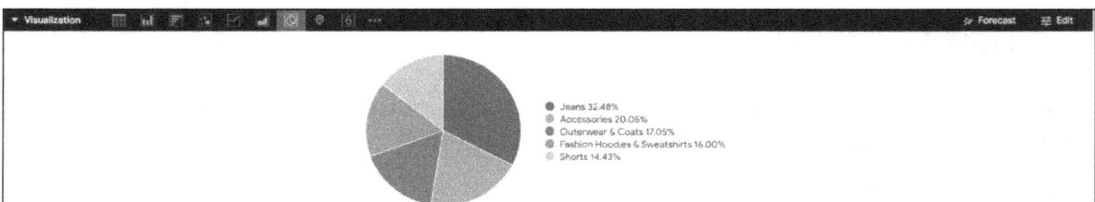

Figure 2.28: *Pie chart visualization*

7. To change this to a **Donut chart**, you can edit the visualization and mention the inner radius as 60. This Donut chart can be saved on the existing **Training Dashboard**:

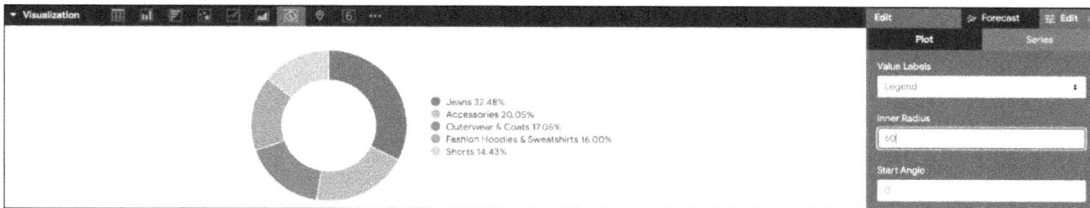

Figure 2.29: Edit Visualization options

Maps

Geographic data can be visualized on responsive and interactive maps called Map charts. They provide significant control over the way that map points are plotted.

Note: **For Maps to work, there should be at least one dimension of type location.**

Question: Which zip codes have the most users in USA?

Fields used: Dimensions: Zip Category Measures: Users Count

Steps:

1. From the field picker, select **Explore** and from the list of explores available, select **E-Commerce Training** and select **Order Items**:

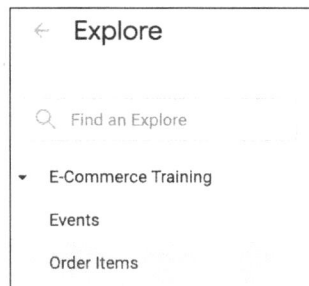

Figure 2.30: Explore Navigation

2. From **Order Items** explore, expand **Users View**, and select **Country**, and click on the **Filter by field**. Enter/Select the value **USA** from the list in the **Filters** section.

3. From **Order Items** explore, expand **Users View**, and select **Zip Dimension** (dimension type is location) and **Count Measure.**

4. In the **Visualization** section, select the **Map** option. This can be further customized using **Edit**.

5. Click **Run**. A USA map with zip codes where the users are present shows. Hovering over the green dots shows the zip codes with user counts:

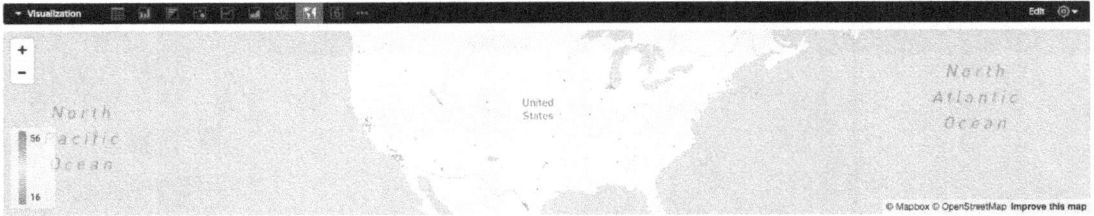

Figure 2.31: *Map Visualization*

The preceding visualizations are provided as examples. However, there are multiple other visualizations available in Looker that can be explored and used as the dashboard needs. Selecting a visualization that can present the data clearly and effectively is important. With effective visualization, you can communicate the results to the audience and empower them to interpret and analyze the data.

Custom fields

So far, you have used the fields created by the LookML developers and used them in the visualizations. However, sometimes you might have to create new fields based on the existing fields (for example, calculating the profit if the sale price and cost are available, or time to ship if the order date time and ship date time is available). Looker explore interface provides capabilities to create such ad-hoc columns.

There are three types of custom fields:

- Custom Dimension
- Custom Measure
- Table Calculation

Custom Dimension

You can create a new dimension using one or more existing dimensions.

For example, we want to know whether there are more orders for items with retail prices under $50 or over $50. This retail Price is available in Product View. However, we need another column that can show whether the price is Over 50 or Under 50. This can be created using Custom Dimension:

1. From the **Order Items** Explore, **Product View**, **Select Retail Price** as a dimension.

2. In the field picker, above all the views, you can see **Custom Fields**. Click on the + **Add** sign and select the **Custom Dimension** option:

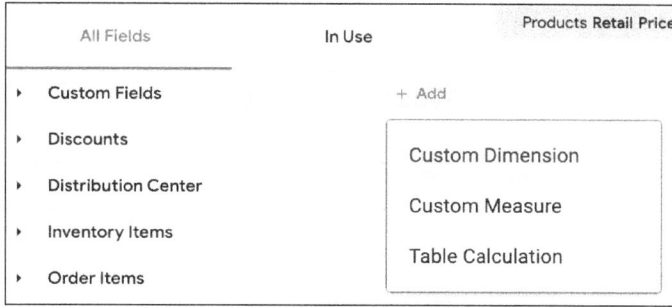

Figure 2.32: Custom Dimension menu

3. The expression window opens. In this window, if you click on the *space bar*, it will show all available options including the fields, functions, and more:

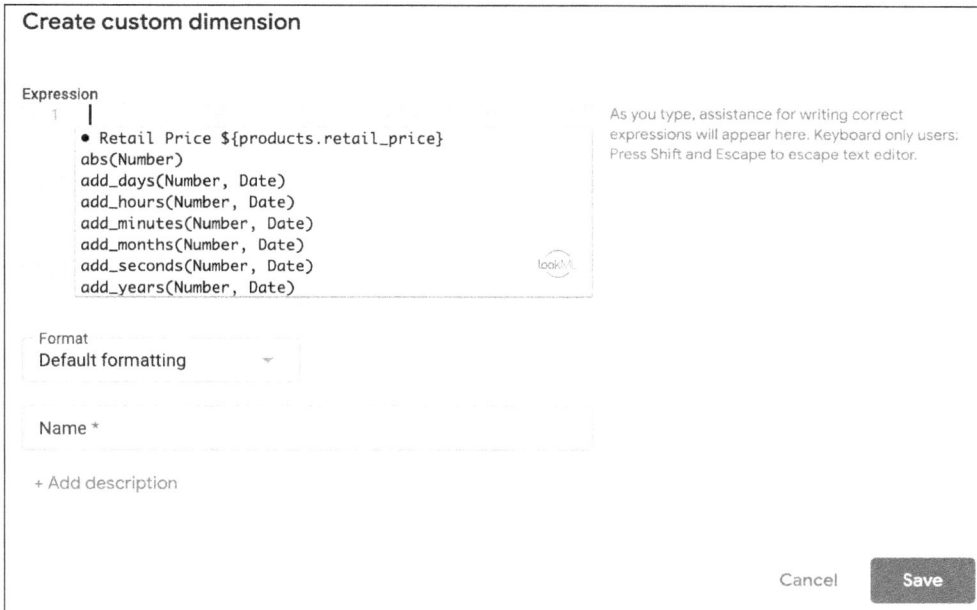

Figure 2.33: Custom Dimension window

4. You can enter the following statement to create new values: **Over 50 and Under 50 by comparing the Retail price with 50**. Name the column as **Retail Price Group** and **Save**:

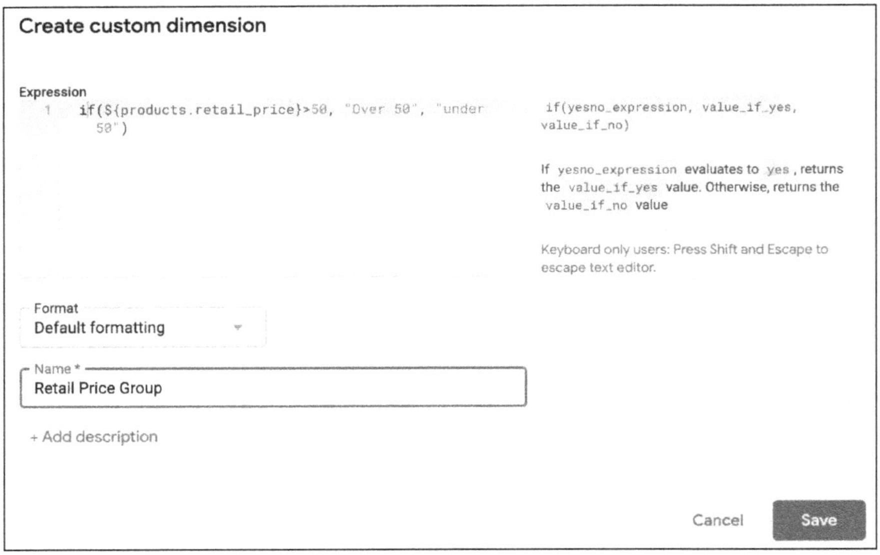

Figure 2.34: Custom Dimension creation

5. A New column will be added in the **Custom Fields** section and also the data section on the right.

6. Add the **Order Count**. Remove the field **Retail Price**

7. Select the **Table visualization** and click **Run**:

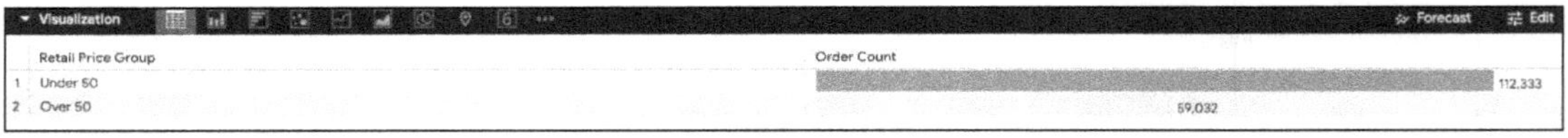

Figure 2.35: Table Visualization

8. From the numbers we can see the under $50 products have more orders than over $50

Custom Measure

There are two types of Custom Measures you can create in the Explore interface:

- **Custom Measure based on an existing dimension**:

  There are two ways this can be done which are as discussed a follows:

  o Using the '...' menu from the dimension: This is a quick way to aggregate the **Dimension** fields and create a measure that will be added to the custom fields.

  For example: To find the average **Retail Price** of the **Products**, you can click on the '...' dots of retail price and select **Aggregate | Average**:

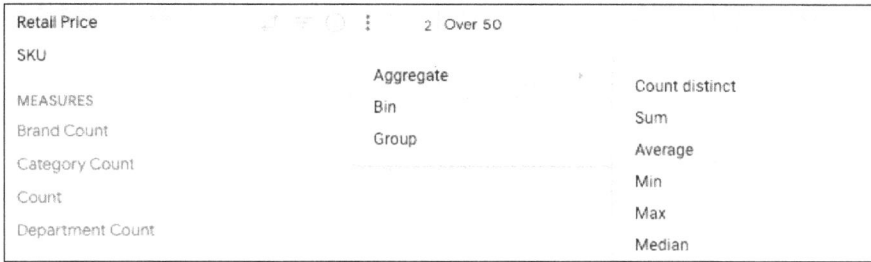

Figure 2.36: Custom Measure Aggregation

A new column with the name **Average of Retail Price** will be added to the **Custom Fields** section and also the **Data section**.

o   Using the **Custom Fields** section similar to **Custom Dimension**: To create a Custom Measure in this way for the preceding example:

1.   Click on **Add next** to **Custom Fields** and select **Custom Measure**.

2.   A new window pops up. In this window, select **Retail Price** for **Field to Measure** and select **Average for Measure Type**:

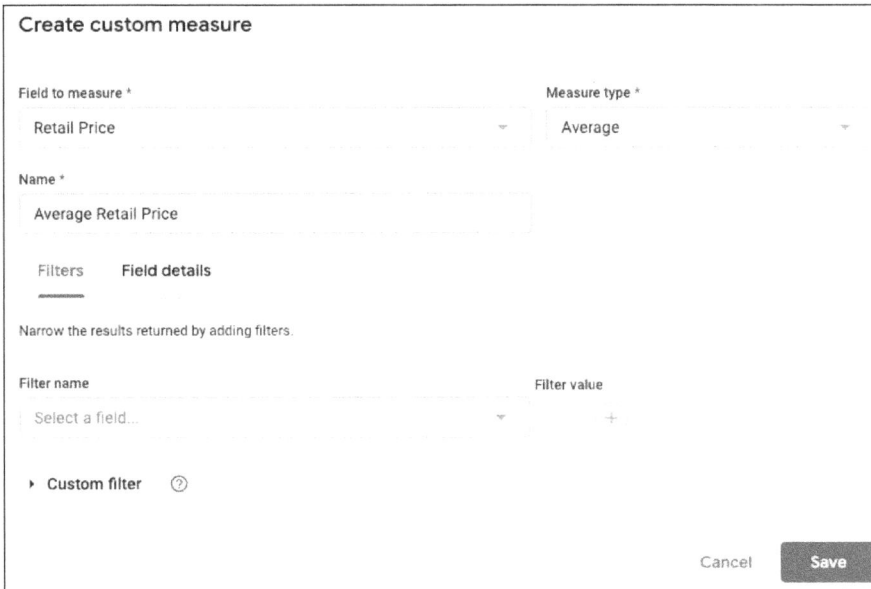

Figure 2.37: Custom Measure creation

- **Filtered Measure based on an existing Measure**: We can also create a filtered measure based on an existing measure by applying a filter on a dimension column.

For example, if we have a measure for total sales, to find the sales for a particular year like 2022, you can create a filtered measure. There are two ways:

o Using the '**…**' menu from the measure: Go to the measure **Total Sales Price** and click on the '**…**' dots menu and select **Create a Filtered Measure**:

Figure 2.38: Filtered Measure option

o Using the **Custom Fields** section similar to **Custom Dimension**: Click on **Add** next to **Custom Fields** and select **Custom Measure**. A new window pops up.

In this window, select **Total Sales Price** from **Order Items View** for **Field to measure** and select **Created Year** for **Filter Name** and **is in the Year 2022** for **Filter Value**:

Figure 2.39: Filtered Measure creation

Discussing Table Calculations

As the name suggests, these are calculations that are performed on the fields in the data table.

Table Calculations can be mathematical, logical, Boolean, date-based, or string/text-based. These can be on both dimensions, measures, or other Table Calculations.

There are some key differences between Custom Fields and Table Calculations:

- Custom fields (in the preceding section) do not need to include the columns in the data table. Table Calculations, on the other hand, need the columns to be included in the data table.

- Custom Fields are executed along with the query (LookML-defined fields). However, Table Calculations are executed post query, which means the calculations are performed on the results that the query returns in the datatable.

For example: To know the percentage of user count by traffic source:

1. We can first create a data table with **User Count** and **Traffic Source** as the fields from **User View** of the **Order Items**.

2. Table Calculation can be created in one of two ways:

   a. Quickest way is to click on the *gear icon* of the measure and select **Calculations** and choose the appropriate calculation - **% of column** in this case. You can observe that there are other calculations readily available that can be selected when you need them:

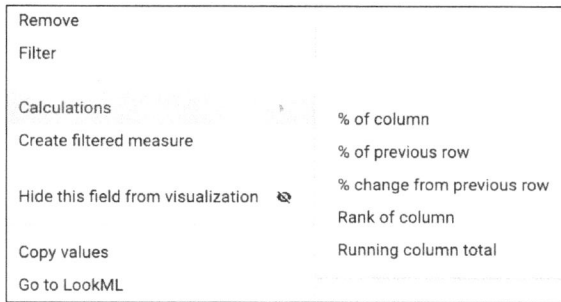

Figure 2.40: Table Calculation menu

   b. Second option is in the field picket above all views, you can see **Custom Fields**. Click on the +**Add** sign and select the **Table Calculation** option. A new window pops up. Enter **the % of column** in **Calculation** and choose **User Count** in **Source Column**:

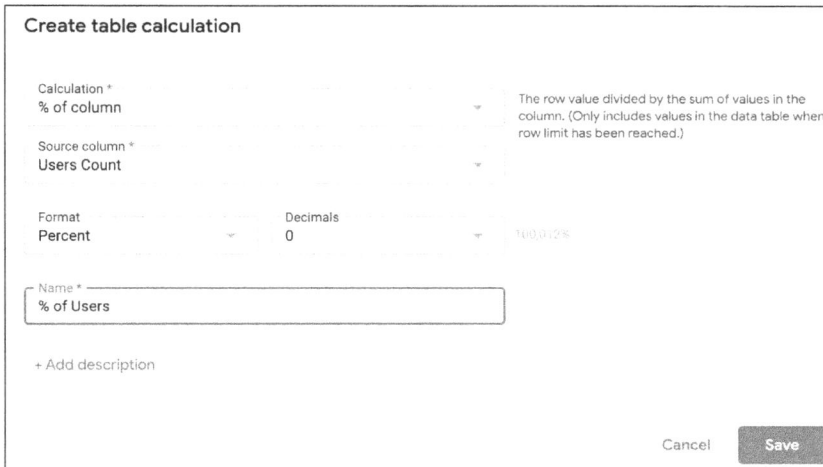

Figure 2.41: Table Calculation creation

3. A new column - % **of Users** in light green color will be created and added to the data table:

Figure 2.42: *Table Calculation result*

Another example: To know the basket size of the Order:

1. We can first create a data table with **Order Count** and **Total Sale Price** from the **Order Items View**.

2. In the field picker above all views, you can see **Custom Fields**. Click on the **+Add** sign and select **Table Calculation** option. A new window pops up.

3. Select **Custom Expression** in the **Calculation** and Enter the Expression: **${order_items.total_sale_price}/${order_items.order_count}**

4. Select the **U.S. Dollars** from Format and **2** decimals and name the column as **Basket Size** and **Save**:

Figure 2.43: *Table Calculation creation*

5. A new column - **Basketsize** in light green color will be created and added to the data table:

Figure 2.44: *Table Calculation Result*

Looker SQL

In the Explore interface, data section, you will see two tabs, one is **Results** and another tab is **SQL**. This will display the SQL generated by the Looker to get the results. The SQL will be generated based on the LookML explore that is being used and sent to the database to get the results. You can also see how the SQL changes when you add or change the explore fields or filters:

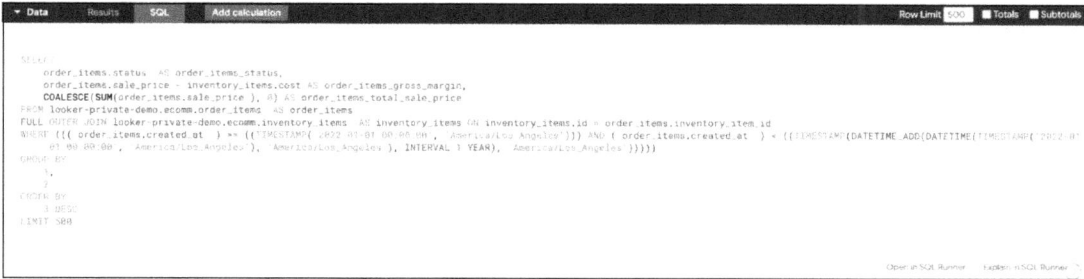

Figure 2.45: Explore SQL

SQL Runner

In the preceding window, as shown in *Figure 2.45*, on the bottom right corner, you can see the links to open or explore in **SQL Runner**. Clicking on the link opens another SQL interface/editor, as shown in *Figure 2.45*, that is mainly used to build and run SQL queries. On the left-hand side, you will see options to browse the databases, the LookML models, and select the tables/views under them. On the right-hand side, you will see a similar interface, like the Explore interface.

SQL Runner can also be opened with the main navigation window under **Develop Menu**:

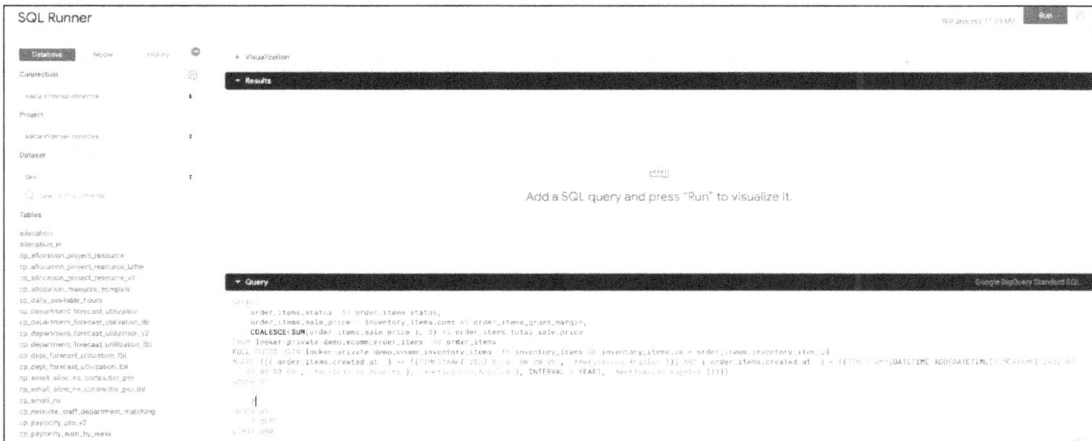

Figure 2.46: SQL Runner interface

The same SQL Runner interface can be used to create, run, debug queries and create derived tables. Next to the Run button on top, it also shows the amount of data it processes. This will be helpful for cloud data warehouses to make sure the query is not going to cause cost overages. After the query is run, it will display rows returned and the time it took to run the query.

Explain in SQL Runner will execute the explain plan on the query that is supported by many database dialects. It shows the steps taken by the database to complete the query that includes the number of records scanned, time to execute and order of steps etc. This is useful to diagnose the query, identify the problem areas of the query and optimize it.

Exploring Merge Results

Sometimes you might need to Merge Results from two different reports, or from two different explores where the tables are not actually joined in the LookML. In those scenarios, you can use the feature called **Merge Results**, which lets you join the results from two different queries.

For example, we want to find out the percentage of the Brand Sales in each category of the products. For this, we need the total sales numbers for each category level and also at Brand level.

Steps:

1. The brand level sales can be created from **Order Items** explore by simply using **Category, Brand** as dimensions and **Total Sales Price** as the measure as shown in *Figure 2.47*:

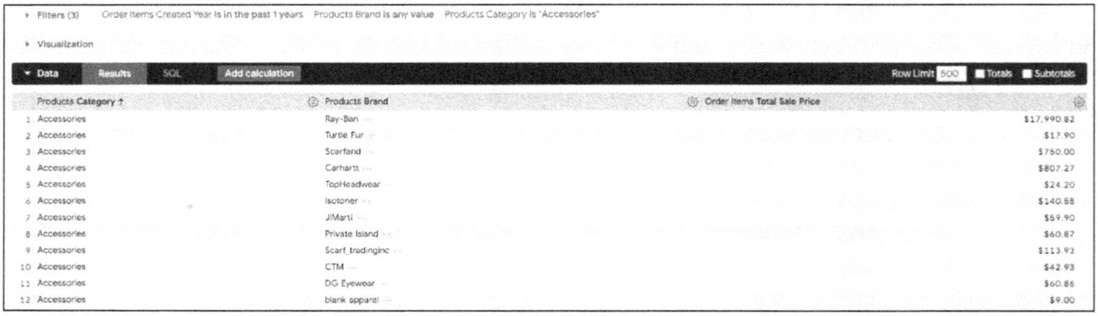

Figure 2.47: First Query in Merge Results

2. On the top menu icon, click on the **Merge Result**:

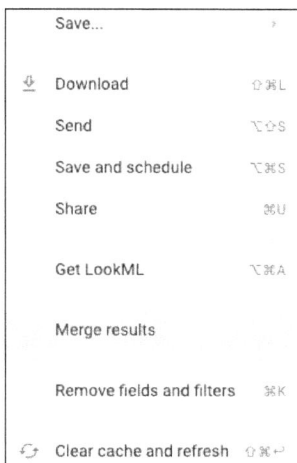

Figure 2.48: Merge Results Menu

3. A new window opens with gray color. Select the **Order items** Explore again.

4. Here you can select **Category and Sales Price** as the columns and click **Run**. Results will be as shown *Figure 2.49*:

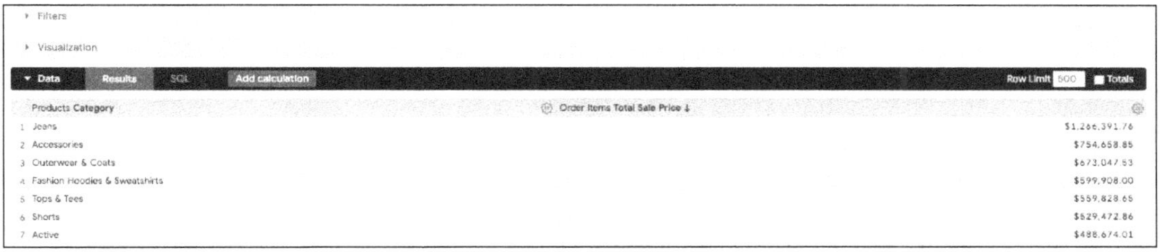

Figure 2.49: Second query in Merge Results

5. When you click on **Save**, you can see the two queries are joined/merged by the common column—**Category** in our case. In cases where the column name is not the same in both queries, you can choose the columns that can be used to merge:

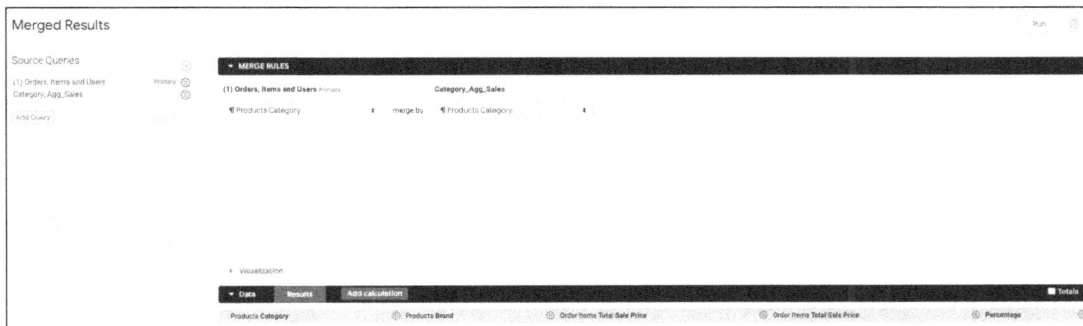

Figure 2.50: Both Queries in Merge Results

6. Click on the **Add calculation** and enter the below calculation and select the **format** and name the column as **Percentage**:

Edit table calculation

Calculation *
Custom expression

Expression

1. ${order_items.total_sale_price}/${q1_order_items.total_sale_price}

Total Sale Price `order_items.total_sale_price`

Type: Number

Keyboard only users: Press Shift and Escape to escape text editor.

Format
Percent

Decimals
2

100,012.35%

Name *
Percentage

+ Add description

Cancel   Save

Figure 2.51: Table Calculation in Merge Results

7. Select **Table Visualization** and click **Run**. You can see the table visualization with both sales and the percentage as shown in *Figure 2.51*. You can format this visualization further using the **Edit** menu:

	Category	Brand	Order Items	Order Items	Percentage
1	Accessories	Ray-Ban	$536,913.82	$754,658.85	71.15%
2	Accessories	TrendsBlue	$20,515.78	$754,658.85	2.72%
3	Accessories	Scarfand	$19,972.00	$754,658.85	2.65%
4	Accessories	Carhartt	$19,686.61	$754,658.85	2.61%
5	Accessories	Oakley	$11,128.80	$754,658.85	1.47%
6	Accessories	Isotoner	$6,007.13	$754,658.85	0.80%
7	Accessories	Seirus Innovation	$5,200.59	$754,658.85	0.69%
8	Accessories	Levi's	$5,085.27	$754,658.85	0.67%
9	Accessories	180s	$5,010.91	$754,658.85	0.66%

Figure 2.52: Final Merge Results Table

8. Explore other options in the definition of this visualization like setting primary query, editing columns, and more.

In the preceding example, we used the same explore twice. However, we can use the same feature for joining results from two different explores (from same model or different model), even if the data is from two different databases.

- Merge results is actually a post-query-processing feature, which means the merges are not sent to the Database. However, they are processed after getting the results from the individual queries that are part of the Merge Results. So, it should not be used for large result sets. Otherwise, you might encounter performance issues.

- Not all visualization features may be available with the merge results. So, use this feature with a caution.

Looks

In the preceding example, we created the visualizations on a dashboard. However, the visualizations can also be saved as stand-alone objects called Looks from the same Explore interface. Looks can also be stored and accessed from the folders similar to dashboard. Looks also have filters on top, download, schedule, and other options that can be accessed from the gear icon on the right. As the functionality is similar to dashboards, we will not discuss more details about Looks.

Exploring dashboards

There are two types of dashboards in Looker:

- User Defined Dashboards, which are created on the Looker UI.
- LookML dashboards which are code versions of the dashboards.

In this section, we will learn about **User Defined Dashboards**. Dashboard is a place where we can put together multiple visualizations, filters, text and images. Usually, charts and visualizations that are part of the same subject/analysis are put together. For example, Sales might have one dashboard with multiple visualizations, and customer analytics visualizations might be in another dashboard.

In Looker, you can create a dashboard in multiple ways, which are as follows:

- You can create a blank dashboard from a folder and add tiles to the dashboard.
- Another way is to start with an explore and add the results/visualizations to a new or existing dashboard. We discussed this option in the above section while creating visualizations.

Steps to create a dashboard from a folder:

1. Go to the desired folder and on the '**…**' **menu** on right, click on **New** | **Dashboard**:

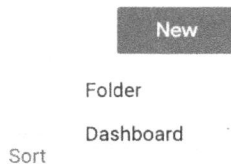

New

Folder

Dashboard

Sort

Figure 2.53: Dashboard creation menu

2. **Create Dashboard** window pops up. Give a name to the dashboard and click on **Create Dashboard**. A dashboard with the name will be created:

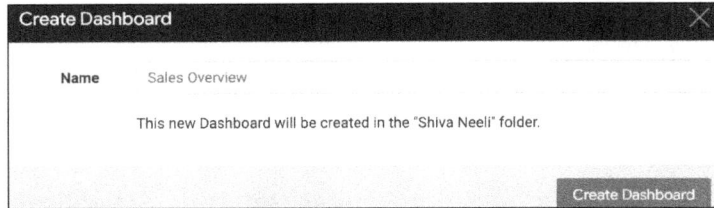

Figure 2.54: Dashboard Name

3. On the new dashboard, click on the **Add** button on top left side. You will see options to add different content including visualizations, text or buttons on the dashboard:

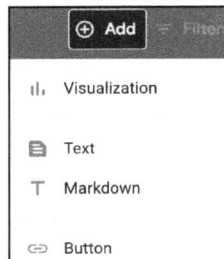

Figure 2.55: Dashboard Add menu

The following is the purpose of each options:

- **Visualization**: Here you can create a visualization by selecting the fields, filters and visualizations similar to the steps mentioned in the previous sections.

- **Text**: Along with visualization, you can also add a text tile. This is mainly used to describe/analyze the visualizations or put notes for users.

- **Markdown**: This lets you add some HTML style text. This is mainly used to display some images or links on the dashboard.

- **Button**: This option lets you add a link to another Looker dashboard/look URL or an external URL.

4. Edit Dashboard option on the right hand can be used to edit the existing content on the dashboard:

Figure 2.56: Edit Dashboard option

Dashboard filters

Once a visualization is added, you can see the option for filters enabled. You can choose the required fields as filters. For example, you can select the created year from **Order Items** explore and apply/not apply to the visualizations or tiles on the dashboard:

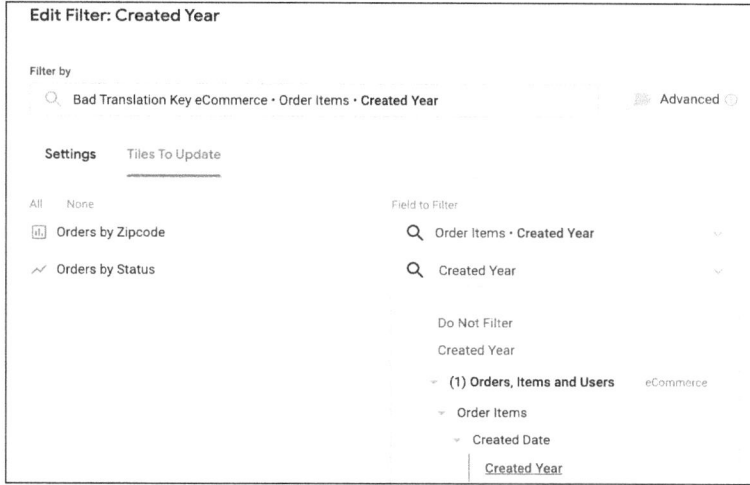

Figure 2.57: Dashboard Filter Creation

There are multiple Dashboard filter controls options available, for example, radio button, check boxes, button and more:

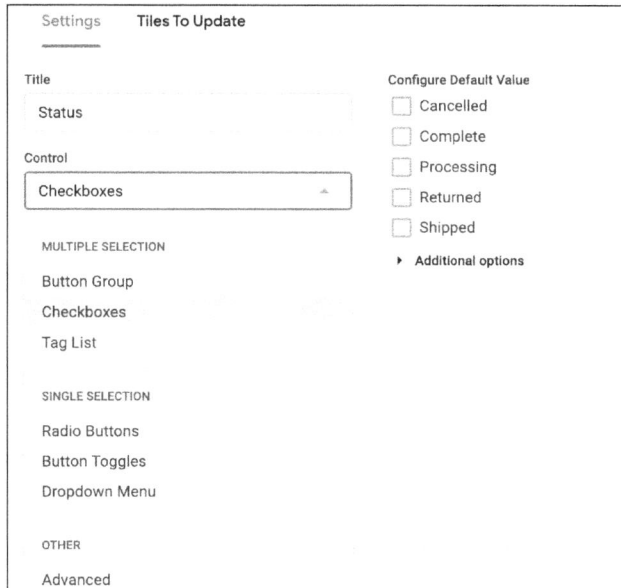

Figure 2.58: Dashboard Filter Setting options

With the **Advanced filter** option, you can select the fields from another model and explore.

Linking filters

Dashboard filters can also be linked so that values for one filter can be narrowed by selecting the value of the linked filter. For example, we can have **State** and **City** as two separate filters. These two filters can be linked with **select filters to update when this filter changes** option on the State filter and selecting the other filter—City:

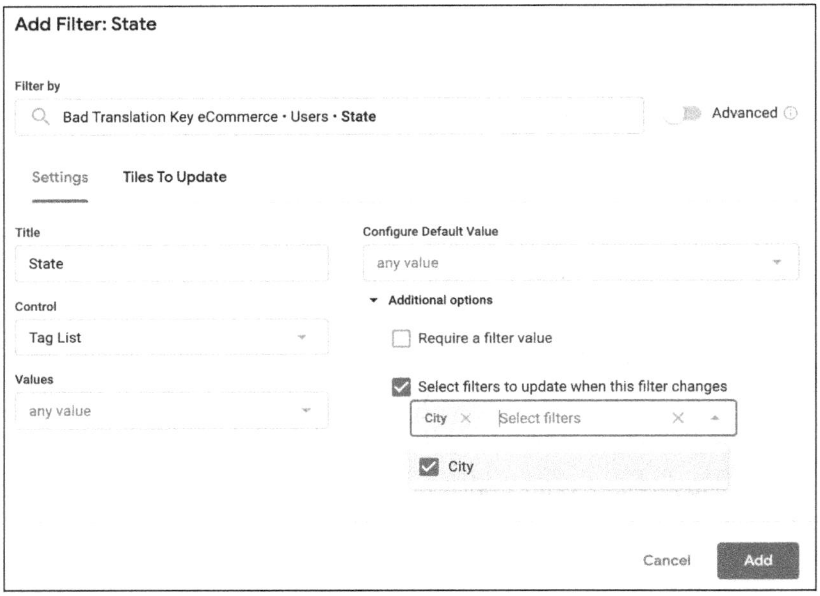

Figure 2.59: Linking filters

On the dashboard, when we select a state, the cities from the selected state will only be displayed. Notice that there is a link symbol on top of the **City** filter:

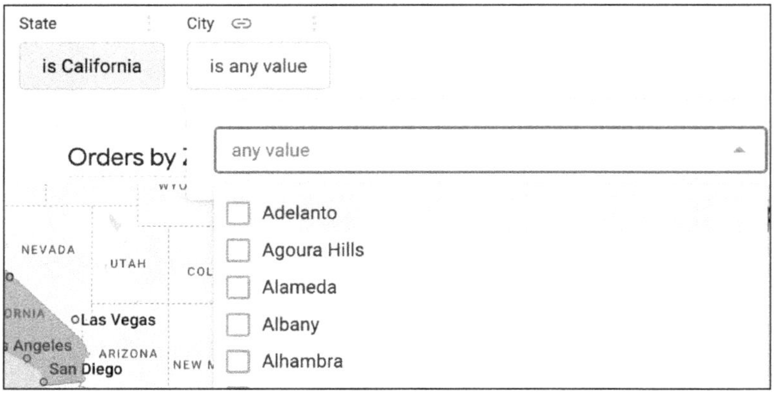

Figure 2.60: Sample Linked Filters

Cross-filtering

If all the tiles on the dashboard are from a single explore, the option—**Cross-filtering** can be enabled. With this, if you click on a data point on one tile, it will automatically apply the filter to the other tiles on the same dashboard:

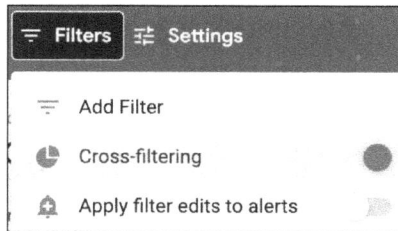

Figure 2.61: *Cross-filtering option*

Dashboards have many formatting options including:

- Tiles can also be resized or moved
- Filters can be shown on top or side
- Filters can be hidden or shown

Visualization best practices

While many options are available in Looker for visualizations, you should choose the visualizations that can:

- Effectively present the data
- Achieve your analytical goals
- Consider audience perspectives

Data can be of different types:

- **Categorical**: Data constraints groups of similar patterns and sets
- **Ordinal**: Classifies data while introducing an order or ranking
- **Continuous**: Data that occurs over a long period of time

For each of these types, you can choose the appropriate visualization type. The following table shows the best appropriate visualization depending on the type of data:

Chart	Type of data
Bar	Categorical data with long Category titles
Column	Categorical data and few categories to compare
Scatterplot	Highlighting correlation between two variables

Chart	Type of data
Line	Continuous data over time
Area	Shifts in quantities over time
Pie	Proportional values
Donut Multiples	Proportional values with multiple components
Funnel	Sequential stages
Timeline	Progression of time
Waterfall	Sequential positive and negative values
Single Value	Isolated piece of data
Single Record	Limited data pieces
Word Cloud	Show data frequency
Google Maps	Geographic data with heatmaps
Map	Interactive geographic data
Static Maps (Regions)	Regional data
Static Maps (Points)	Geographic point-specific data
Boxplot	Data distribution through statistical summary

Table 2.1: Appropriate visualization for type of data

Conclusion

We learned about the components of Looker the creator users can use to create content including Explore interface, different types of visualizations and customization options for those available out of the box with examples. After this chapter, you should be able to create dashboards using basic visualizations. We also learned about the Custom Dimensions, measures and Table Calculations how we can use those features to create on the fly metrics that are not readily available in the explore. Other types of visualizations can also be explored in the same interface. We will learn about additional visualizations that can be imported into Looker in the coming chapter. Try to follow best practices to present the visualizations in an effective manner.

In the next chapter, we will learn the LookML, a modeling language to create the explores where we can write the business logic for dimensions and measures used for creating dashboards.

CHAPTER 3
LookML Development

Introduction

In the previous chapters, we learned how to view and organize Looker content, and create Looker reports and dashboards using Explores. In this chapter, we will learn how to create those Explores using a lightweight modeling language called LookML. LookML tells Looker how the database and its tables are structured and what additional logic is needed so it can prepare SQL queries, allowing everyone in the organization to create reports and dashboards without needing to understand the SQL.

Structure

In this chapter, we will be talking about the following topics:

- LookML files
- Looker integrated development environment
- Development mode versus production mode
- Creating a project
- Git and version control
- LookML code
- Caching

- Derived tables
- Persistent derived table
- LookML dashboards
- Moving dashboards outside of LookML dashboards folder

Objectives

In this chapter, we will explore LookML terminology and concepts and learn how to write LookML code in order to define things like dimensions, measures, and explores. We will cover how LookML generates SQL code, how LookML code is organized, and how to create derived tables. Additionally, we will discuss how to persist derived tables, their role in advanced SQL functions, and how they can enhance performance. We will also explore LookML dashboards, learn how to create them, and how to filter them at different levels.

LookML files

LookML code is written in different files. The files have a hierarchy and are organized as shown in the following figure:

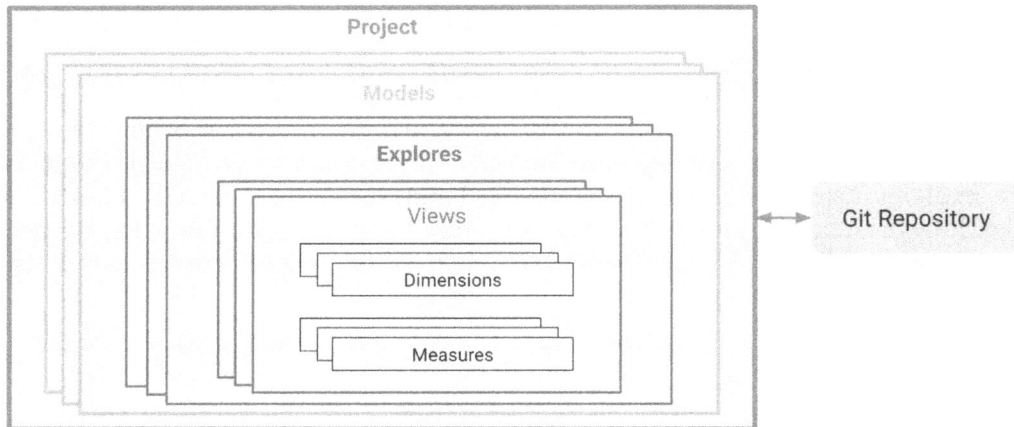

Figure 3.1: LookML file hierarchy

A **Project** is the highest level of container and hosts all LookML files. Each project can be configured to host the files on a git repository. Generally, a project is 1:1 to a connection. A project might also contain a few other files such as manifest file, LookML dashboard, explore file, data files, document files, etc. Projects can have one or more model files.

A **Model** is a set of Explores. Each **Explore** is a set of pre-joined views. Explores group tables by subject area or business need. For example, there might be one explore for marketing and another for sales.

A **View** in LookML corresponds to a database table or view. Each view defines dimensions and measures, which correspond to columns in the database. We learned about dimensions and measures in the previous chapters.

A **Dimension** is an attribute, and **Measure** is an aggregate/calculation like total sales, number of users, etc.

Looker integrated development environment

In the previous chapters, we learned about the Explore menu item in the main interface. In this chapter, we will learn about the **Develop** menu, where all LookML development happens. Looker facilitates development through its own **integrated development environment** (**IDE**), which can be accessed using this menu item (Develop) and selecting the desired project. For example: **lookml_demo** in the following *Figure 3.2* click on **Develop**:

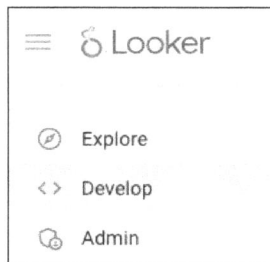

Figure 3.2: *Develop Menu navigation*

Select the Project, as shown in the following figure:

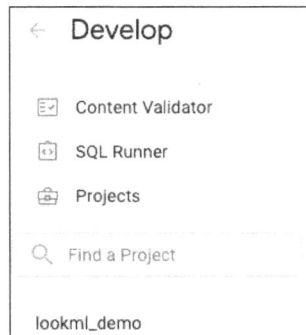

Figure 3.3: *Develop menu options*

Once the project is selected, you can see the navigational menu items on the left with options for File Browser, Object Browser, and Find and Replace icons. The central part shows the code from the file that was selected. In this case, the content of **lookml_demo**. Model files are shown in *Figure 3.4*.

On the right side, you can see **quick help**, which shows the syntax, which provides assistance when writing or editing the code:

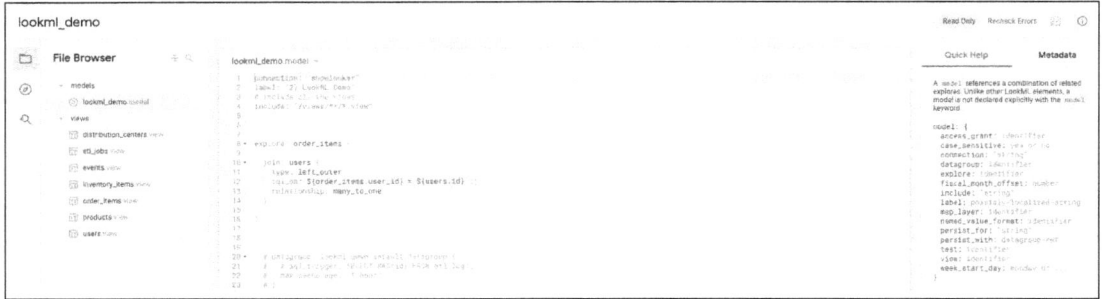

Figure 3.4: File Browser

Development mode versus production mode

Looker has two states: **production mode** and **development mode**. Production mode displays the instance's production version, in which the project files are in read-only mode. Explore users creating dashboards and looks, and also the viewers will use this mode.

Development mode is for making changes in LookML code and previewing them without affecting the other user's content. Only after the LookML developer pushes the changes to production mode, will other users see those changes.

To switch to development mode, turn on the toggle at the bottom of the navigation bar. A blue bar will appear at the top, indicating that you are in development mode. Development mode toggle is shown in *Figure 3.5:*

Figure 3.5: Development mode

To exit the development mode, turn the toggle off or click on the exit development mode option on the blue bar, as shown in the following figure:

Figure 3.6: Exit development mode

Creating a project

A project in Looker is a collection of LookML files that includes the logic of how the tables in the database are related to each other, and how the Explore objects (views, dimensions, measures, etc.) are defined. Looker generates the SQL based on the logic defined in these files. Projects can have different files that can be organized into folders, as we saw in *Figure 3.1*.

The following are the steps to create a project:

1. Toggle on the development mode.

2. Navigate to the **Develop** section and select a project.

3. On the Projects page, select a new LookML Project. A new page opens where you can enter the project name and configure project options:

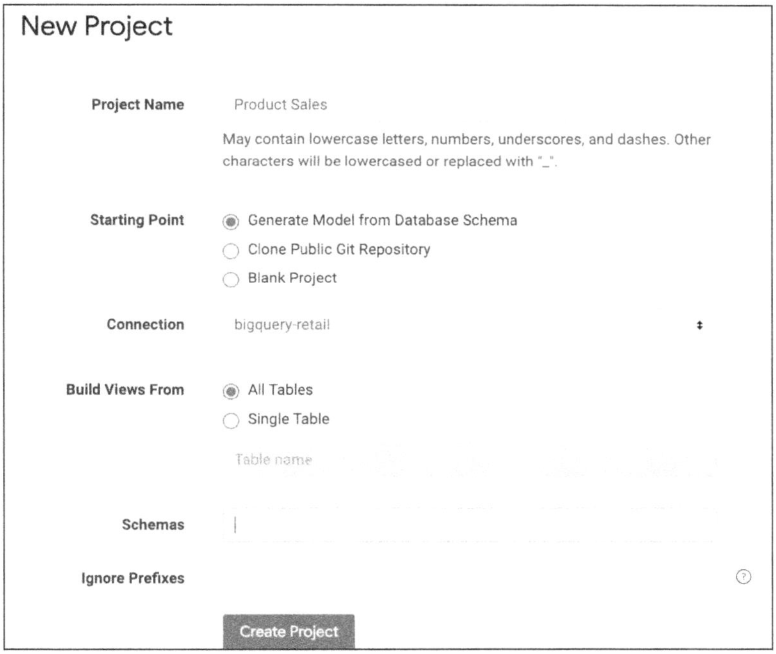

Figure 3.7: *New Project creation*

4. There are three configuration options for a project:

   - **Generate Model from Database Schema**: If there is a database from which you want to generate a model, select this option. Looker will automatically generate model and view files based on the tables in the database.

   - **Clone Public Git Repository**: Looker will copy the files from a public Git repository into your new project.

   - **Blank project**: No files will be created with this option.

5. For this section, we can start with option three and build all the files manually to understand the process better:

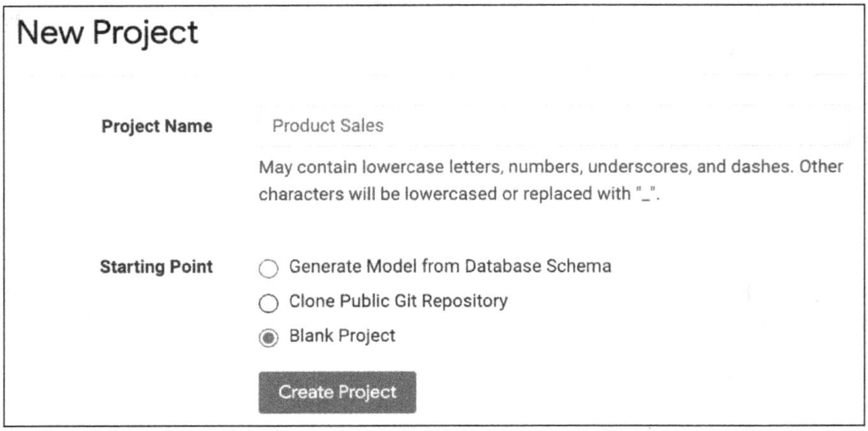

Figure 3.8: Blank Project creation

6. A new project will be created once you click on the **Create Project**.

7. Once a project is created, it needs to be configured on the model page. Open the main menu and select **Develop | Projects**. This will open a page of all projects and their allowed connections.

8. Configure the project and select the database connection that you want to your project to be able to access. If your connection does not yet exist, you can create connections through the **Admin** section:

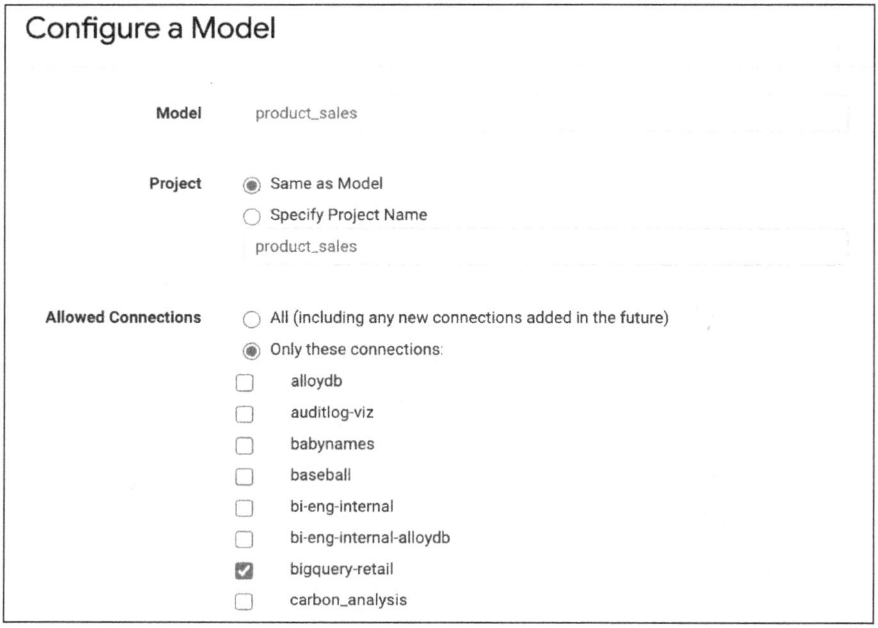

Figure 3.9: Configuring a Project

Git and version control

Looker uses Git as a version control system to track changes to the files and manage file versions. Each Looker project has a **Git Repository** when a user turns the development mode on and makes changes to the files, the changes will be applied to the user's own Git branch.

There are multiple Git providers in the market (GitHub, GitLab, and Bitbucket) that can be configured with Looker. We will use **GitHub** as an example here. However, configuration steps using other providers follow similar steps.

To configure the Git for a project, refer to the following steps:

1. Click on the **Configure Git** button on the right-hand side:

Figure 3.10: *Configure Git button*

2. A new page opens where you can enter the URL for Git repository.

3. To get the Git URL, navigate to the git repository on github. Under code section, select SSH option.

   Note: **HTTPS can also be used to set up the git connection. This will require all users to log into a git account in order to make changes to the project. The following steps assume we are using the SSH method.**

4. Copy the URL. For example: **git@github.com:shivaneeli/product_dales.git**

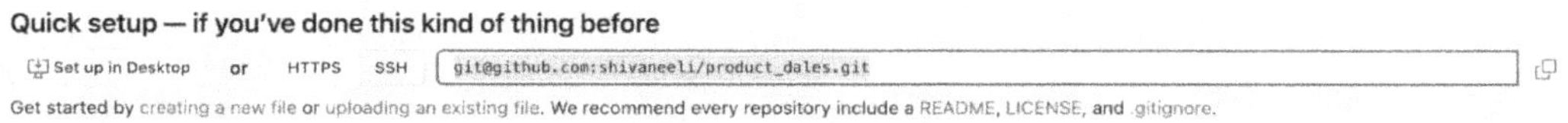

Figure 3.11: *GitHub URL*

5. Enter the URL in the **Repository URL** section on Looker page you opened in step 1 and click on **Configure Git**:

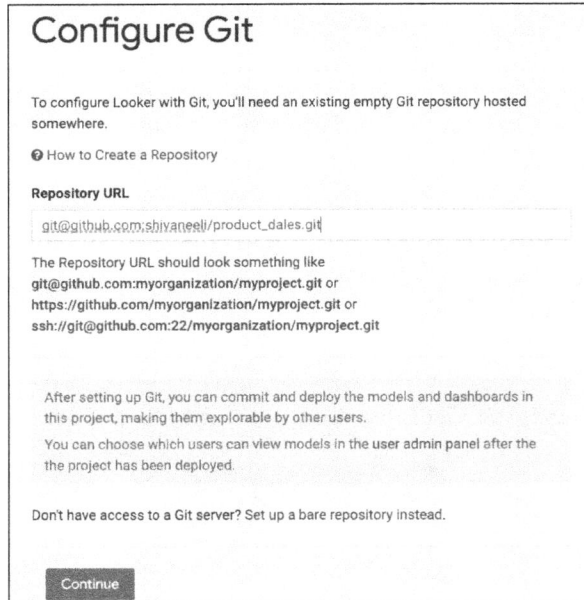

Figure 3.12: Configuring Git

6. Looker will generate an SSH deploy key for you, as shown in *Figure 3.13*. Copy the deploy key from the window and navigate back to Git.

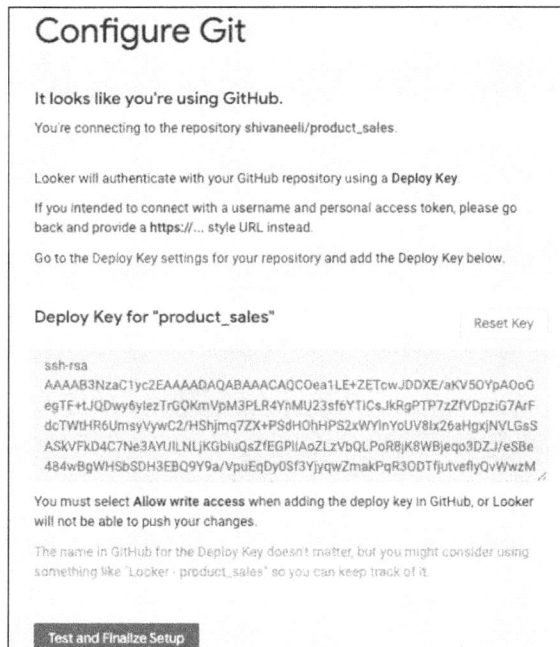

Figure 3.13: Deploy Key

7. In the settings page of the repository, select **Deploy Key**. If you do not see **Settings** or **Deploy Key** as an option, you may need to contact your Git admin to acquire the correct permissions to add a deploy key.

8. Add the Deploy Key you copied in *step 5* and give it a name. Select **Allow write access** and click **Add Key**:

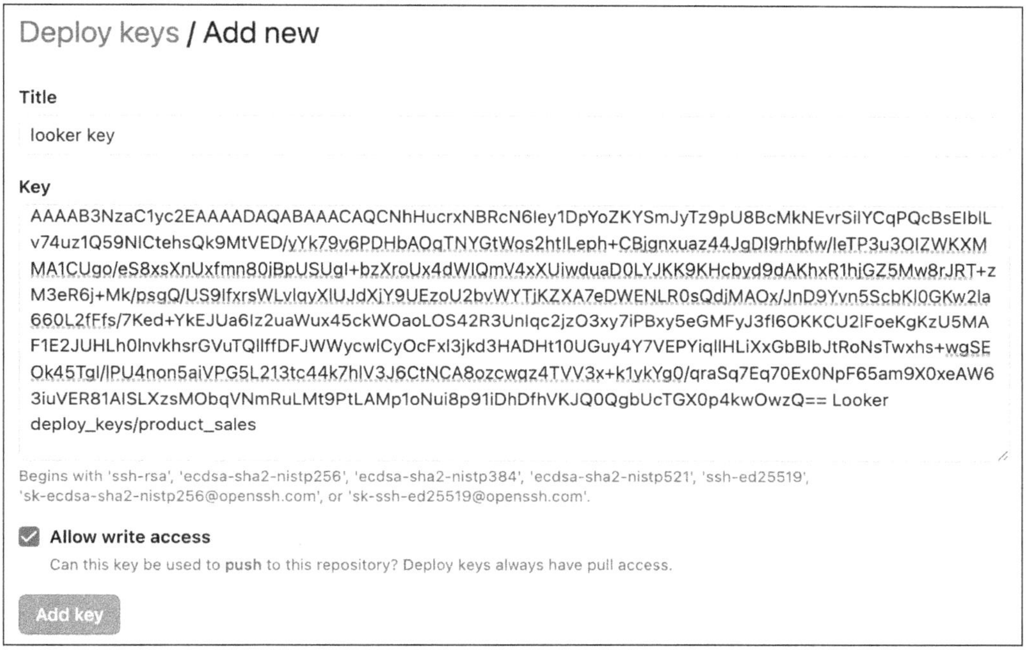

Deploy keys / Add new

Title

looker key

Key

AAAAB3NzaC1yc2EAAAADAQABAAACAQCNhHucrxNBRcN6ley1DpYoZKYSmJyTz9pU8BcMkNEvrSilYCqPQcBsElblL
v74uz1Q59NlCtehsQk9MtVED/yYk79v6PDHbAOqTNYGtWos2htlLeph+CBjgnxuaz44JgDl9rhbfw/leTP3u3OIZWKXM
MA1CUgo/eS8xsXnUxfmn80jBpUSUgl+bzXroUx4dWIQmV4xXUiwduaD0LYJKK9KHcbyd9dAKhxR1hjGZ5Mw8rJRT+z
M3eR6j+Mk/psgQ/US9IfxrsWLvlqyXlUJdXjY9UEzoU2bvWYTjKZXA7eDWENLR0sQdjMAOx/JnD9Yvn5ScbKl0GKw2la
660L2fFfs/7Ked+YkEJUa6Iz2uaWux45ckWOaoLOS42R3Unlqc2jzO3xy7iPBxy5eGMFyJ3fl6OKKCU2lFoeKgKzU5MA
F1E2JUHLh0InvkhsrGVuTQllffDFJWWycwlCyOcFxl3jkd3HADHt10UGuy4Y7VEPYiqllHLiXxGbBIbJtRoNsTwxhs+wgSE
Qk45Tgl/IPU4non5aiVPG5L213tc44k7hlV3J6CtNCA8ozcwqz4TVV3x+k1ykYg0/qraSq7Eq70Ex0NpF65am9X0xeAW6
3iuVER81AISLXzsMObqVNmRuLMt9PtLAMp1oNui8p91iDhDfhVKJQ0QgbUcTGX0p4kwOwzQ== Looker
deploy_keys/product_sales

Begins with 'ssh-rsa', 'ecdsa-sha2-nistp256', 'ecdsa-sha2-nistp384', 'ecdsa-sha2-nistp521', 'ssh-ed25519',
'sk-ecdsa-sha2-nistp256@openssh.com', or 'sk-ssh-ed25519@openssh.com'.

☑ **Allow write access**
   Can this key be used to **push** to this repository? Deploy keys always have pull access.

Add key

Figure 3.14: Adding Looker Key to GitHub

9. Return back to the Looker setup page where you copied the deploy key as shown in *Figure 3.13* and click on **Test and Finalize set up**.

Now, the Looker project is configured with the git provider GitHub and all the branch management deployment actions can be performed within Looker IDE.

Project Configuration has other git integration options, such as pull requests, advanced deploy mode, and webhooks, is configurable.

LookML code

Now that the project is set up and configured with Git, we can begin creating LookML code.

1. To auto-generate the LookML code for your database tables, click on the + sign next to the file browser and select **Create View** from **Table** option, as shown in *Figure 3.15* (if this has not already been done):

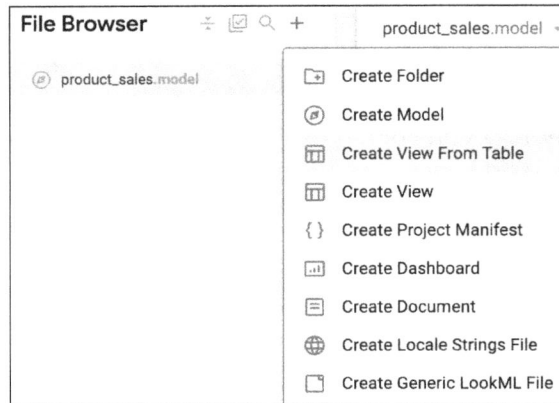

Figure 3.15: Creating View from Table

2. Select the list of tables you would like to generate view files for. In our example, we are selecting the tables from a sample e-commerce database in BigQuery:

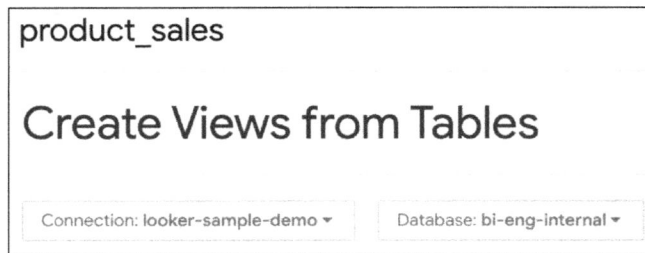

Figure 3.16: Selecting the Connection and DB/Schema

From the selected database, the tables will be displayed as shown in the following figure:

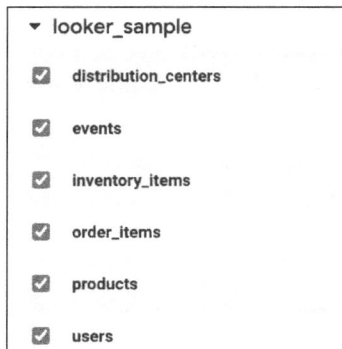

Figure 3.17: Selecting the Views

3. Click on **Create Views**. The selected views will be added to the **Project**.

Each table creates a view file under the views folder:

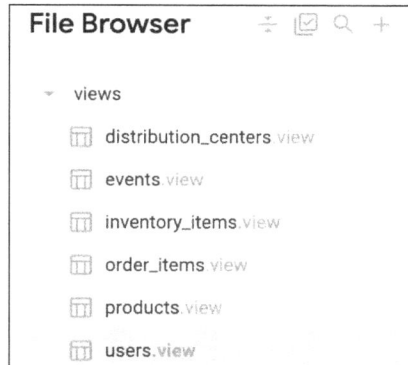

File Browser　　÷　▣　Q　+

▾　views

🔳　distribution_centers.view

🔳　events.view

🔳　inventory_items.view

🔳　order_items.view

🔳　products.view

🔳　users.view

Figure 3.18: Imported Views

Before going to create the code, let us define some key LookML terms and learn about their use.

LookML uses different parameters to define the objects in the different files we learned previously: model files, view files, explore files, and manifest files. While the Looker documentation and IDE quick help provide the list of available parameters in each file, we will learn a few basic ones here to understand the code:

- **Model**: LookML model references a combination of related explores and dashboards. The model object is not explicitly declared with the model keyword. However a file is created with the **.model** extension in the Looker IDE. The model name is taken from the file name. For example: **product_sales.model** file means the model name is **product_sales**. Model names must be unique across the instance. Model names cannot be repeated even in different projects.

  At a minimum, each model file has a connection parameter that shows the database connection and one or more explore parameters.

- **Explore**: An explore is a starting point for a query in Looker. Explores reference views and shows the relationship between views using joins. Explores are declared with the parameter explore and the explore name, and the definition for explore is within curly brackets, beginning parentheses { and ending parentheses } :

```
explore: explore_name {}
```

The following code shows a sample explore code:

```
explore: order_items {
  join: orders {
    relationship: many_to_one
    sql_on: ${orders.id} = ${order_items.order_id} ;;
  }
```

```
join: users {
  relationship: many_to_one
  sql_on: ${users.id} = ${orders.user_id} ;;
}
}
```

- o The name of the Explore is **order_items**, which references the view file **order_items**. Whatever view is used as the Explore name is considered the base view and will be included in every query Looker sends to the database when users interact with this explore.

- o The Orders table is joined on **orders.id = order_items.order_id**, and the relationship is many to one, i.e., there can be many order items for each order.

- o The User's table is joined on **users.id = order_items.order_id**, and the relationship is many to one, i.e., there can be many orders for each user.

Each Explore defines the relationship between the views, and what views are exposed to end users. Views, defined by themselves, and without being added to an explore, are not available to users.

- **Views**: We also generated the view files from tables in the database. A view in LookML corresponds to a table in the database. Each view file has field definitions, which typically correspond to a column in the underlying table or a calculation. Views are defined with the parameter view, and the file name also contains the extension **.view**. However, a single **.view** file can have multiple view definitions.

A view name generally matches the table name in the database. In case you want to use a different name for the view, **sql_table_name** parameter can be used to reference the database table name.

For example:

```
view: users {
  sql_table_name: `bi-eng-internal.looker_sample.users`
    ;;
```

- **Fields**: There are different types of fields that are part of views:

  - o **Dimensions** usually represent a column in a table or a value based on some sort of column manipulation.

    There can be different types of dimensions:

    - ▪ **string**: This is used for text dimensions like name, product name, category etc.

    - ▪ **number**: This is used for numeric dimensions like age, distance etc.

- - **yesno**: This is a Boolean dimension type. It becomes yes or no based on the condition.

  - **tier:** This is used to define the tiers/buckets based on case statements. for example: Age tier can be defined with **tiertype** dimension.

  o **Dimension Groups** are only used with time-based data, and enable you to create different levels of granularity, such as day, week, month, year, etc.

  o **Measures** are fields with aggregate functions like count, sum, average in SQL, and operations performed on multiple rows.

  o **Filters** create a filter-only field that users can use to provide input based on a dimension to a templated filter or a conditional join.

  o **Parameters** create a filter-only field users can use to provide input created by developers while using the explore.

Substitution operator

Looker uses **${}** syntax in order to denote a variable. There are a few reserved words that are already-defined global variables. The substitute operator **${TABLE}**, for example, will be replaced by the table mentioned in the **sql_table_name** in the file. Other fields in the same file can be referenced with substitute operator **${<fieldname>}**. For example, if there is a dimension named **first_name**, it can be referenced in another field as **${first_name)**. You can also reference fields in another view file if they are joined together in an explore. If the variable is located in another view file, it can be referenced as **${view_name.field_name}**. If it references an object in another view, the two views *must* always be joined at the explore level, otherwise Looker will throw an error during validation.

Let us take a look at the sample code that was generated by looker for a table called users:

```
view: users {
  sql_table_name: `bi-reporting.looker_sample.users`
    ;;

  dimension: id {
    primary_key: yes
    type: number
    sql: ${TABLE}.id ;;
  }

  dimension: first_name {
    type: string
    sql: ${TABLE}.first_name ;;
  }

  dimension_group: created {
    type: time
    timeframes: [
      raw,
```

```
      time,
      date,
      week,
      month,
      quarter,
      year
    ]
    sql: ${TABLE}.created_at ;;
  }
..
  measure: count {
    type: count
    drill_fields: [id, last_name, first_name, order_items.count, events.
count]
  }
}
```

In the preceding code, the view name is users. It references the table in the database - **bi-reporting.looker_sample.users (using sql_table_name)**. It has several columns such as ID of type number, **first_name** of type string, dimension group created and measure **namedcount**.

The previous code was generated by Looker automatically, but it can be changed at any time to edit existing fields or create any additional fields:

- **Example one**: Assume we have two columns called **first_name** and **last_name**. We need a new field that has both names in a single column. Looker allows functions to be part of the SQL definition, in this case, we can use CONCAT syntax. The code for doing it will be:

  ```
  dimension: full_name {
    type: string
    sql: ${first_name}||' '||${last_name} ;;
  }
  ```

  We referenced both fields and concatenated them using the | | symbol in SQL.

- **Example two**: Say, we can create a new column named Region that groups countries into two groups called domestic and international. In order to achieve this, we can use a **CASE WHEN** statement:

  ```
  dimension: region {
    type: string
    sql: CASE WHEN ${country} = 'United States' THEN 'Domestic' ELSE
  'International' END ;;
    }
  ```

Measures are created by defining an aggregate function, and the column to aggregate on. For example, to create a measure that shows the total number of units sold based on the **item_id**:

```
measure: total_units_sold {
    type: sum
    sql: ${item_id} ;;
}
```

Measures using other measures: Measures can also used in other measures to create complex measures, but **only** for simple arithmetic. For example, we can calculate the percentage of category sales by dividing category sales and total sales. It is **not** possible to create another measure that aggregates measure:

```
measure: percentage_product_category_sales {
    type: number
    sql: ${product_category_sales}/ ${total_sales} ;;
}
```

Other parameters

There are parameters that we can use to organize the fields in the explore so that it is easier to find and understand:

- **label**: Changes the field name in the field picker.

- **description**: Adds additional information about the field, which become visible to Explore users when hovering over the field.

- **group_label**: Sorts fields into custom groups within an Explore.

- **Group_item_label**: Customizes how the individual fields are shown in the Explore field explore when they are grouped together. Often used in tandem with **group_ label**.

- **view_label**: Changes the name of the view is listed under in the Explore field picker.

- **hidden**: Hides a field from the user interface while still allowing it to be available for reference in other fields or modeling.

Value formatting

The **value_format_name** parameter is used to format the values of fields. Values can be formatted into different currencies, like USD or Euros by assigning **value_format_name** to **usd** or **euro**, respectively decimals and percentages are the standard formats available by assigning it as decimal or percent. The exact precision of the decimal or percent can be defined by adding "_#", such as **decimal_0** or **percent_3** to denote how many decimal places it should round to (if applicable). The **value_format** parameter can be used instead if you want to use the Excel style formatting.

Note: **Formatting does not affect calculations and are solely used to format values for end users.**

Both of the following examples will convert a raw integer value into a USD-format (e.g. the value 10.34 will be formatted as $10.34):

```
dimension: field_name {
   value_format_name: usd
 }
dimension: field_name {
   value_format:"$#.00;($#.00)"
 }
```

drill_fields

drill_fields parameter allows you to configure the fields to display, when users drill down on a value. For example, in the **users.view** file you can see the count field has a **drill_field**:

```
measure: count {
    type: count
    drill_fields: [id, last_name, first_name]
}
```

Clicking on count will display the fields mentioned in the **drill_fields** parameter in a table pop-up.

Link

The link parameter turn values of the table into a clickable link. This link lets you navigate to ta URL directly from the visualization or table:

```
    link: {
label: "Desired label name"
url: "string"
icon_url: "string"
}
```

For example, if you are showing an account number from Salesforce or other systems, you can navigate to that application using link parameter from Looker.

Explore

Explores are the fundamental way in which end users interact with the data. How an explore is defined determines what users can query from the database.

To create an Explore, perform the following steps:

1. Go to **Develop**, select the **product_sales** project we created previously, and ensure you are in development mode.

2. In the file browser, you will see the file **product_sales.model**. If not, you can create the file by selecting the create model option.

3. Open the **product_sales.model** files and enter the connection name, include all view files and create an Explore by entering **explore: users{}**. This is the simplest **Explore** you can create using a single table.

connection: "bigquery-retail"

include: "/views/*.view.lkml"

include all views in the **views/** folder in this project

explore: users{}

4. Save the file and click on validate LookML. If there are no errors found, you can see the message: No LookML errors found:

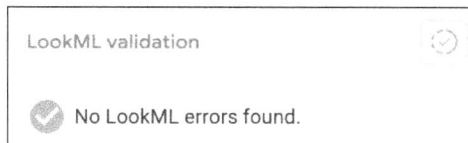

Figure 3.19: *LookML Validation*

5. To test the Explore, you can go to the top section where it shows the filename **product_sales.model** and select the drop-down **Explore Users**:

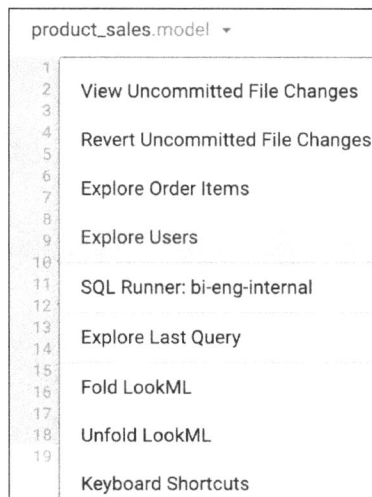

Figure 3.20: *Viewing the Explore*

6. A new user **Explore** window opens. Here, you can follow the steps for creating a look in the last chapter and test whether you can see the results:

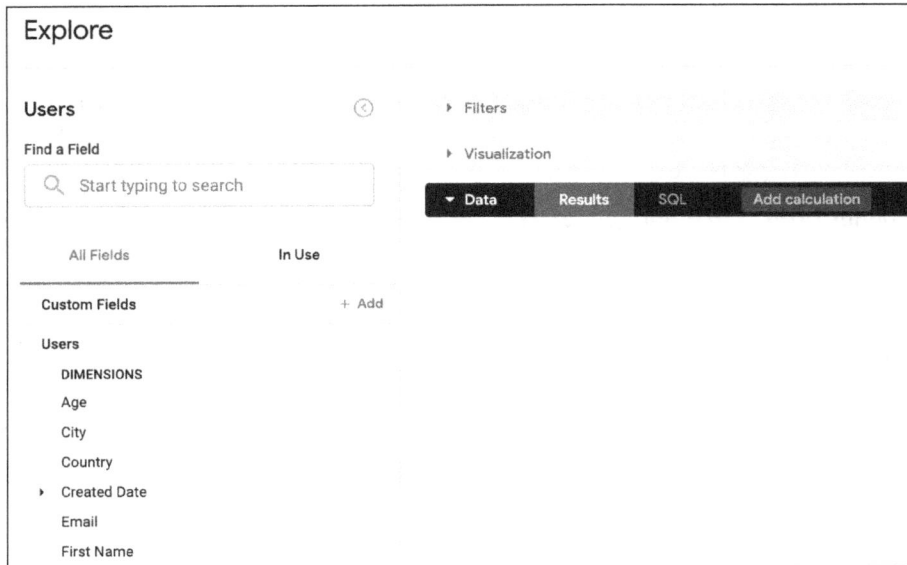

Figure 3.21: Explore interface

7. Optionally, you can also create another explore with joins like the one shown as follows and test similar to the preceding Explore:

```
explore: order_items {
  join: users {
    relationship: many_to_one
    sql_on: ${users.id} = ${order_items.user_id} ;;
  }
}
```

8. At this step, you can still see the blue bar on top. That means you are still in development mode. All the changes you made in LookML are visible only to you. This is because the changes are made only in your branch. So, to make these changes visible to others, you have to check-in these changes to the main branch which will appear in the production copy. Users will be able to use the explores to build dashboards or looks.

   a. Click on **Commit changes & Push**:

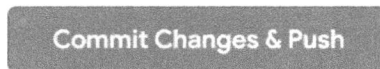

Figure 3.22: Commit Changes button

   b. A new window pops up. Here, you can enter a commit message and click on commit.

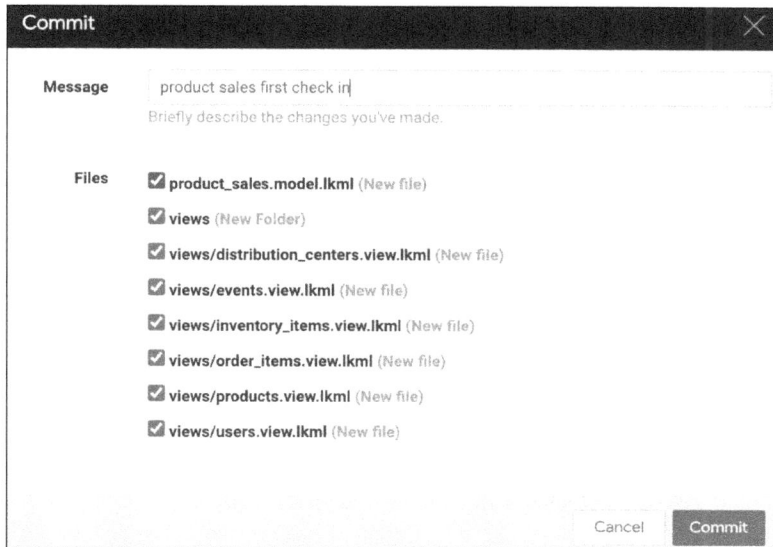

Figure 3.23: *Commit the changes in files*

c. Click on **Deploy to Production**:

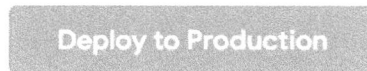

Figure 3.24: *Deploying to Production*

b. After deploying to production, your local changes are in sync with the production branch, and you will see a grayed-out button showing **Up to Date**:

Figure 3.25: *Production changes in local*

Explore files: In the preceding example, we created the explores with in a model file. However, you can also create an explore file just to keep the explore code for better organization of code. To do this, you need to create the generic file and name the file with an extension `.explore`.

To create a separate explore file:

1. Go to **Develop**, select the `product_sales` project we created previously, and ensure you are in development mode.

2. In the file browser, click the + sign. A menu opens. Select **Create Generic LookML File** as shown in *Figure 3.26*:

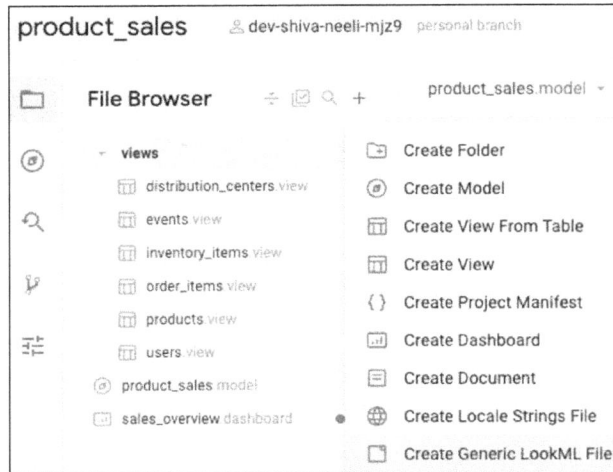

Figure 3.26: Generic LookML File option

3. Enter the file name as **order_items.explore** as shown in *Figure 3.27*. Looker automatically adds **.lkml** to this file:

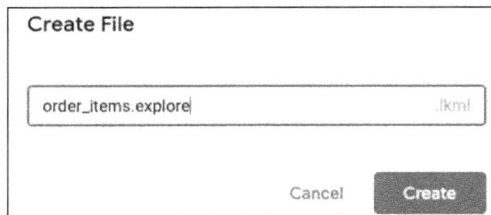

Figure 3.27: Naming an explore file

4. For better organization and easy navigation, create a folder named **explores** and drag the **order_items.explore** file into it as shown in *Figure 3.28*:

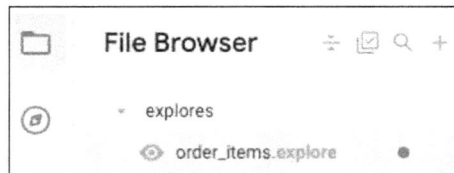

Figure 3.28: Explores folder

5. Create the explore code (or copy and paste the code from **product_sales.model**) into the **order_items.explore** file. Use the same code as in *step 11* in the **Explore** section above.

6. Add the include statements needed for the view files referenced in the Explore. For example, here we need the following two views:

```
include: "/views/order_items.view.lkml"
include: "/views/users.view.lkml"
```

7. Save the file by clicking the blue save button.

8. In the **product_sales.model** file, add the include statement to include the .**explore** file, and save:

```
include: "/explores/order_items.explore.lkml"
```

Filters

In Looker, there are many ways to filter the data. However, each filter works differently; Developers will need to know what kind of filter to use and when to use it for a particular use case. In the preceding chapters, we learned about filters that can be added as part of a look or dashboard UI. Here, we will learn about LookML filter parameters that allow you to filter the data at different object granularities, such as explores, measures, etc.:

- **sql_always_where**: If you want to add filter(s) to an explore that explore and dashboard users cannot change, use **sql_always_where**. Multiple filters can also be added using AND/OR condition. This is used on dimension fields:

```
explore: explore_name {
  sql_always_where: ${created_date} >= '2017-01-01';;
}
```

The **sql_always_where** filter, defined at the Explore level, applies a permanent condition to all queries within that Explore. Only one **sql_always_where** condition is allowed per Explore. This is often used to exclude test data, restrict data access, or optimize query performance.

- **sql_always_having**: This field is similar to **sql_always_where**, but this filter is used with measures instead of dimensions.

- **always_filter**: If you want a filter that is required for the explore, but allows users to select the value, use **always_filter**. A default value can be defined in the filter that acts as the initial filter value:

```
explore: explore_name {
  always_filter: {
    filters: [field_name: "filter expression", field_name: "filter
expression", ...]
  }
}
```

- **conditionally_filter**: Developers define a filter that acts similarly to an **always_filter**, meaning a filter that, by default, is applied whenever a user enters the explore. In the unless field, developers can add fields that, if selected as a filter, will allow users to remove the first initial filter. In both cases, users can change the value of the filter:

```
explore: explore_name {
  conditionally_filter: {
    filters: [field_name: "filter expression", field_name: "filter
expression", ...]
    unless: [field_name, field_name, ...]
  }
}
```

This filter is commonly used to prevent users from accidentally running queries without any filters on large tables, which could potentially cause performance and cost overrun issues.

The scope of these filters: `sql_always_where`, `sql_always_having`, `always_filter`, `conditionally_filter` is the explore itself. They affect all queries using that specific explore but do not extend to other explores, regardless of whether they belong to the same model.

- **Filter parameter**: You can create a filter-only field within a view file, enabling users to utilize it as a filter during exploration and visualization creation. The syntax incorporates optional parameters like `'suggest_explore'` and `'suggest_dimension'`, which draw values from separate fields:

```
View: view_name {
    Filter: filter_name { }
}
```

Filter fields affect only the specific query they are used in. Other queries within the same Explore are not impacted unless they also include that filter field.

- **Filtered measures**: In the preceding examples, we saw filter parameters that were used to automatically add filters on Explores. The filters parameter can also be used in measures to create filtered measures:

```
view: view_name {
  measure: field_name {
    filters: [dimension_name: "filter expression", dimension_name:
"filter expression", ... ]
  }
}
```

This is equivalent to applying a filter using a case statement in a dimension and creating a measure on the dimension.

For example, if there is a regular measure, the total number of users, and you want to create a measure that counts the total number of users in the state of California, you can create the filtered measure by simply including a filter in the definition:

```
measure:  california_user_count {
   type: count_distinct
   sql: ${TABLE}.user_id ;;
   filters: [state: "california" ]
}
```

You can also use numeric conditions and ranges in filters. Some examples are shown as follows:

```
measure: total_big_ticket_sales {
  type: sum
  filters: [orders.item_price: ">1000"]
  sql: ${orders.item_price} ;;
}
measure: total_sales_priced_50_to_100 {
  type: sum
  filters: [orders.item_price: ">=50 AND <=100"]
  sql: ${orders.item_price} ;;
}
```

The **filters** parameter within a filtered measure defines the criteria applied *only* to that specific measure's calculation, not to other measures or the overall query.

The following table compares these filters and will be useful to determine when to use what kind of filter:

Feature	sql_always_where	sql_always_having	always_filter	conditionally_filter	Filter Parameter (for fields)	filters Parameter (in measures)
Syntax	sql_always_where: condition	sql_always_having: condition	always_filter: { field: field_name, value: value }	conditionally_filter: { field: field_name, value: value, condition: expression }	filter: field_name	filters: [{field: field_name, value: value},...]
Scope	Explore	Explore	Explore	Explore	Query	Measure
Rules	Applied to the WHERE clause of all queries. Use AND/OR to add multiple conditions.	Applied to the HAVING clause of all queries. Use AND/OR to add multiple conditions.	Default filter, user can modify values but not remove.	Filter applied only when the condition is met.	Applies only to the specific field in the query.	Applies only to the specific measure's calculation.

Usage	Data security, strict data governance, performance.	Filtering aggregated results.	Data consistency, guided analysis, performance.	Dynamic filtering based on conditions (parameters, etc.).	Ad-hoc filtering within a query.	Filtering data within a measure calculation.
Permanence	Permanent (cannot be changed by users).	Permanent (cannot be changed by users).	Semi-permanent (values can be changed by users).	Conditional (depends on the condition).	Temporary (for the current query).	Permanent (for the measure).
User modification	No	No	Yes (values only)	Potentially (if based on user-defined parameters)	Yes (fully modifiable)	No
Visibility	Hidden (unless user views SQL).	Hidden (unless user views SQL).	Visible.	Usually visible.	Visible.	Not directly visible (affects measure calculation).
Applied to	All queries in the Explore.	All queries in the Explore.	All queries in the Explore.	All queries in the Explore (when condition is met).	The specific field in the query.	The specific measure's calculation.
Key features	Row-level security, data access control.	Filtering after aggregation.	Data consistency, performance defaults.	Dynamic filtering, flexible data exploration.	Quick filtering, ad-hoc analysis.	Conditional metrics, specific calculations.
Example	sql_always_where: region = 'US'	sql_always_having: COUNT(*) > 10	always_filter: { field: order_status, value: 'Shipped' }	conditionally_filter: { field: discount_percent, value: 0, condition: ${is_discounted} = 'Yes' }	filter: order_date	filters: [{field: order_status, value: 'Shipped'}, {field: order_date, value: '2023-10-26'}]

Table 3.1: Compared filters

Caching

Looker maintains a cache of the results of the queries in order to reduce database load and improve dashboard performance.

Let us look at how the Looker cache works:

- Whenever a query is run for the first time, Looker checks the cache to see it has run the query before. If it finds no matches for the query, it runs the query against the database, gets the results, and stores it in cache.

- When the query is run again, Looker will check the cache, and if the results are still valid from the query's previous run (as defined by the cache policy), then Looker uses the cached results instead of sending the query to the database again.

- If Looker finds a match but the results are no longer valid, it runs the query against the database, receives the results, and stores them in the cache.

Looker cache results are stored in an encrypted file in the Looker instance. By default, Looker caches query results for 60 minutes. Looker caching policies can be configured to change the retention time.

There are two ways the cache can be configured:

- Using the **persist_for** parameter, which can be set at the model or explore level. Assigning a numerical value and time unit (e.g. 12 hours) will determine how long data will be retained in the cache for:

  ```
  persist_for: "5 hours"
  ```

- Using the **data_groups** parameter, which let you define the caching policies. Data groups allow for more robust policies and are recommended over **persist_for**. Datagroup are defined at the model level and can be assigned to Explores and persistent derived tables (we will explore these in the next section).

  Datagroup requires the following fields:

  ```
  datagroup: datagroup_name {
    max_cache_age: "24 hours"
    sql_trigger: SELECT max(id) FROM my_tablename ;;
    interval_trigger: "12 hours"
    label: "desired label"
    description: "description string"
  }

  explore:explore_name {
    persist_with: datagroup_name
  }
  ```

- **Max_cache_age**: This parameter specifies the maximum time the cached results are valid, similar to **persist_for**. If the data in the cache exceeds the set time, results will be invalidated.

- **sql_trigger**: This field requires a SQL query that returns a single value. Ideally, developers should create a query that returns a new value whenever there is an update to the data. Looker will store the value and rerun the query. If the latest query result is different from the last run result, the **dataroup** goes into a triggered state and will invalidate the cache. The query is run at intervals specified in the **persistent derived tables** (**PDT**) and Datagroup Maintenance Schedule field of the database connection. By default, the query will be run every five minutes.

Typically, this is used to check if there is any new data in the database to guarantee that end users are not served stale data by the cache. Common SQL triggers include querying **max(ID)** or the **max(timestamp)**.

- **interval_trigger**: This is an alternate parameter that can be used instead of **sql_trigger**. It specifies an interval for rebuilding. A **datagroup** cannot have both **sql_trigger** and **interval_trigger** parameters. If both are defined, **interval_trigger** will override the **sql_trigger** value.

- **persist_with**: This parameter is not part of the **datagroup** definition, instead, it is added to explores or models to apply the **datagroup** policy. If the parameter is defined at the model level, all Explores in the model use the same data group. If it is used at the Explore level, the policy is applied only to that explore.

There are a few things to know when creating data groups:

- If different explores need different caching policies, you can create separate datagroups and apply them using the **persist_with** parameter

- When you define both **max_cache_age** and **sql_trigger_value/interval_trigger**, if the **sql_trigger/interval_trigger** is not triggered, query results will be automatically invalidated by the time specified, which will avoid showing the stale results. When used in tandem, developers can maximize cache usage (therefore reducing queries to the database), while minimizing the amount of stale data served by the cache.

- Looker does not perform **timezone** conversion for **sql_trigger**. So, make sure you either include the **timezone** conversion in the query or set the trigger in the database **timezone**.

See the following sample **datagroup** definition for caching. The policy will keep results for 24 hours unless there is new data detected in the database:

```
datagroup: order_items_datagroup {
  sql_trigger: SELECT max(id) FROM order_items ;;
  max_cache_age: "24 hours"
  label: "New ID added"
  description: "Triggered when new ID is added table"
}

    explore: order_items {
        persist_with: order_items_datagroup
    }
```

Cache and datagroup options in explore

In the Explore interface, when a look or dashboard is created, there is an indicator that tells whether the query results are coming from the cache and other result details:

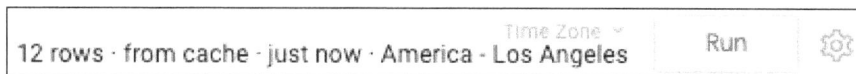

Figure 3.29: Dashboard results details

If you want to refresh results from the database and clear the cache, select **Clear Cache** and **Refresh** option, located in the gear icon found on the top left **Explore** interface:

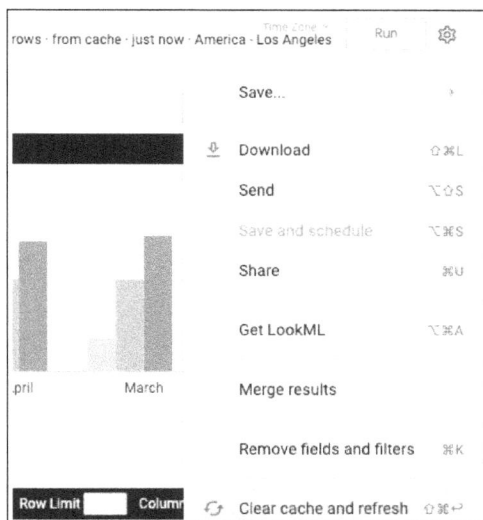

Figure 3.30: Clearing cache and refreshing

Datagroups can be used to schedule the delivery of the dashboard. For this, select the Datagroup Update option in the / Recurrence section of the schedule and select the desired datagroup from the dropdown.

Derived tables

So far, we have used tables that already exist in the database, in LookML using the parameter `sql_table_name`. Sometimes, the database tables may not be sufficient or may not be in the desired form. In such cases, we can create custom SQL queries and and use those queries to build logic in LookML. These custom views are called derived tables.

There are two types of derived tables:

- **Ephemeral derived tables**: These are temporary in nature, compile at run time, and are generated as **common table expressions** (**CTEs**) in Looker-generated SQL.

- **Persistent derived tables**: These tables are created in the underlying database and stored as long as you want. These are similar to materialized views. These help reduce the query time, improve performance, and can reduce costs.

Both types of derived tables can be written in two ways:

- **SQL derived table**: The derived table is defined by SQL. You can write complex joins, unions and analytic functions, etc. using this method. This is the preferred way for most developers who are already familiar with SQL.

  To create this derived table, you can use **sql** parameter inside the derived table parameter, which is used in lieu of **sql_table_name**.

  Sample SQL derived table code:

```
view: customer_order_fact {
  derived_table: {
    sql:
      SELECT
      order_items.user_id  AS user_id,
      COUNT(*) AS count
    FROM order_items
    GROUP BY user_id ;;
  }
}
```

- **Native derived table**: The derived table defined by LookML. This method requires an already built model. It is recommended if the derived table uses a set of fields that is already defined into an Explore. This will reuse the code and can have concise LookML code. Looker can also auto-generate this code in the Explore interface which makes it easy in some use cases.

  To create a native derived table, you can use **explore_source** parameter inside the **derived_table** parameter of a view parameter.

  Sample native-derived table code to create a **customer_order_fact**:

```
view: customer_order_fact {
 derived_table: {
    explore_source: order_items {
      column: user_id {}
      column: count {}
    }
  }
}
```

The LookML code for the derived table is generated using an Explore. The following steps are used to create it:

1. Select the desired **Explore** and select the desired fields and filters. The process is similar to creating a normal look.

2. Click on the gear menu and select **Get LookML** option:

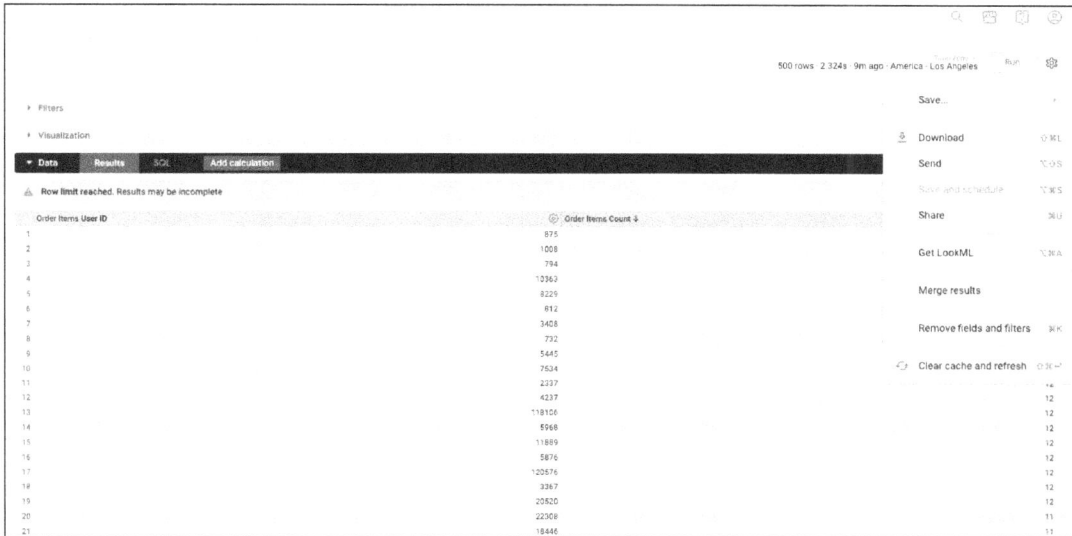

Figure 3.31: Get LookML option

3. Select the third tab in the window, called **Derived Table**. Copy the LookML code from here to the corresponding view file, as shown in the following figure:

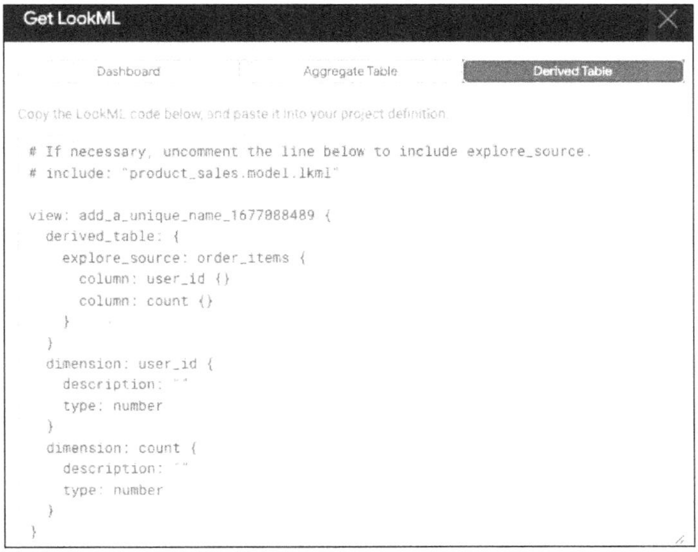

Figure 3.32: LookML code

There are a few additional parameters that we should be aware of when dealing with native-derived tables:

- In the preceding example, the column name is the same as the field name. You can change the column name but reference the underlying explore field using **field** parameter.

- You can also create derived columns in the native SQL using **derived_column** parameter.

- You can also use filters for the derived table.

The following example includes the preceding three parameters:

```
view: customer_order_facts_1_year {
  derived_table: {
    explore_source: order_items {
      column: customer_id {
field:order_items.user_id
}
      column: sales_count {
field:order_items.count
}
      column:total_sales{}
      derived_column:  average_basket_size {
sql: total_sales/ sales_count ;;
}
      filters: [order_items.created_date: "1 year"]
    }
  }
}
```

Persistent derived table

So far, we learned about ephemeral derived tables, where the derived table query is run at runtime to get the results. Every time a user requests data from an ephemeral derived table, Looker must send the derived table's query to the database, as well as the actual query that has the selected fields by the end user. The initial SQL query that defines the derived table can be expensive and take some time to run. In such scenarios, persisting the derived table results, i.e., storing the results in a table, is a better option. If the results persist, they can be reused—removing the need to re-run the derived table query, thus reducing the query run time and database load. Looker has a way to persist the derived table in the database using datagroups.

When creating a database connection, admins have the option to define the scratch/ temporary schema. PDTs are created in the defined scratch schema of the database connection.

There is a list of databases that support looker SQL-based PDTs and LookML based PDTs. Check if your database supports it by visiting the looker documentation/support page.

There are a couple of ways to persist the derived **table:**

- **datagroup_trigger**: This uses data group and applies the datagroup policy to the derived table. We learned about datagroups in the preceding section: **Caching**. Whenever the datagroup is triggered, the derived table will be persisted (or refreshed, if it already exists) into the database. This is the robust and recommended way to **persist.**

  Example: **datagroup_trigger: order_items_datagroup**:

- **sql_trigger_value:** This works similarly to **sql_trigger** in datagroups. The PDT will be rebuilt if the query returns a different value than the last run. This is recommended when derived tables need to be persisted on a very specific interval or time.

  Example: **sql_trigger_value: SELECT current_date ;;**

- **persist_for**: This is the maximum time the PDT should be stored before dropping from the database. Typically, **persist_for** will be used in conjunction with **sql_ trigger_value**

  Example: **persist_for: "12 hours";;**

We can also create indexes, partition keys, cluster keys, sort keys, and incremental PDTs if Looker supports your database dialect, which will help in optimizing the Looker PDT performance.

Derived tables use cases are as follows:

- Restructure the data and build complex logic.
- Nested aggregations or multi-step aggregations, often in the case where developers need to create an aggregation on top of a measure.
- Use window functions to create calculations.
- Union different queries to results. For example: getting similar data from two tables and combining the results.
- Roll up the data at a dimension level. For example, month or product category, etc.
- You can also use PDTs to test different indexes, distributions, and other optimizations and finalize and use the strategy in the database when building the permanent table.

Example PDT code:

```
view: customer_order_facts_1_year {
  derived_table: {
```

```
    explore_source: order_items {
      column: customer_id {
field:order_items.user_id
}
      column: sales_count {
field:order_items.count
}

      column:total_sales{}
      derived_column:  average_basket_size {
sql: total_sales/ sales_count ;;
}
      filters: [order_items.created_date: "1 year"]
datagroup_trigger: order_items_datagroup
 }
  }
}
```

In the above example, **order_items_datagroup** is used to persist the derived table.

LookML dashboards

In the previous chapter, you learned how to create dashboards using the GUI. Those are called **user-defined dashboards**. Looker maintains another type of dashboards called LookML dashboards, which are code representation of the dashboards.

User defined dashboards are not part of the project folder and will not be included in the Git repository. As a result, user-defined dashboards lack version control.

LookML dashboards are version-controlled and can be edited using code. These will be included in the looker project folder and are part of the Git repository. The files work like other project files and can take advantage of the Git features.

LookML dashboards, when first created, are available in a separate folder with the name **LookML Dashboards**, which can then be imported or moved to the regular shared folders.

They can also be extended to create a second dashboard that inherits the first dashboard elements. Some settings can be overridden, and additional elements can be added. Any changes in the original dashboard are inherited by the second one, eliminating the need to make changes in multiple places. We will learn about extensions in the upcoming chapter.

Following are the steps to create a LookML dashboard:

1. Turn on the development mode.

2. In the **Develop** menu, select the project. In the file browser, click on the plus sign and select create dashboard:

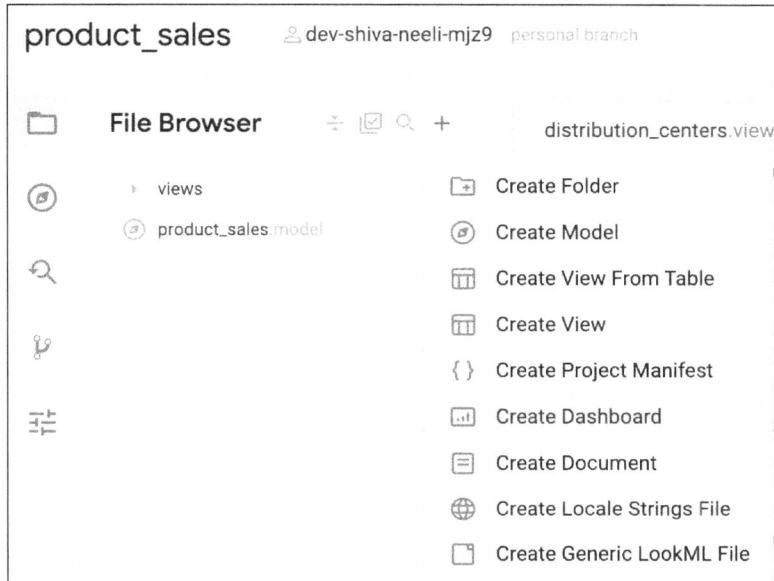

Figure 3.33: Creating a dashboard

3. Enter the dashboard name in the next window. A dashboard file will be created. You can also see the file in the file browser:

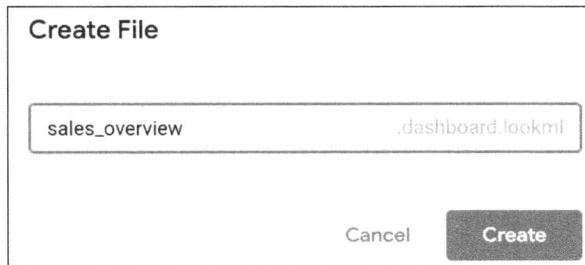

Figure 3.34: Naming the dashboard

4. Here, the code can be added manually, or Looker auto-generated LookML code from looks or dashboard can be added to this file. To add the dashboard code to this file, open a user-defined dashboard in another browser window and click on the three dots menu and select get LookML:

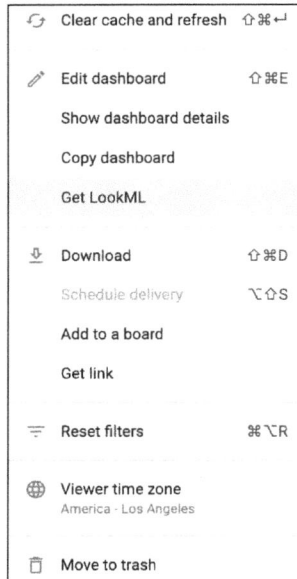

Figure 3.35: *Get dashboard LookML option*

5. In the new window, click on **Copy to Clipboard**:

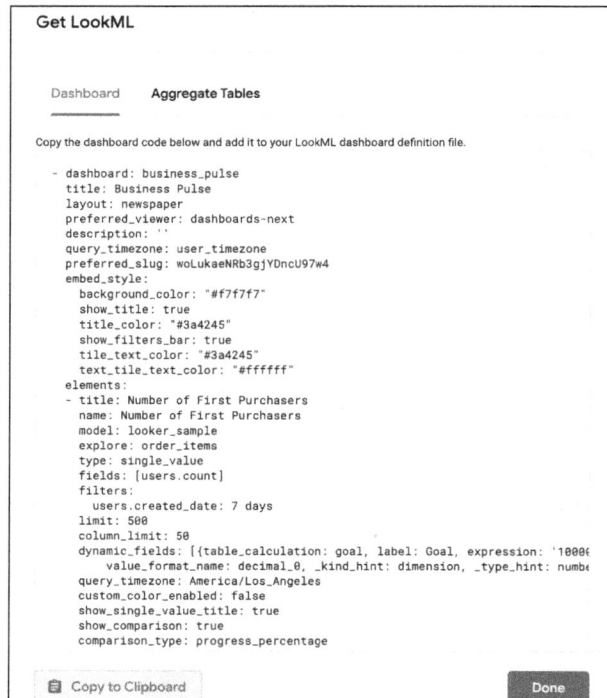

Figure 3.36: *Copying the LookML*

6. Come back to the dashboard file you just created in *step 3*, paste the code in the file, replacing the existing code, and save the file.

7. In the model file, include the dashboard file by adding the include statement.

   `include: "/path/*.dashboard.lookml`:

   This will add all dashboard files.

8. Save the contents, validate, and check in the changes like other LookML content.

9. You can view the dashboard in the LookML dashboards folder under **All folders** in the Main navigation menu:

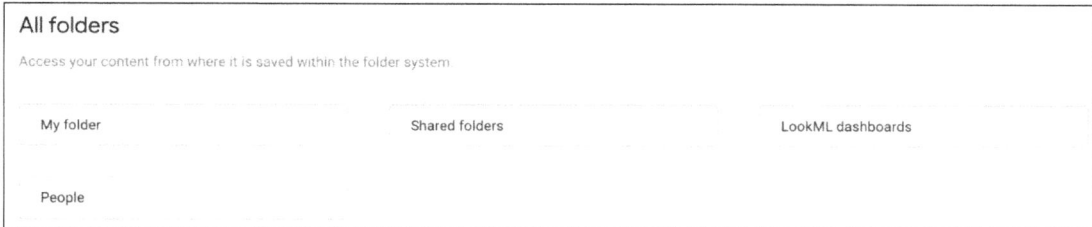

All folders

Access your content from where it is saved within the folder system.

| My folder | Shared folders | LookML dashboards |

People

Figure 3.37: LookML dashboard folder

Moving dashboards outside of LookML dashboards folder

To move the LookML dashboards, we need to have **lookml_dashboards** and develop permissions, and have access to the LookML model, in which the dashboard is included. We should also have mange access and edit permissions to the folder you are moving to.

There are two ways you can move:

- In production mode, select the dashboard in the LookML dashboard folder, click on the move button on top (or on the three-dot menu of the dashboard, select move option) and select the folder you want to move to. The dashboard will show in the LookML dashboard section of the destination folder.

- In production mode or development mode, select the dashboard in the LookML dashboard folder, click on the import button at the top, and select the folder you want to import the dashboard to. Import will create a copy and convert the dashboard to a user-defined dashboard, and it will let you edit the dashboard. However, changes to the user-defined dashboard will need to be copied manually to the LookML dashboard or a new LooML code can be generated using the steps we learned from the previous section.

Conclusion

In this chapter, we explored the fundamentals of LookML development, including different file types used, Looker's IDE for LookML creation, and key building blocks such as various field types and useful parameters. We also covered caching and derived tables, which enhance performance and support advanced SQL functions not directly implementable in view files. Additionally, we examined LookML dashboards, which are version-controlled and assist in managing dashboards across multiple environments.

In the next chapter, we will delve into advanced LookML concepts, including extends and refinements, the LookML Marketplace, parameterized and templated filters, and Liquid.

Join our book's Discord space

Join the book's Discord Workspace for Latest updates, Offers, Tech happenings around the world, New Release and Sessions with the Authors:

https://discord.bpbonline.com

CHAPTER 4
Advanced LookML

Introduction

In the last chapter, you learned about how to model data in Looker using LookML, how Looker generates the SQL, how Looker organizes the code in different files, how caching works in Looker, and how to use LookML dashboards. By now, you should be able to create explores and dashboards for most basic use cases. Some use cases will arise where you will also want to make dashboards dynamic to user input or specific data values. As you keep developing more LookML, you will come across situations where you want to reuse the code to maintain a cleaner code repository. In this chapter, we will learn how to make LookML both dynamic and reusable.

Structure

This chapter covers the following topics:

- Extends
- Refinements
- Looker Marketplace
- Parameters and Templated filters
- Liquid
- Aggregate awareness

Objectives

In this chapter, we will learn about extends and refinements, which allow you to reuse the code, thus facilitating easier code management. We will also learn about Looker blocks, which are pre-written pieces of code that can be reused, especially for commonly used data-sources, such as Salesforce, Google Analytics, and LinkedIn.

We will also review ways to create dynamic content in Looker. We will go over how to use Parameters, Templated filters, and Liquid (an open-source template language created by Shopify and written in Ruby). We will learn about these concepts and some basics of Liquid and how to use Liquid with some examples.

Extends

As you develop LookML code, you will come across situations where you need to repeat the same code for different use cases. LookML has a parameter called **extends** which allows developers to reuse the code. Extends are available for files at different levels: **views**, **explores** and **dashboards**. Extends allow us to modularize the code—we can build upon those modules to expand the model. Using Looker extends help you write **Don't Repeat Yourself** (**DRY**) code.

Extends make maintenance of the code easier. It reduces the number of places you need to update the code, if any part of the code does change.

When you extend a LookML object (view, explore, or dashboard), a copy of the object will be made, resulting in two objects: the base version (parent) and copy (extended/child) version of the object. The extended object includes all the parameters and code of the base object. Any new objects/parameters added to the extended version is only added to the copy, not the base.

There are four steps that Looker takes when extending a LookML object:

1. **Copy**: Looker makes a copy of the LookML object.

2. **Merge**: Looker merges the LookML of the extended object and the base object.

3. **Resolve conflicts**: If there is any element that is defined in both the base and the extended object, the one in extended object will be used (except for additive parameters), meaning extended object parameters override the base parameters. For additive parameters, it will combine the code.

4. **Apply the LookML**: Once the code is merged and all conflicts are resolved, Looker interprets the code in a standard way and the object can be used like any other LookML object.

There are several different ways extends can be used and defined:

- **Requiring extension**: Developers can require that an object only be used as an extend if you use **extension: required**, it ensures that this object cannot be used unless it is extended. It denotes that it is a container of code that will need to be merged into something else—the object is also not visible to the users on its own. Common use cases for requiring a block of code as an extension is in a hub and spoke model, wherein developers create a common base that serves as a hub, and each object that extends the hub is the spoke that personalizes it to a department, topic, etc.

- **Chaining extensions**: An extended object can also be further extended, which is referred as chaining extends. If there are any conflicts, the chain of extends, the last extended object overrides the preceding objects.

- **Extending multiple objects**: An object can extend multiple other objects at the same time. The extended object includes the merged code of all base objects. If there is any conflict between the base objects, the object listed last in the list overrides the ones before.

- **Extending views syntax**:

```
view: view_name {
   extends: [view_name, view_name,…]
}
```

The following are the common use cases for extending views:

- o   Adding more fields and/or updating the logic of the existing fields:

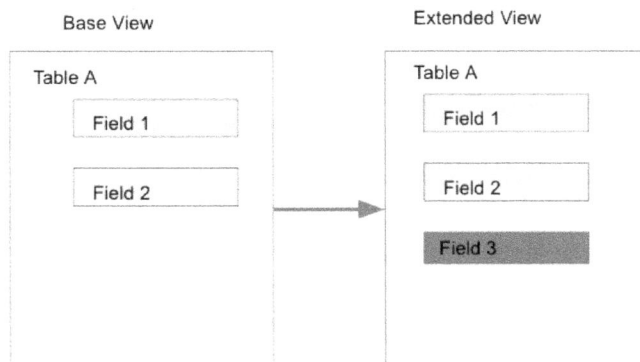

Figure 4.1: Looker View extends—adding an additional field

- o   Change the database table specified in the **sql_table_name** parameter:

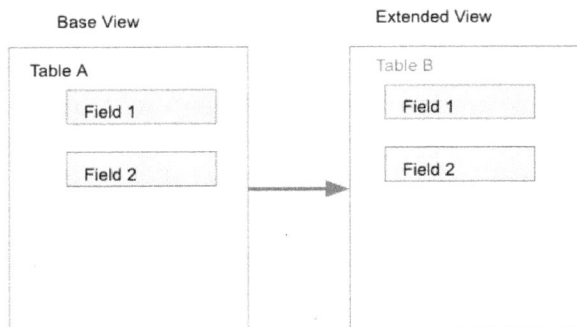

Figure 4.2: Looker View extends—replace the table name

In the preceding examples, we will add additional fields and set the source table without changing the original view, using extends.

Let us say we have a customer view, which includes the fields customer ID, name, and address. For our example, we would like to create a new subscribed customer view, based off customer, that adds the subscription start state and total purchase amount. In this case, we can extend the original customer view to create subscribed customer view and add the additional fields in the newly created subscribed customer view:

```
File: customer.view
Base view: customer {
     extension:required
     dimension: customer_id {}
     dimension: customer_name {}
     dimension: address {}
}

File: subscribed_customer.view
     include: "customer.view.lkml"
     view: subscribed_customer {
          extends: customer
          sql_table_name: project.dataset.subscribed_customer
          dimension: subscription_start_date { }
          measure: total_purchase_amount{}

     }
```

Observe that in the preceding example, the base object has **extension: required** and no **sql_table_name** parameter. This setup was designed so that the customer view cannot be used by itself, it must be extended. The extended view (**subscribed_customer** view) has **sql_table_name**, which sets the source table for the view. Note, the views do not have to be defined in the same file, they can also be in separate files as mentioned previously.

Additive parameters

If the extended view has the same parameter as the base parameter, the extended view overrides the base parameter unless it is additive. When a field is additive, it means both the base and the extended parameters will be combined. The following are the additive parameters:

- **Dimension fields**:
    - o action
    - o filters
    - o link
- **Views fields**: extends
- **Explore fields**:
    - o access_filter
    - o aggregate_table
    - o extends
    - o join
    - o query

Extending explores: Explores can also be extended in a way that is similar to views

Syntax:

```
explore: explore_name{
    extends: [explore_name, explore_name, …]
}
```

Common use cases of extending explores:

1. Include joins to more views:

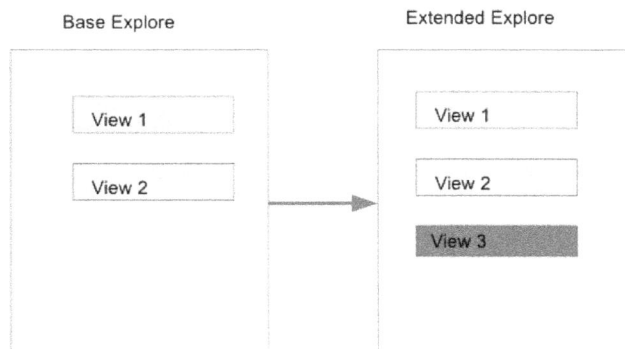

Figure 4.3: *Looker Explore extends—additional view joins*

2. Change the base view of the original extend.

3. Limit fields for different users/groups:

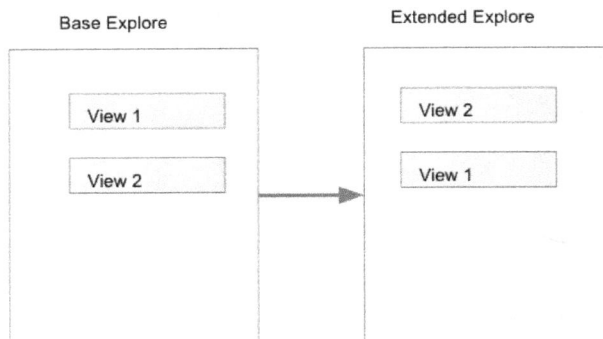

Figure 4.4: *Looker Explore extends—start with a different view*

Explores can be extended within the same model or across models:

- To extend explores within the same model, define both the base explore and the extending explores in the same model file.

- To extend explores across model files, create a separate explore file and write the base explore code in the file. After that, the extended explore should include the explore file in the model file/explore file (using **include** statement). If the extended explore is also in an explore file, include that in the model file. Explore will use the connection mentioned in the model file where the explore is included.

Here is an example where we used extends to add an additional join to the base explore. Let us say we want to include product reviews, which is a separate table than the products; we can extend **order_items** explore and add the additional table with a join:

```
explore: order_items {
  label: "Base Explore"
  view_name: order_items

  join: products {
    view_label: "Products"
    type: left_outer
    relationship: many_to_one
    sql_on: ${products.id} = ${inventory_items.product_id} ;;
  }
}
```

The preceding base explore can be extended to include additional joins:

```
explore: orders_with_product_reviews {
  extends: [order_items]
```

```
  label: "order Items Extended"
  join: product_reviews {
    view_label: "Reviews of Products"
    sql_on: ${order_items.product_id} = ${product_reviews.product_id} ;;
  }
}
```

Extending dashboards

Earlier, we learned that there are two types of dashboards: user defined dashboards and LookML dashboards. We also learned how to create a LookML dashboard from a user defined dashboard. LookML dashboards can be reused by extending similar to views or explores. To extend a LookML dashboard, both the base dashboard and the extended dashboard files must be included in the model file.

Extending dashboards syntax:

```
Dashboard: new_dashboard_name
      extends: [dashboard_name]
      Title: Title of the extended/new dashboard
      elements:
            title: tile_name
            model: model_name
            explore: explore_name
            …
```

Extended dashboards can add more tiles than the base dashboard. The tiles are part of the elements section in the LookML dashboard.

To be able to use the extends dashboards effectively, understanding the different parameters in the LookML dashboard is essential.

Refinements

Refinements allow modification of the original object (view/explore) without editing the original file that contains the object. A refinement code can be written in any LookML file: view, model, explore or its own file.

Refinements versus extends:

- The biggest difference to note between refinements and extends is that an extend creates a copy, whereas refinements edit the original code.

- Refinements are useful when you want to modify the existing view or explore, but do not have access to or do not want to modify the original file.

- Extensions are needed when you want to create a new copy of an existing view or explore and want to more parameters/objects.

Refinement syntax +

Reference the desired object to refine and simply add a + (plus sign) in front of the object name

For example, say there is a base view called **users.view**:

```
view: user {
      sql_table_name: db_name.user_tbl
      dimension: user_id{…}
      dimension: user_name {…}
      …
}
```

With a refinement, we can add additional dimensions and/or measures:

```
view: +user {
        dimension: city {…}
        measure: user_count {
                type:count_distinct
                sql: ${user_id};;
        }
}
```

Note: +user exists as its own view object, completely separate from user.

The following are the refinement rules:

- Refinements override most parameters, except for a few parameters where it is additive instead. The last refinement takes precedence over the base object or previous refinements. There are some additive parameters in refinements (similar to extends), listed as follows:

    o For dimensions and measures: **action, filters, link**

    o For views: **extends**

    o For explores: **access_filter, aggregate_table, extends, join** and **query**.

- Refinements can be defined in any file and in multiple places, but they are applied in the order they are defined.

    o If refinements are defined in separate files and included in the model (with include statements), they are applied in the order of the includes. Refinements farther down will take precedence over the ones before it, in case of any conflict.

    o If refinements are defined in a single file, they are applied line by line going downwards. Refinements farther down in the page will take precedence over the one before in case of any conflict.

- You can use **final: yes** to prevent further refinements. If anyone tries to refine the object that has this flag set to yes, Looker will throw an error.

- Refinements can contain extends. If a refinement contains an extend, it adds the extension to the original object. Looker combines the extends and refinement principles and overrides the parameters in case of any conflicts. Here is the order of precedence where each subsequent step overrides the previous one:

  1. Values from the extends specified in the object

  2. Values from the extends specified in the refinement object

  3. Values from the object

  4. Values from the refinement object

Here are some common use cases of refinements:

- If the database tables change often, you can create a base view file by importing the table from the database. Any additional changes like measures, dimensions with additional logic can be added in a separate file using refinement.

- Use refinements if you are using Looker Blocks (prebuilt pieces of Looker code) and want to modify the logic in the original object.

- When importing files from another project, refinements can be used to make changes to imported files without needing to change the files in the underlying project.

- Views with PDTs should use refinements over extends. The PDTs cannot be extended as the copy creates another table in the database.

Looker Marketplace

Looker Marketplace is a central location for finding, deploying, and managing Looker Blocks, Visualizations, and Applications. Everything on the Looker Marketplace can be added to an instance without any additional cost. Think of Looker Marketplace as a collection of additional plug-ins for the instance.

To access the Marketplace, perform the following steps:

1. Click on the **Marketplace** icon (as shown in the underlying figure) on the top right-hand side of the Looker landing page and select the **Discover** option. If this option is not available to you, it is either disabled on the instance and needs to be enabled by a Looker admin, or you do not have sufficient permissions to view it:

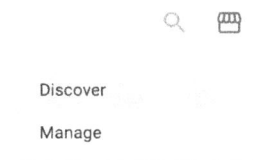

Discover

Manage

Figure 4.5: *Looker Marketplace search option*

2.　You can see that there are many prebuilt blocks available:

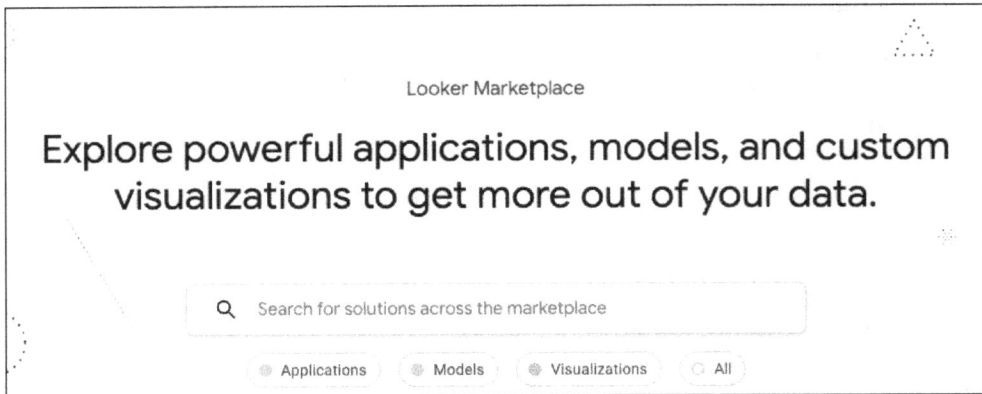

Looker Marketplace

Explore powerful applications, models, and custom visualizations to get more out of your data.

Q　Search for solutions across the marketplace

○ Applications　　○ Models　　○ Visualizations　　○ All

Figure 4.6: Looker Marketplace search option

There are three different types of content in Marketplace:

- **Applications**: Applications are completely built/plug and play and provide a specific feature. For example:

    o　**LookML diagram**: Shows the visual representation of the model.

    o　**Data dictionary**: Reads from the LookML code and provides a searchable application that lists the Looker fields and descriptions.

- **Visualizations**: Visualizations from Marketplace are additional visualizations that you can install and select immediately from the Explore interface when building a dashboard. Histogram, Calendar Heatmap, Multiple Value, and Sankey are a few examples of the visualizations available through the Marketplace.

- **Blocks/Models blocks**: Looker Blocks are prebuilt data models for common analytical patterns and data sources. These include LookML model, views and dashboards. With blocks, you can reuse the code that someone has already developed on commonly used data structures. You can leverage the expert knowledge and modeling best practices of the authors/publishers. Google Analytics 360, Salesforce Analytics, BigQuery Performance are a few examples of Looker Blocks/models.

3.　You can install blocks by simply clicking the install button on the individual Marketplace object page. Some features may require some set up (for example, blocks will often ask what dataset to use), but otherwise, features are immediately available for use after installation.

4.　Already installed marketplace items can also be updated whenever there is a code update using **Manage** option in the **Marketplace** menu:

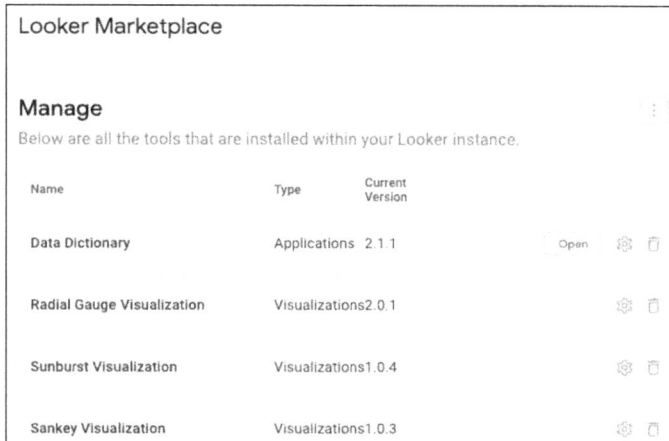

Figure 4.7: *Looker Marketplace Manage page*

You can also customize the Looker Blocks by installing/importing the code and refining. After installing the block, Looker adds the code in to the project and will have a read only version of the model, view files. By using LookML refinements mentioned previously, you can add custom edits to the block. If the original code ever gets updated in the future, you can simply update it without disturbing the custom code you created in the refinements (although any objects referenced by the refinements may be interrupted).

Parameters and Templated filters

We learned about different types of filters that are used in explores, view files, visualizations, dashboards, etc. All of these filters, when converted to SQL, will be part of **WHERE** or **HAVING** clause of the outer most SQL. However, there are times when you may need to apply the filters based on user input, or create a dynamic SQL based on a particular value selection from the user. Parameters and templated filters are useful in these scenarios.

Parameters

Parameters let the user select or insert a value, which can then be used in filters in different places like Explores, Looks and Dashboards.

To use parameters, do the following:

1. Define the parameter for the users to interact with

2. Apply the input taken from the user from the created parameter.

    Parameters: Basic syntax for creating a parameter:

```
Parameter: paramter_name {
        type: string/yesno/unquoted/date_time
        allowed_value: {
```

```
                        value: "value selected1"
                        label: "value_displayed_to_user_1"
                }
                allowed_value: {
                        value: "value selected2"
                        label: "value_displayed_to_user_2"
                }
                ...
        }
```

These parameters can be used anywhere in a derived table SQL or SQL part of the LookML. The syntax for referencing the parameter is **{% parameter parameter_name %}**

For example, say we want to give users the ability to select a different dimension within the same chart/visualization, we can use parameters to accomplish this:

```
parameter: slice_by_dimension {
  type: unquoted
  allowed_value: {
    value: "Country"
    label: "Country"
  }
  allowed_value: {
    value: "Product_Type"
    label: "Product Type"
  }
  allowed_value: {
    value: "Status"
    label: "Status"
  }
  default_value: "Status"
}
dimension: dynamic_column {
  type: string
  sql:  ${TABLE}.{% parameter slice_by_dimension %};;
}
measure: total_sale_price {
  label: "Total Sale Price"
  type: sum
  value_format_name: usd
  sql: ${TABLE}.sale_price ;;
}
```

The parameter will show as **Filter** only **Field** in the **Field Picker**. We can create an analysis, as shown in the following figure:

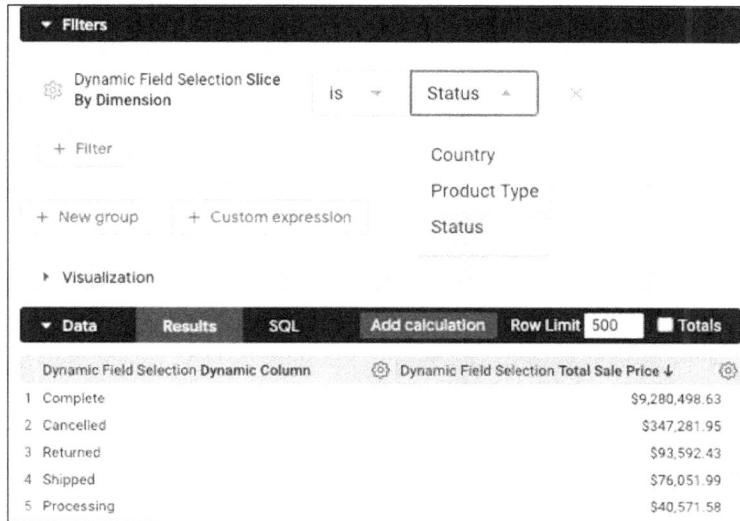

***Figure 4.8**: Looker parameters — Dynamic column*

Looker will present the options for the filter **Slice by dimension**. Once the user selects the value, it will substitute in the dimension: Dynamic Column. In the preceding example, we can see that the **Status** dimension is selected and also used in the results. If the user selects another value, the respective field will be used as the dimension in the SQL/results.

Parameter values can also be referenced with the syntax `parameter_name._parameter_value` in liquid logical statements that can be used in various places in LookML, including `sql_table_name`, `liquid`, SQL parameters etc. We will learn about liquid templating language later in this chapter.

Templated filters

With templated filters, users can enter the values that can be passed into SQL queries using conditional logic in Liquid templated language.

The difference between parameters and templated filters is that Parameters allow a fixed set of values out of which, the user can pick one value. Templated filters allow the users to enter any value and also allow multiple operations on the values entered. For example: for string inputs we can do LIKE, CONTAINS, for dates comparisons etcetera.

Parameters and templated filters provide more flexibility to the users and will help write complex, dynamic SQL queries for advanced use cases.

Syntax for using the templated filters is:

`{% condition filter_name %} field_to_affect {% endcondition %}`

Similar to parameters, first we need to create something that the users can interact with/ give input. We can either create a filter or use a regular dimension. After that, we can use the preceding syntax to use the templated filter either in the LookML or in the derived table SQL.

For example, consider the following derived table that calculates the total orders and revenue for US:

```
derived_table: {
    sql: {
SELECT    users.country
        , COUNT(DISTINCT order_id) AS total_orders
        , SUM(sale_price) AS total_revenue
    FROM ecommerce_sample.order_items AS order_items
    LEFT JOIN ecommerce_sample.users AS users
    ON order_items.user_id = users.id
    WHERE users.country = 'USA'
    GROUP BY 1 ;;
}
}
```

If you want to give the user an option to select the country and pass the value to the derived table, you can use the following code:

```
derived_table: {
    sql:
SELECT    users.country
        , COUNT(DISTINCT order_id) AS total_orders
        , SUM(sale_price) AS total_revenue
    FROM ecommerce_sample.order_items AS order_items
    LEFT JOIN ecommerce_sample.users AS users
    ON order_items.user_id = users.id
        WHERE {% condition country_selection %} users.country {%
endcondition %}
        GROUP BY 1 ;;
}
filter:  country_selection {
        type: string
}
```

In the explore, it shows up as follows:

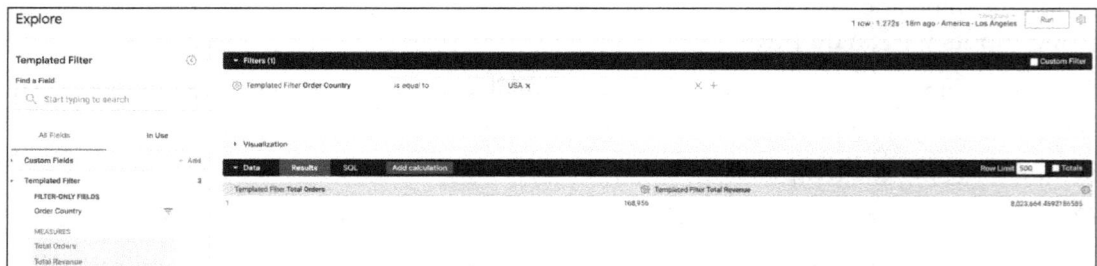

Figure 4.9: Looker Templated Filter

Users can enter a value in the order country filter.

The SQL generated replaces the country filter:

```
WITH templated_filter AS (SELECT     users.country as country
        , COUNT(DISTINCT order_id) AS total_orders
        , SUM(sale_price) AS total_revenue
      FROM ecommerce_sample.order_items AS order_items
      LEFT JOIN ecommerce_sample.users AS users
      ON order_items.user_id = users.id
     WHERE (users.country = 'USA')
      GROUP BY 1
      )
SELECT
COALESCE(SUM(templated_filter.total_orders), 0) AS templated_filter_total_
orders,
COALESCE(SUM(templated_filter.total_revenue), 0) AS templated_filter_total_
revenue
FROM templated_filter
LIMIT 500
```

In the preceding example, you can use the regular dimension instead of filter. However, if you use regular dimension, it will be applied both in the derived table SQL as well as the outer table **WHERE** clause SQL:

```
WITH templated_filter AS (SELECT    users.country country
        , COUNT(DISTINCT order_id) AS total_orders
        , SUM(sale_price) AS total_revenue
      FROM ecommerce_sample.order_items AS order_items
      LEFT JOIN ecommerce_sample.users AS users
      ON order_items.user_id = users.id
     WHERE (users.country = 'USA')
      GROUP BY 1
      )
SELECT
 COALESCE(SUM(templated_filter.total_orders), 0) AS templated_filter_total_
orders,
 COALESCE(SUM(templated_filter.total_revenue), 0) AS templated_filter_total_
revenue
FROM templated_filter
WHERE (templated_filter.country ) = 'USA'
LIMIT 500
```

You can also use the templated filter in different places of the view file, wherever SQL is required. For example, you can use it in the **CASE** statement like so:

```
CASE WHEN {% condition order_country %} users.country {% endcondition %}
THEN   users.country END as country
```

It will just replace the templated filter with (**users.country = 'USA'**)

If you want to have a filter on the date column, you can simply use the date column in the filter. Looker can detect the date and provide an appropriate selection filter.

To test how the date templated filter works in the same example as before, you can perform the following steps:

1. You can create a date filter in the view:

   ```
   filter: date_range {
     type: date
   }
   ```

2. Replace the derived table **WHERE** condition with the following SQL:

   ```
   WHERE {% condition date_range %} order_items.created_at {%
   endcondition %}
   ```

The filter look, as shown in the following figure, with different date options:

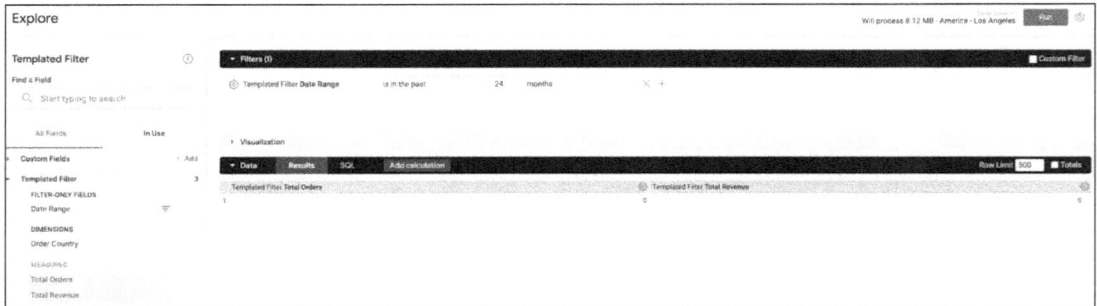

Figure 4.10: *Looker Templated Filter — Date*

Looker automatically provides date options in the filter. Let us say you selected 24 months as shown in *Figure 4.10*.

The SQL will look as follows:

```
      WITH templated_filter AS (SELECT    users.country country
      , COUNT(DISTINCT order_id) AS total_orders
      , SUM(sale_price) AS total_revenue
    FROM ecommerce_sample.order_items AS order_items
    LEFT JOIN ecommerce_sample.users AS users
    ON order_items.user_id = users.id
     WHERE ((( order_items.created_at ) >= ((TIMESTAMP(DATETIME_
ADD(DATETIME(TIMESTAMP_TRUNC(TIMESTAMP_TRUNC(CURRENT_TIMESTAMP(), DAY,
'America/Los_Angeles'), MONTH, 'America/Los_Angeles'), 'America/Los_
```

```
Angeles'), INTERVAL -23 MONTH), 'America/Los_Angeles'))) AND ( order_items.
created_at ) < ((TIMESTAMP(DATETIME_ADD(DATETIME(TIMESTAMP(DATETIME_
ADD(DATETIME(TIMESTAMP_TRUNC(TIMESTAMP_TRUNC(CURRENT_TIMESTAMP(), DAY,
'America/Los_Angeles'), MONTH, 'America/Los_Angeles'), 'America/Los_
Angeles'), INTERVAL -23 MONTH), 'America/Los_Angeles'), 'America/Los_
Angeles'), INTERVAL 24 MONTH), 'America/Los_Angeles')))))
      GROUP BY 1
      )
SELECT
 COALESCE(SUM(templated_filter.total_orders), 0) AS templated_filter_total_
orders,
 COALESCE(SUM(templated_filter.total_revenue), 0) AS templated_filter_total_
revenue
FROM templated_filter
LIMIT 500
```

You can see that Looker automatically converts the templated filter to the complex date logic in the SQL generated.

Liquid

Liquid is a templating language that allows developers to create dynamic content. It is an open sourced, Ruby-based language created by Shopify, used in many web applications including Looker. Liquid can be used mainly in the following LookML parameters:

action, **html**, **label**, **link**, **sql**, **sql_on** and **sql_table_name**

Different Liquid fields have different levels of usability for LookML fields, please reference the official documentation for the detailed list of uses.

Liquid is very simple and easy to use. We will learn some basics and see how it can be used in LookML, with some examples:

- **Variables/Objects**: These are represented using double curly braces **{{ value }}**. They are used to output dynamic content.

    For example, you can use a Liquid variable to create/build the URL of the product in a company website using **sku_id** from the database:

    ```
    dimension: product_sku {
        sql: ${TABLE}.sku_id ;;
        link: {
            url:"http://www.companywebsite.com/sku={{ value }}"
    }
        }
    ```

    Here, the value will be replaced by the **sku_id** from the database. Clicking on the **product_sku** link from the dashboard/look takes the user to the webpage of the product.

Variables from other fields can also be accessed with the fully qualified syntax like:

```
{{ view_name.field_name._value }}
```

- **Tags**: Tags create the logic and control flow for templates. Tags start with a curly brace and a percent sign (**{%**), and end with a percent sign and curly brace (**%}**). You can assign variables and write control statements like if...then statements and for loops. Liquid code/logic written within the tags does not show up in the SQL code generated from the LookML.

  Assigning value: We can assign a value to a variable like:

```
{% assign var1 = 20 %}
{% assign var 2 = "apple" %}
```

  Control statement: if- else, case- when or for loop can also be written in tags.

  Syntax of if else statement:

```
        {% if variable == 'value1' %}
        {% elsif variable == 'value2'%}
        ….
        {% endif %}
```

- **Filters**: Filters change the output of the Liquid object or variable. Vertical pipe |
  is used with in the double curly braces to append the filter to the object/variable.
  These are different from filters that restrict the output in SQL/Looker.

  Example 1: **{{ 3.578 | round: 1 }}** will output: **3.6**

  Example 2: **{% assign fruits = "apples, bananas, oranges, grapes" | split: "," %}**

  {{ fruits.size }} will give an output: 4

  Example 3: **{{ "This product is new" | replace "new", "latest" }}**

  Will give an output: **This product is latest**

In the following example, you can see another way of using the parameters in the **sql_table_name**. Here, we use liquid to select the database and table we are querying from. This is useful in case you want to query different databases/schemas like Dev, QA and Prod for the same dashboard or Look. Make sure all the databases accessible through the same database connection:

```
sql_table_name:
    {% if environment._parameter_value == 'Dev' %}
  `dev_project.dataset.table_name`
  {% elsif environment._parameter_value == 'Prod' %}
  `prod_project.dataset.table_name`
    {% elsif environment._parameter_value == 'QA' %}
```

```
 `dev_project.dataset.table_name`
{% else %} -- Default to production
``dev_project.dataset.table_name`
{% endif %}
;;
    parameter: environment {
      type: unquoted
      default_value: "Prod"
      allowed_value: {
        label: "Dev"
        value: "Dev"
      }
      allowed_value: {
        label: "Prod"
        value: "Prod"
      }
      allowed_value: {
        label: "QA"
        value: "QA"
      }
    }
```

Another example that follows shows the use of liquid within the HTML tag of the measure. If you want to format the data on the dashboard using different colors. We can see the reference to value and rendered value also here:

```
measure: total_sales {
  type: sum
  html:
    {% if value > 1000000 %}
      <span style="color:green;">{{ rendered_value }}</span>
    {% elsif value > 500000 %}
      <span style="color:goldenrod;">{{ rendered_value }}</span>
    {% else %}
      <span style="color:red;">{{ rendered_value }}</span>
    {% endif %} ;;
}
```

Aggregate awareness

You may encounter slowness of queries when Looker is using the raw tables/derived tables that contain large amounts of data. In these cases, you may need to create aggregate tables.

With Looker's aggregate awareness feature, you can create aggregate tables that are essentially smaller versions of the original table that Looker can use to query instead of the original table. Users need not make a selection between the aggregate or original explore—Looker automatically selects the appropriate table based on the query and the dimensions used.

For example, say we have a very large ecommerce store that is getting orders and storing all the order details in a table called **order_details**. As the number of orders increase, the original table becomes incresingly big, causing slow performance for summary reports at daily and monthly levels. To speed up the results, we can create a daily table (that summarizes the orders at a day level (**orders_daily**)) and a monthly sales table (**orders_monthly**). If you designate these tables as aggregate tables, Looker will automatically aggregate awareness. Looker will use the smallest, appropriate aggregate table possible to resolve user's queries. For any queries that are at a month or above levels, for example yearly sales or quarterly sales, it uses the **orders_monthly**, and any query that is at a day or week level, it uses **order_daily**. If there are queries that need the details that are not available in the aggregate tables, it uses the most detailed table, the original table **order_details**.

Aggregate table is defined using the parameter **aggregate_table** under explore parameter in LookML.

Aggregate tables are a type of **persistent derived tables** (PDTs), so they have the same requirements as PDTs.

Syntax of **aggregate_table**:

```
explore: explore_name {
  aggregate_table: table_name {
    query:  {
      dimensions: [dimension1, dimension2, ... ]
      measures: [measure1, measure2, ... ]
      sorts: [field1: asc, field2: desc, ... ]
      filters: [field1: "value1", field2: "value2", ... ]
      timezone: timezone
    }
    materialization:  {
    }
  }
}
```

The syntax includes the **aggregate_table** parameter followed by the name of the aggregate table. It has the query sub parameter that defines the aggregate table. The query includes dimensions, measures, sorting options, filters and also the time zone for time fields. The materialization subparameter specifies the persistence strategy for the aggregate table. It can include a datagroup, **sql_trigger_value**, or persist for values. Other options **incremental_key** and **increment_offset** can also be used for incremental aggregate table.

For ecommerce sales explore example we described above, the aggregate table looks like the following:

```
explore: order_items {
  view_name: order_items
  description: "This explore includes Orders, Items and Users"
  join: order_facts {
    type: left_outer
    view_label: "Orders"
    relationship: many_to_one
    sql_on: ${order_facts.order_id} = ${order_items.order_id} ;;
  }

  join: inventory_items {
    view_label: "Inventory Items"
    type: full_outer
    relationship: one_to_one
    sql_on: ${inventory_items.id} = ${order_items.inventory_item_id} ;;
  }
  join: users {
    view_label: "Users"
    type: left_outer
    relationship: many_to_one
    sql_on: ${order_items.user_id} = ${users.id} ;;
  }
  join: products {
    view_label: "Products"
    type: left_outer
    relationship: many_to_one
    sql_on: ${products.id} = ${inventory_items.product_id} ;;
  }

  # roll up table for commonly used queries
  aggregate_table: simple_rollup {
    query: {
      dimensions: [created_date, products.brand, products.category, products.department]
      measures: [count, returned_count, returned_total_sale_price, total_gross_margin, total_sale_price]
      filters: [order_items.created_date: "6 months"]
    }
    materialization: {
      datagroup_trigger: ecommerce_etl
```

```
        }
    }
}
```

If any of the fields Created Month, Product Band, Total Sales Price and Order Items Count are selected in the corresponding explore, it will use the aggregate table instead of the original table. Looker will also notify users through the SQL when an aggregate table has been used. The aggregate table's use status is displayed on the SQL comments at the top of the query like so:

```
-- generate derived table order_items::simple_rollup
-- running the following sql through the bigquery API to create table as
select:
-- Building aggregate table looker_blueprint::order_items::simple_rollup on
instance 5a0cb53c8577a3a0cdc483efbc309196

-- finished order_items::simple_rollup => `looker_temp.
LR_5N00V1727380015083_order_items_simple_rollup`
```

The actual query will show that it is using the already built PDT:

```
-- use existing order_items::simple_rollup in `looker_temp.
LR_5N00V1727380015083_order_items_simple_rollup`
SELECT
    products_brand,
    COALESCE(SUM(order_items_total_sale_price), 0) AS order_items_total_
sale_price,
    COALESCE(SUM(order_items_count), 0) AS order_items_count
FROM `looker_temp.LR_5N00V1727380015083_order_items_simple_rollup`
WHERE ((( order_items_created_date) >= ((TIMESTAMP(DATETIME_
ADD(DATETIME(TIMESTAMP_TRUNC(TIMESTAMP_TRUNC(CURRENT_TIMESTAMP(), DAY,
'America/Los_Angeles'), MONTH, 'America/Los_Angeles'), 'America/Los_
Angeles'), INTERVAL -1 MONTH), 'America/Los_Angeles'))) AND ( order_items_
created_date) < ((TIMESTAMP(DATETIME_ADD(DATETIME(TIMESTAMP(DATETIME_
ADD(DATETIME(TIMESTAMP_TRUNC(TIMESTAMP_TRUNC(CURRENT_TIMESTAMP(),
DAY, 'America/Los_Angeles'), MONTH, 'America/Los_Angeles'), 'America/
Los_Angeles'), INTERVAL -1 MONTH), 'America/Los_Angeles'), 'America/Los_
Angeles'), INTERVAL 2 MONTH), 'America/Los_Angeles')))))
GROUP BY
    1
ORDER BY
    2 DESC
LIMIT 500
```

This confirms that Looker is building the associated persistent derived table and using it for the queries. Any other query above the date level, for example, month level, will also use the same PDT.

If you include any other field that is not part of the **aggregate_table** definition, for example, average age of the user, it sends the query to the base table instead of using the aggregate table. Similarly, Looker will note in the SQL comments when an aggregate table is not used.

For your explore queries to use the aggregate tables, there are some design considerations, like:

- The explore query must include all fields specified in the aggregate table definition. Only trimeframe roll ups are an exception to this rule. For example: if a date column is included, you can query at a month or year level.

- Supported measure types for aggregate awareness include **SUM**, **COUNT**, **AVERAGE**, **MIN**, and **MAX**. However, ***_DISTINCT** measures (e.g., **SUM_DISTINCT**), as well as medians and percentiles, are not supported.

- The timezone of the explore query must align with the timezone of the aggregate table.

- Filter fields must be either dimensions or filters defined in the aggregate table. Additionally, fields used in explore filters, such as **access_filters**, **always_filter**, and **conditionally_filter**, should also be present in the aggregate table.

The aggregate table definition is created using an explore query—Looker does not permit custom SQL to define the aggregate table. By using the explore query, Looker guarantees that developers only select columns that already exist in the explore.

To create an aggregat table, on the Explore interface, go to Explore actions next to Run button, you can see the menu. Click on **Get LookML**:

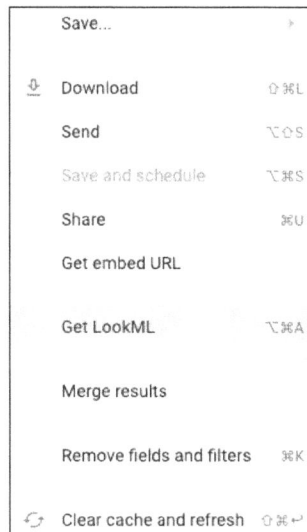

Save...	▸
Download	⇧⌘L
Send	⌥⇧S
Save and schedule	⌥⌘S
Share	⌘U
Get embed URL	
Get LookML	⌥⌘A
Merge results	
Remove fields and filters	⌘K
Clear cache and refresh	⇧⌘↵

Figure 4.11: Get LookML option in Explore actions menu

By default, the first tab, Dashboard, shows up. Alongside the **Dashboard** option, there is **Aggregate Table** option in this window. Select this option and it will display the aggregate table definition. This code can be copied into the explore definition to essentially turn on aggregate awareness for the explore:

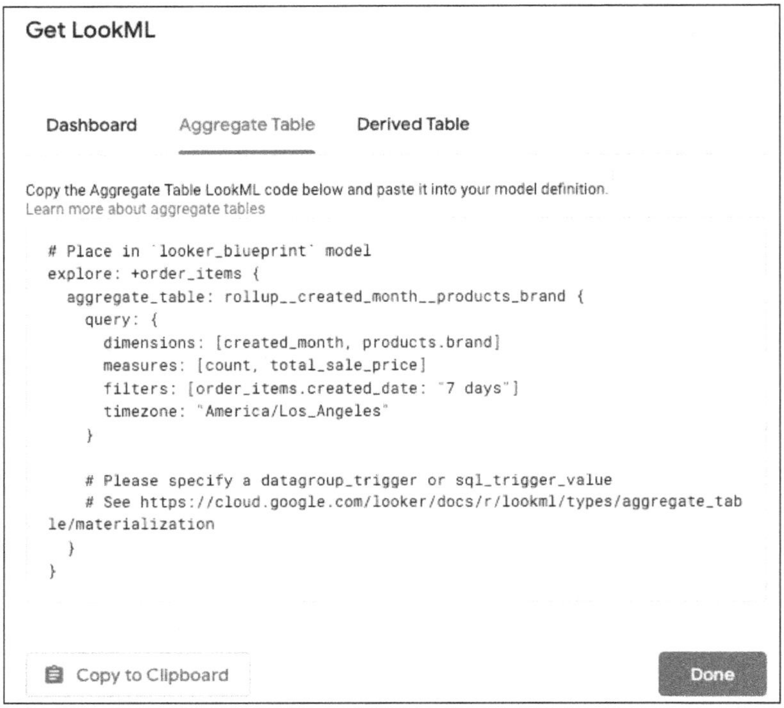

Figure 4.12: *Aggregate Table definition in Get LookML*

Conclusion

In this chapter, we explored advanced LookML concepts, including extends, refinements, parameters, templated filters, and the basics of the Liquid templating language. We also covered aggregate awareness and the marketplace. Utilizing these concepts enhances code reusability and readability, while aggregate awareness aids in performance and cost optimization. The marketplace allows us to leverage out-of-the-box features and code developed by others, accelerating our development process.

In the next chapter, we will delve into integrating Looker with external tools and applications beyond the native Looker interface. This integration will enable us to harness Looker's powerful modeling capabilities and present results in diverse ways.

CHAPTER 5

Beyond Looker

Introduction

In the previous chapters, we discussed the user interface and the native features of Looker. Apart from those out-of-the-box Looker features, Looker can also be accessed using other applications, including Google products like Connected Sheets, Looker Studio, and the Looker mobile application. Non-Google products such as Power BI can also be connected to Looker, to use the powerful modeling layer and take advantage of the definitions created in the explores. In this chapter, we will explore these tools and learn how we can connect other tools to Looker and use them. We will also learn how we can extend Looker's functionality using various integrations and third-party tools.

Structure

In this chapter, we will go through the following topics:

- Looker mobile application
- Connected Sheets
- Looker Studio
- Deliver data through Action Hub
- Data actions

- Building custom visualizations
- Third party tools

Objectives

In this chapter, we will discuss how Looker works with other tools namely, Looker mobile application, connected sheets, and Looker Studio; how we can use those tools and get data out of Looker, and how we can extend Looker's native functionality.

Additionally, we will discuss how to use Action Hub, data actions, custom visualizations, and how we can use third party tools like LAMS, Gazer, etc. to enhance usability and provide better customer experiences.

Looker mobile application

Looker mobile application is available on both AppStore (iOS) and Google Play Store (Android). With this application, you can browse, view Looker dashboards and Looks, View Favorite and recently viewed content, share, and follow. Admins can enable the Looker Mobile app on the Looker Instance.

Enabling the Looker mobile application

The following steps will enable mobile application users to be able to view Looker content in the application:

1. Go to **General**, **Settings** page in the **Looker Admin** page, then under the **Feature Configuration** section and select **Enabled**, in **Mobile Application Access**, as shown:

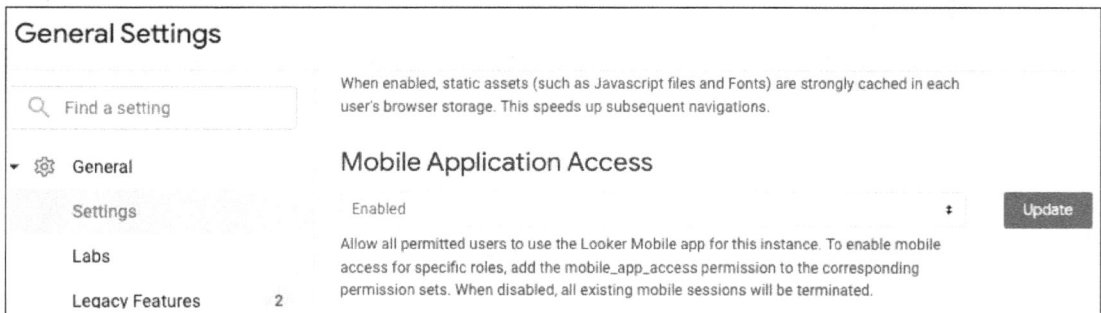

General Settings

	When enabled, static assets (such as Javascript files and Fonts) are strongly cached in each user's browser storage. This speeds up subsequent navigations.
🔍 Find a setting	
▾ ⚙ General	**Mobile Application Access**
Settings	Enabled ‡ [Update]
Labs	Allow all permitted users to use the Looker Mobile app for this instance. To enable mobile access for specific roles, add the mobile_app_access permission to the corresponding permission sets. When disabled, all existing mobile sessions will be terminated.
Legacy Features 2	

Figure 5.1: Setting to enable mobile application

2. Assign the user or group a role with a permission set that includes the **mobile_ app_access** permission.

Installing the Looker mobile application

To install the Looker mobile application on your smart device:

1. Open the **App Store** on your Mobile and search for **Looker Mobile**. You can find the application on Google, as shown in the following figure:

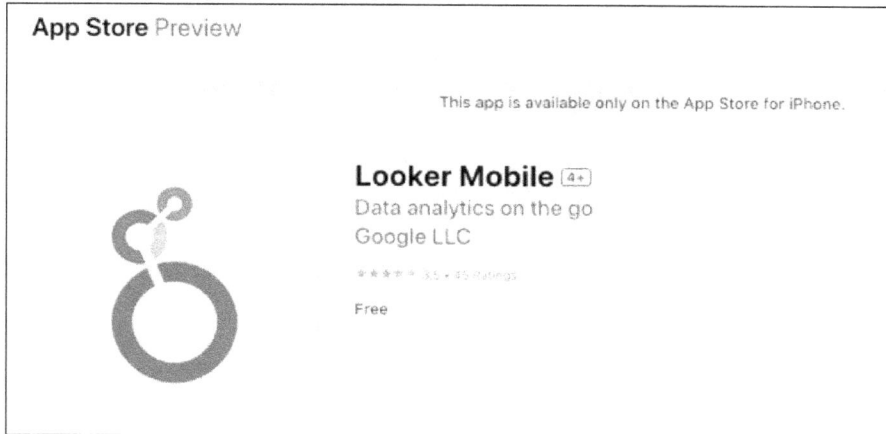

App Store Preview

This app is available only on the App Store for iPhone.

Looker Mobile [4+]
Data analytics on the go
Google LLC

★★★★★ 3.5 • 35 Ratings

Free

Figure 5.2: Looker mobile application in App Store

2. Install the application and open it, once the installation is done.

Login to Looker mobile application

On the first screen, you will see two options, as follows:

- **Sign in with email**: This option is like Looker on a browser, where you can simply log in using your email and password.

- **Sign in with QR Code**:

  o To sign in, **Open Looker** on your computer and go to **Account** on the top right-hand.

  o Select the **QR Code** button next to the mobile application login.

  o On your mobile phone, select the **Scan QR code** in blue. Your camera opens.

  o You can point the mobile camera to the QR code opened on the computer browser. You will log in to the Looker application through Mobile.

The following figure clearly shows the login options:

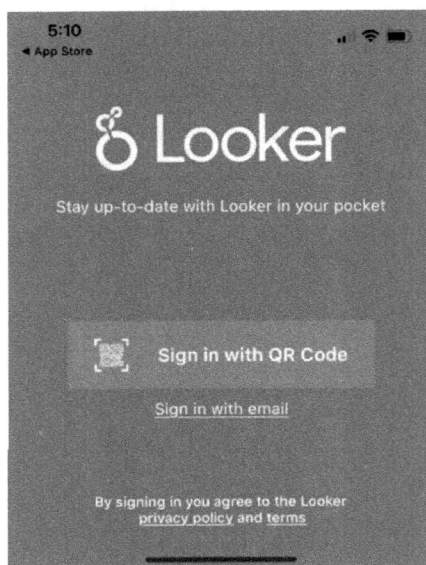

Figure 5.3: Looker mobile application login screen

Note: The QR code works only for 5 minutes. After 5 minutes, you must generate a new QR code following the same instructions mentioned before.

Navigation

The main page on mobile has a navigation menu, as shown in the following figure:

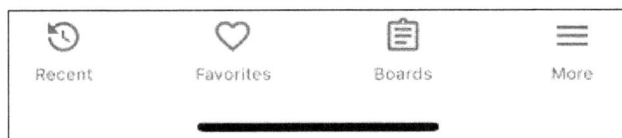

Figure 5.4: Navigation menu

- **Recent**: This section shows the most recent dashboards (up to 20) and Looks (up to 20). This list includes the most recent content you have viewed in either the mobile application or the web browser on the computer.

- **Favorites**: It includes all favorite content you have marked as favorites. (Includes both web application and mobile application favorites).

- **Boards**: Boards that you have followed (Includes both web application and mobile application).

- **More**: This has a few options as shown in the following figure:

Figure 5.5: More options in navigation menu

o **All folders**: This displays **All folders** which further takes you to a personal folder, shared folder, and any other folder you have access to on the web application.

o **My account**: Displays account details.

o **Privacy and legal**: Shows privacy policy and terms.

o **Report a problem**: You can also send an email to customer service regarding issues.

o **Sign out**: This will log you out of the Looker application and you will have to log back in to access any content again.

o **Search option**: This is available in Recent and Favorites.

o **Sort option**: This is available in all menus and sub-menus

o **Alerts**: You can also receive alerts that were created with the web application on your mobile application. In the upper right-hand corner of the navigation menu, you can see alerts under the *bell icon,* as shown in the following figure:

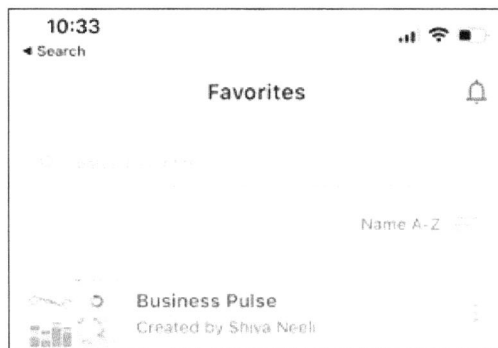

Figure 5.6: Alert bell icon

To enable this, you need to enable the Firebase under **Action Hub** | **Admin** | **Action**, as follows:

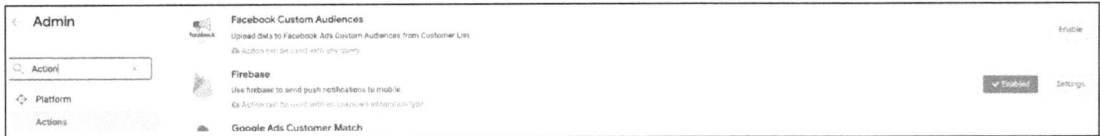

Figure 5.7: Enabling push notifications in the Looker mobile application

Viewing the content

You can view the content (dashboards and Looks) using the navigation menu and selecting the dashboard or Look. You can see that the same dashboards that you have access to on the web application, are also available through mobile. The only difference is that the tiles are adjusted to fit the mobile application:

Figure 5.8: Viewing dashboard in Looker mobile application

On each dashboard or Look, you can see that the dashboard filters are available on top.

On the three dots menu of the dashboard, you can also:

- Add to favorites
- Share the dashboard through different means (emails, other applications) on your mobile

- Copy the link and send it through, text or other applications
- Get info displays more dashboard info like the one on the web application

Connected Sheets

Google Sheets can be used to access the LookML model, charts, and formulas, offering a flexible interface for analysis. You can also create pivot tables within Sheets, enabling more dynamic insights. Instead of storing data directly in the sheet, it connects to Looker, leveraging the LookML model to pull data from the database and display the results in Sheets. This approach combines the single source of truth provided by the Looker model with the flexibility of Google Sheets for analysis and reporting.

Enabling Google Sheets

Let us look at the steps to enable the Connected Sheets feature within your Looker instance:

1. To enable connected sheets, go to **Admin | Platform | BI Connectors** and enable the **Google Sheets** option, as follows:

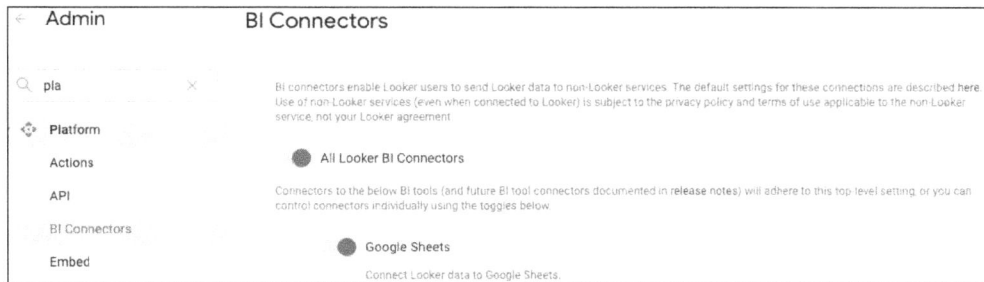

Figure 5.9: Enabling Google Sheets

2. Users should use the same email address to access the Google Workspace account and Looker.

Connecting to Looker from Sheets

To connect to Looker:

1. Open Google Sheets, under the **Data** menu and select **Data Connectors | Connect to Looker**:

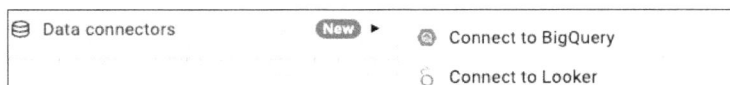

Figure 5.10: Enabling Google Sheets

2. In the next popup window, enter your Looker URL. A new window opens asking to link both Google and Looker accounts. You can then link both accounts.

3. In the next window, it shows the Looker model and explores what you want to query. Select the **Explore** you want to use, as shown in the following figure:

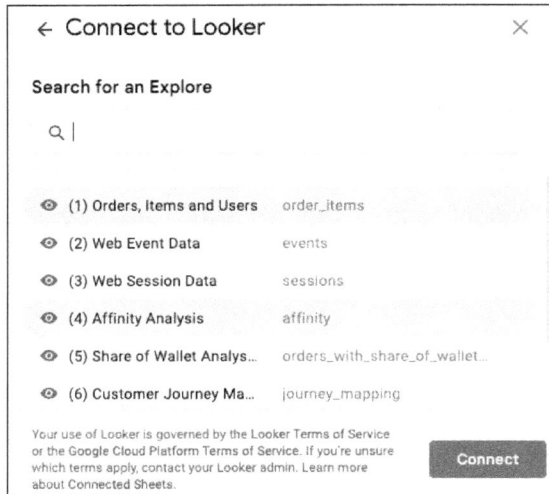

Figure 5.11: Connecting to Looker Explores

After the connection, sheets will open a new sheet that shows the explore details including the views, dimensions, and measures, as follows:

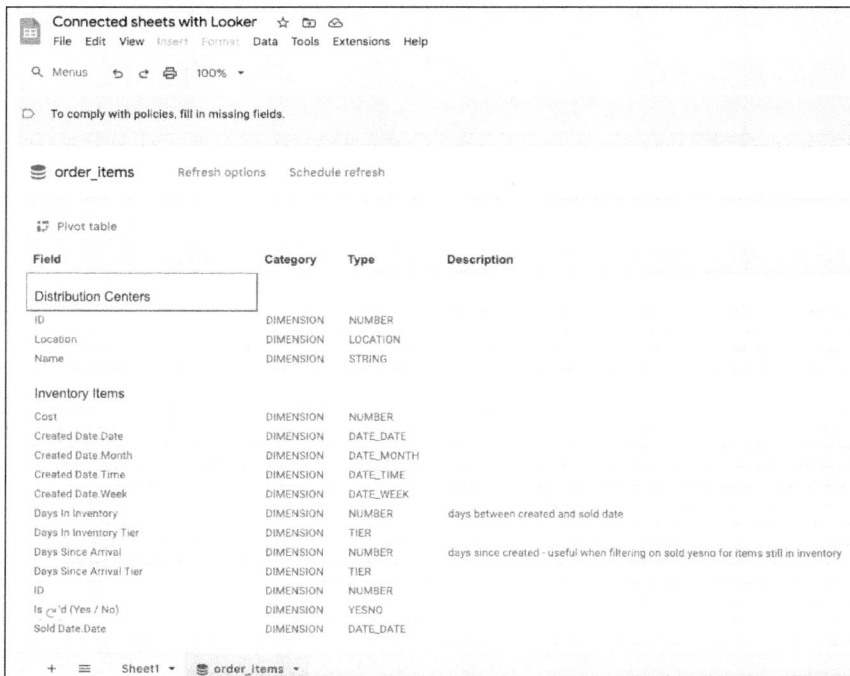

Figure 5.12: Connecting to Looker Explores

Using sheets to query Looker Explores

This section outlines the steps to use Connected Sheets to query Looker explores with few examples:

1. On the Explore sheet, you can see the **Pivot table** option on top. Click on it and select the sheet where you want to **Create** the pivot table, as follows:

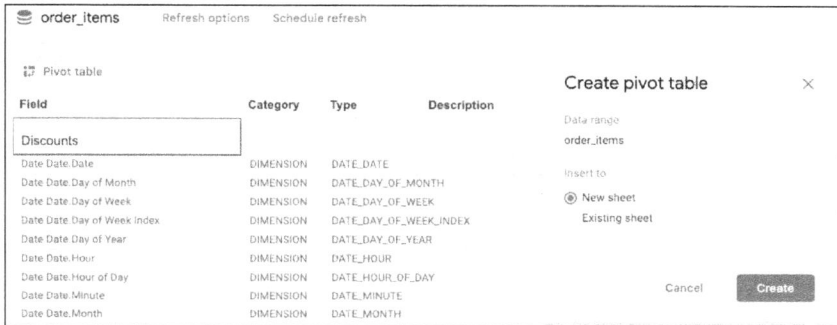

Figure 5.13: *Using connected sheets to create a pivot table from Looker Explore*

On the new sheet, you can see options for pivot table rows, columns, values, and filters.

For example, the **Product Category** under **Rows**, **Created Year** under **Columns**, and **Total Sale Price** under **Values** and, the years 2021, 2022, and 2023 under **Filters**, as shown in the following figure:

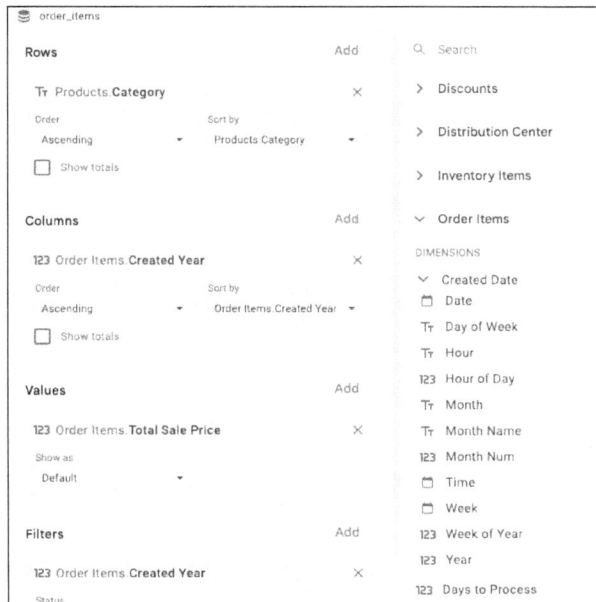

Figure 5.14: *Pivot table definition in sheets*

2. Once the selection is done, click on **Apply**. This will run the query against **Looker Explore** and get the results in sheets, as follows:

Total Sale Price	Created Year		
Category	2021	2022	2023
Accessories	72738.38994	130037.2399	173748.5599
Active	73966.88999	148413.1101	178214.6
Blazers & Jacket	46167.66006	93283.83018	122134.6002
Clothing Sets	2472.970016	6180.54001	6827.539997
Dresses	69796.62018	152766.4904	192687.9204
Fashion Hoodies	111521.5002	201536.9902	256517.59
Intimates	75410.52009	140955.8502	186647.7903
Jeans	214231.4603	391267.7604	497122.1308
Jumpsuits & Ror	6823.740017	13194.85005	17695.13006

Figure 5.15: Pivot table results in sheets

3. Once the pivot table has results, you can do normal analysis and further tasks in sheets, like building further visualizations. For example, we can select the pivot table and add a chart visualization from the **Insert | Chart** option in the sheet, as follows:

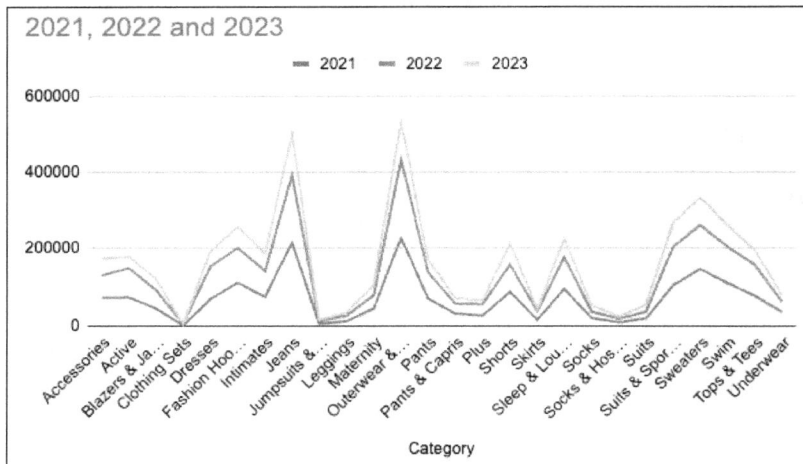

Figure 5.16: Chart in Google Connected sheet

4. The pivot table can also be refreshed to get fresh data, as shown in the following figure:

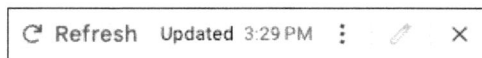

Figure 5.17: Refresh option for pivot table in Google sheet

If there are multiple tables you built from the same Explore, all those can be refreshed from a single place under the **Refresh options**:

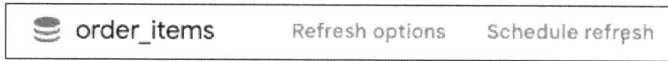

Figure 5.18: Refresh and schedule refresh menu items in Google Sheet

We can also schedule the **Refresh** by selecting the frequency interval:

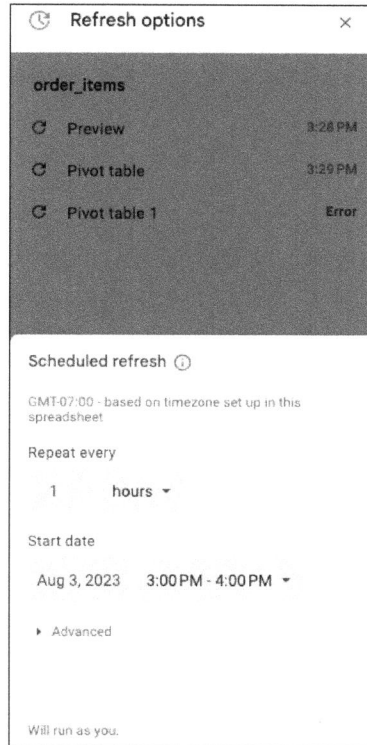

Figure 5.19: Refresh and Schedule refresh options in Google Sheet

Looker Studio

Looker Studio (formerly known as **Data Studio**), another Google visualization tool can also connect to Looker and make use of the powerful Looker modeling layer and build reports and dashboards. Data from Looker can also be merged with other sources within Looker Studio.

Enabling Looker Studio

This section outlines the steps to enable Looker studio in Looker.

1. To enable Looker Studio, under **Admin** | **Platform** | **BI Connectors**, enable the **Looker Studio** option, as follows:

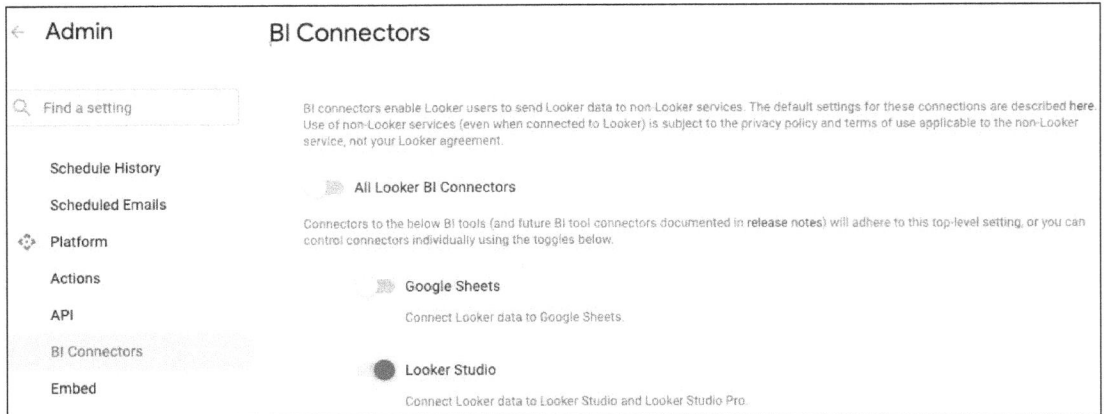

Figure 5.20: Enabling Google Sheets

2. Users should have explore permissions for at least one model, Looker studio users must have **access_data** and **clear_cache_refresh** permissions in Looker.

Connecting to Looker from Looker Studio

The steps to connect to Looker from Looker Studio are as follows:

1. Open Looker Studio, under the **Create** menu, and select **Data source**, as follows:

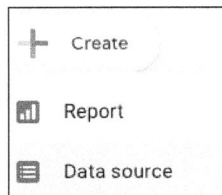

Figure 5.21: Looker Studio Data Source Option

2. You will see different connectors. Select **Looker** from the list of connectors:

Figure 5.22: Looker connector in Looker Studio

3. In the next pop-up window, enter your Looker URL. A new window opens asking to link both Google and Looker accounts. You can link both accounts.

   In the next window, it shows the Looker model and explores you want to query. Select the explore you want to use:

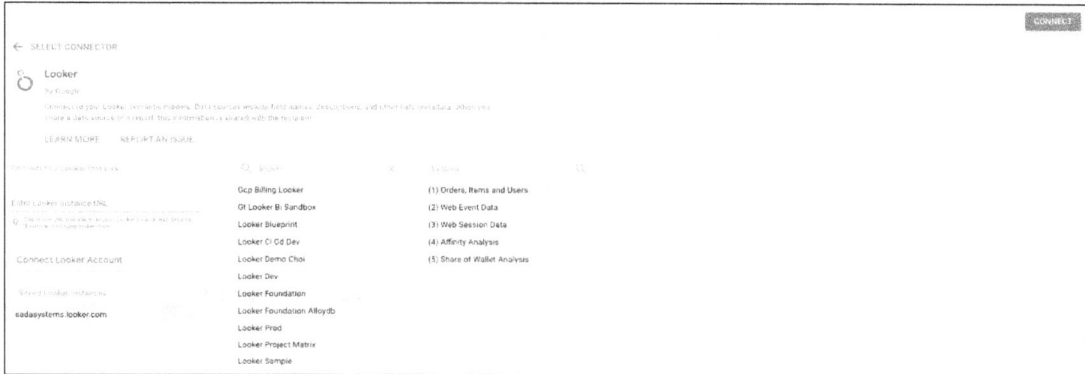

Figure 5.23: *Connecting to Looker Explores from Looker Studio*

4. After the connection, Looker Studio will open a new sheet that shows the Explore details including the views, dimensions, and measures.

Deliver data through Action Hub

We learned about some built-in destinations to deliver data, like scheduling email. In addition to the built-in options, we can also deliver Looker content to external or third-party services through Action Hub (also called **integrations**). Looker hosts and provides a server called Action Hub that implements Looker Action API and exposes popular actions. Any data Looker users send using the Action Hub will be processed temporarily on the Looker Action Hub server rather than the Looker server.

In addition to the Looker Action Hub server, we can also build custom actions and publish those actions to the Looker Action Hub for public use or publish them to a separate private Action Hub server for private use.

The services available through the Action Hub server include Slack, Airtable, Azure Storage, Dropbox, Firebase, Google Drive, Google Cloud Storage, Google Sheets, etc.

Action Hub can be accessed through **Admin | Platform | Actions**. Each of the actions can be enabled with the enable button next to the service, as shown in *Figure 5.22*. We already saw one example with Google Sheets:

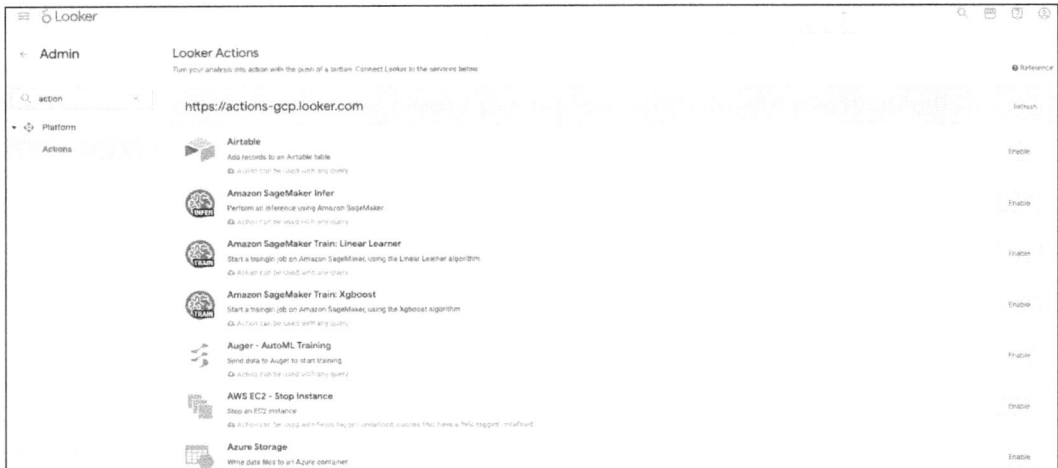

Figure 5.24: Looker Actions page under Admin

Data can be delivered in different ways and levels, depending on the level where the action operates. Actions can be at a field level, query level, or dashboard level. Some actions work at multiple levels.

The description below each service describes at what level the action is performed. So, data delivery can be at the cell or field level or dashboard or query level.

For example, Slack works at the query and dashboard level. Twilio has two services, one at the query level and the other at the field level.

For the services that work at the field level, you need to identify a field with a tag parameter.

For example, **Twilio** needs a field that is tagged with a phone in the LookML model.

So, we can find the field that has phone numbers and add the tag: **[phone]**:

```
dimension: phone_number {
  tags: ["phone"]
   type: string
   sql: ${TABLE}.phone_number ;;
}
```

In the explore, you can use the action from the field's three dots next to the value and select the action, as follows:

Figure 5.25: Twilio action on Looker explore

A new window pops up and you can send the **message** to the phone number, as follows:

Figure 5.26: Sending a text message through twilio action

Another example is Slack, which has a description: action can be used with any query and dashboard. So, this does not need any tags. It works with any query.

On the dashboard, you can schedule a report to send to **Slack** by selecting **workspace** and other options and values like channel or username, as follows:

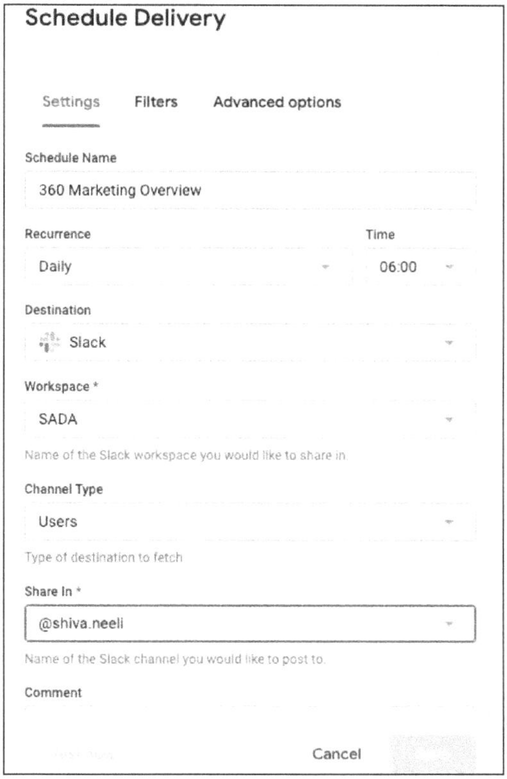

Figure 5.27: Scheduling delivery to Slack

In Slack, you will receive a message as shown in the following figure:

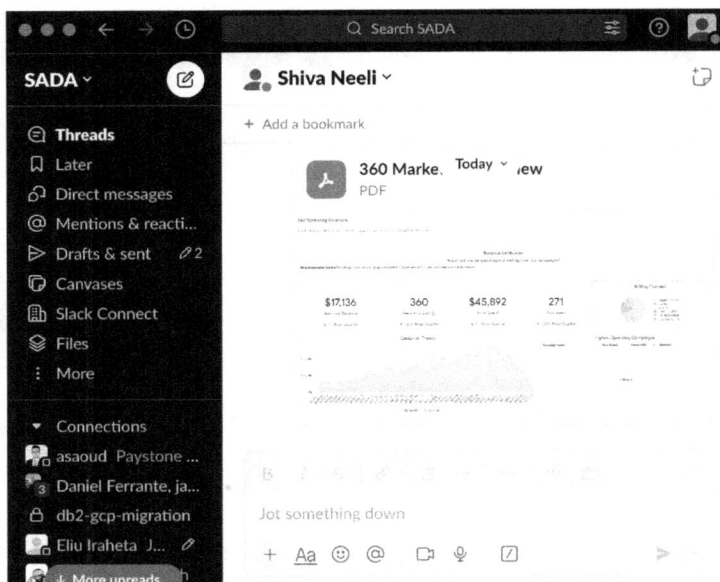

Figure 5.28: *Slack message from Looker example*

Data actions

Like Action Hub, there is another option in Looker to perform field-level actions using action parameters. Some examples include sending an email and updating a record in other applications like Salesforce. So, this is a good option if there is no readily available or custom Action Hub service available.

We can define an action on a dimension or measure. Action will be available on the field in the Look or dashboard or explore the interface.

The action syntax is:

```
view: view_name {
  dimension: field_name {
    action: {
      label: "Label to Appear in Action Menu"
      url: "https://example.com/posts"
      icon_url: "https://looker.com/favicon.ico"
      form_url: "https://example.com/ping/{{ value }}/form.json"
      param: {
        name: "name string"
        value: "value string"
      }
      form_param: {
        name: "name string"
```

```
      type: textarea | string | select
      label: "possibly-localized-string"
      option: {
        name: "name string"
        label: "possibly-localized-string"
      }
      required: yes | no
      description: "possibly-localized-string"
      default: "string"
    }

  user_attribute_param: {
    user_attribute: user_attribute_name
    name: "name_for_json_payload"
    }
   }
  }
 }
}
```

Building custom visualizations

There are many visualization types available in Looker out of the box. You can also add additional visualization types from Marketplace.

If you want to add another completely custom visualization, Looker has a couple of methods to allow this:

- Using visualization parameters in LookML
- Using the visualization page on Admin to add a custom visualization JavaScript file URL

The custom visualizations must be defined in a JavaScript file. Creation of the JavaScript file is not in scope for this book. However, we will learn about how to add the JavaScript file to Looker using the aforementioned two methods.

Using visualization parameters

In LookML, we can use the parameter named visualization. This must be used in the manifest file.

The syntax for visualization is:

```
visualization: {
    id: "unique-id"
    label: "Visualization Label"
    url: "visualization_url" or file: "visualization_file_path" #Use
either the URL or file location. Not both
    sri_hash: "SRI hash"
    dependencies: ["dependency_url_1","dependency_url_2"]
    }
```

The visualization JavaScript file can be either in a separate server or it can be added to the LookML project. If the file is on a server, use the URL parameter. If it is included in the project folder, use the file parameter and mention the file path.

Once you add the visualization, it will be available similarly to other out-of-the-box or native visualizations, or marketplace visualizations, through the Explore interface when you create it.

Add a custom visualization to the project, as follows:

- Create a JavaScript file in the project you want to add the custom visualization and add the JavaScript code in the file.

- Save the contents of the JavaScript file.

- In the manifest file of the project, add the code as follows:

  In this example, we are adding a new visualization: a radar chart:

```
visualization: {
    id: "Radar Chart"
    label: "Radar Chart"
    file: "visualizations/radarchart.js"
}
```

- Commit the changes and deploy them to production (you need to commit the changes for the visualization to show up as an option in the visualization types).

Using the visualization page on the admin

Under **Admin | Platform | Visualizations**, you can see all the additional visualizations that were added to the Looker instance.

The **Visualizations** added through the marketplace and visualization LookML parameter cannot be edited on this page, as shown in the following figure:

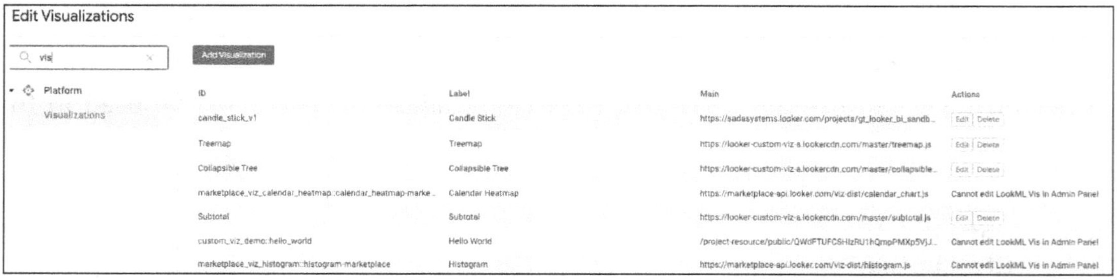

Figure 5.29: Additional visualizations

You can see that there is another option to add visualizations here using the **Add Visualization** button on top. If you click on it, you will see a form to fill out. Here, you can mention the **ID, Label** URL, and other options. Like in the LookML parameter, you can enter details here, to view the new visualization type in the Explore interface, as shown in the following figure:

Figure 5.30: Adding custom visualizations through the admin page

Third party tools

Looker community and other vendors developed a few tools that work with Looker for functionality that is not natively available. We will discuss the following popular tools available and their functionality in brief (detailed explanations and usage of those tools are available on their product page online):

- **LAMS**: It is a style guide and linter for LookML. It is designed to help produce more maintainable LookML projects. It has some built-in rules and allows specific custom rules to be enforced on the LookML.

- **Spectacles**: Spectacles is a tool that runs different validators to perform tests on the LookML and Looker instances. Validations available in this tool are, as follows:

  o **SQL validation**: Tests the SQL field of each dimension for database errors

  o **Assert validation**: For data tests

  o **Content validation**: To test for errors in the Looks and Dashboards

  o **LookML validation**: To check for errors in the LookML

- **Gazer**: It is a command line utility that can be used to manage Looker content, users, schedules, etc. It comes with 11 basic commands and can also be included in scripts. For example, we can migrate the user-defined dashboards between different Looker servers (Dev, UAT, and Prod) using Gazer.

Conclusion

In this chapter, we discussed the capabilities of Looker beyond the native features. We saw how flexible Looker is and how well it integrates and works with other applications and solutions, that are already in place in an organization.

Looker can also be embedded into other applications using different methods.

Embedding requires further explanation, so we will discuss it in the upcoming chapters.

Join our book's Discord space

Join the book's Discord Workspace for Latest updates, Offers, Tech happenings around the world, New Release and Sessions with the Authors:

https://discord.bpbonline.com

CHAPTER 6

Looker Administration

Introduction

In the previous chapters, we learned about the usage and development of dashboards, the central LookML modeling layer, and how Looker content can be integrated and used with other tools.

In this chapter, we will learn how to administer Looker. There are two ways Looker can be hosted, Looker or Google-hosted, or self-hosting. Most companies nowadays are opting for the cloud version of Looker (Looker or Google-hosted) as it reduces the effort to install, configure, and maintain the application. With the Looker-hosted application option, there are certain tasks the administrator must perform to maintain the application for your organization. We will cover these different options in this chapter.

Structure

In this chapter, we will go through the following topics:

- Looker platform editions
- Administration
- System activity

Objectives

In this chapter, we will discuss how to maintain Looker, including changing configuration, connecting to databases, enabling or disabling some features, monitoring Looker alerts, and schedules, diagnosing issues, and queries, and taking actions to improve the performance of the instance.

Looker platform editions

Before going into the details of administering Looker details, we need to understand a few important things, such as hosting types, platform editions, license type, and types of security.

Hosting types

Looker customers also have the option to self-host their Looker instances. If one decides to go this route, they will be responsible for provisioning and managing the server that the Looker application runs on, as well as the network attached to it. The configuration for self-hosting is not in scope for this publication. However, we will briefly go over the difference between Looker-hosted and self-hosted, in the following table:

	Self-hosted	**Looker/Google-hosted**
Infrastructure control	You manage all infrastructure (servers, storage, network), offering maximum control.	Looker/Google handles all infrastructure management and scaling.
Maintenance responsibility	You are responsible for all maintenance, updates, and patching.	Software updates and maintenance are performed automatically by Looker/Google.
Customization flexibility	Full access to the file system and configurations allows for deep customization.	Initial setup is significantly easier and faster. No access to file system.
Feature limitations	Certain newer, cloud-integrated features might be unavailable.	Access to all Looker features, including cloud-native integrations.
Infrastructure cost	You bear the direct costs of hardware/cloud resources and management overhead.	Costs are bundled into a subscription, including infrastructure and maintenance.

Table 6.1: Difference between Looker-hosted and self-hosted

Looker (Google) charges for two components, platform and users:

- Platform costs include the charges to run the Looker application including hardware, software, and platform administration and integrations.
- User costs are for licensing individual users to access the Looker platform. The charges vary depending on the type of user.

Editions

Looker offers distinct editions tailored to varying needs. The Standard edition serves as an entry point, ideal for smaller teams focused on core internal business intelligence. For larger organizations with more complex internal analytics requirements, higher API limits, and advanced security features, the Enterprise edition provides a robust solution. Finally, the Embed edition is specifically designed for companies looking to integrate Looker's powerful analytics directly into their external-facing applications and data products, offering specialized tools and scalability for customer-facing insights. The differences between the editions are outlined as follows:

Standard	Enterprise	Embed
Best suited for small teams and small to medium-sized businesses, typically with up to 50 internal platform users.	Designed for larger organizations with more complex internal BI and analytics requirements and no strict user limits.	Specifically built for organizations that need to embed Looker analytics into external applications and custom-built data products for their customers.
Includes a base of ten Standard Users and two Developer Users. Additional users can be added.	Includes a base of ten Standard Users and two Developer Users, but supports a significantly larger number of users.	Includes a base of ten Standard Users and two Developer Users, with pricing considerations for a potentially large number of viewers of the embedded content.
Lower limits on API calls (e.g., 1,000 query-based and 1,000 admin-based API calls per month).	Higher limits on API calls (e.g., 100,000 query-based and 10,000 admin-based API calls per month).	Highest limits on API calls (e.g., 500,000 query-based and 100,000 admin-based API calls per month), reflecting the demands of embedded analytics at scale.
Offers standard Looker security features.	Includes advanced security features like **VPC Service Controls (VPC-SC)** and Private IP options.	Offers features tailored for embedding, such as signed embedding for secure access, customizable themes (private labeling), and potentially component embedding.
Primarily for internal business intelligence and analytics needs.	Comprehensive internal BI and analytics across various departments and with stricter security needs.	Providing data insights and analytics directly within external-facing applications to enhance product value and user experience.

Table 6.2: Differences between the editions

Users

There are three types of Looker users for licensing, as follows:

- **Developer user**: An end user provisioned on a Looker (Google Cloud core) platform for access to any combination of Looker interfaces including Administration,

LookML Models (including Development Mode), folders, boards, dashboards, Looks (individual reports and charts), explore, SQL Runner, scheduling, the Looker API interfaces, and access to support.

- **Standard user**: An end user provisioned on a Looker (Google Cloud core) platform for access to folders, boards, dashboards, Looks (individual reports and charts), explore, SQL Runner, and scheduling Looker interfaces. Standard User privileges include data filtering, drill-to-row-level detail, data downloads, dashboard or Look creation, and view-only access to LookML. Standard User privileges do not include access to development mode, administration, the Looker API interfaces, or support.

- **Viewer user**: An end user provisioned on a Looker (Google Cloud core) platform for access to Folders, Boards, dashboards, and Looks (individual reports and charts) Looker interfaces. Viewer user privileges include data filtering, drill-to-row-level detail, scheduling, data downloads, and view-only access to LookML. Viewer user privileges do not include dashboard or Look creation, or access to development mode, administration, SQL Runner, Explore, the Looker API interfaces, or support.

Depending on the type of platform your organization purchased, you will have different features enabled.

Should your Looker needs evolve and require an upgrade, please contact Looker or Google Cloud Sales support. Upgrades or downgrades require a change in your Looker plan, which can affect prices. The actual change in edition will be performed by your Looker representative.

Administration

You can access the administrator features from the **Admin** section in the *main menu*, as follows:

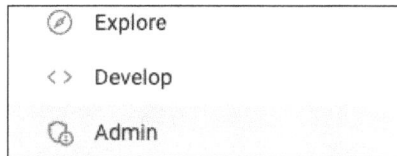

Figure 6.1: Admin navigation menu

Under this menu, there are different options available. Each configuration or function is divided into a group of pages. While most of the settings are obvious, the following are the main purposes of each page:

- **General**: These pages have the general configuration settings. Each page has some settings and an explanation below the setting that has some details, guidance on the functionality, etc.

- **Settings**: Instance-wide settings like application time zone, enablement of some features, default visualization colors, etc. are some options on this page. Many settings on this page are either self-explanatory or a description is available below the setting that explains what happens when the feature is enabled (we will learn about a few settings in the following page).

- **License key**: This shows the license key of the instance. It is unique and enables or disables certain features of the instance based on the license agreement.

- **Use Gravatar**: Gravatar is a free online service that allows users to upload a personal online avatar and associate it with their email address. When this option is enabled, Looker uses the Gravatar image (if an account exists with Gravatar) under **Profile** | account, as follows:

Figure 6.2: *Profile picture using Gravatar*

- **Default visualization colors**: This setting lets you select the default visualization color collection for visualizations. Looker has many color collections, for example, Shoreline, Boardwalk, Breeze, vivid, etc.

If you need to show some custom colors, there is also an option to create a new color collection, as shown in the following figure:

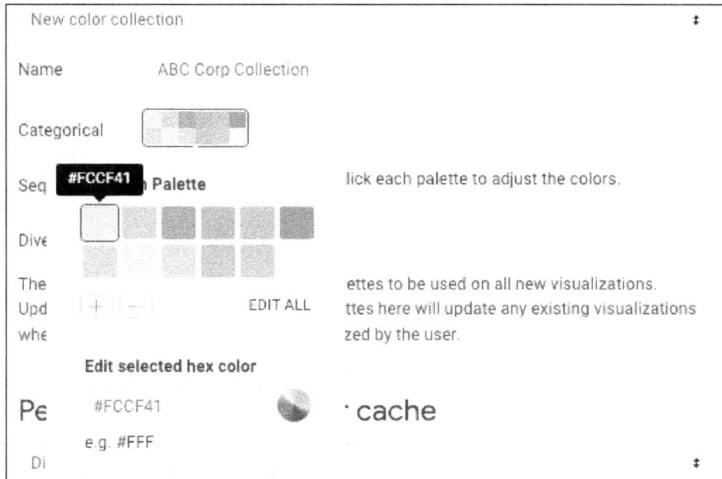

Figure 6.3: *Creating a new color collection*

To create a new color collection:

o   Select a **new color collection** from the drop-down.

o Give a **name** to the color collection

o Select each **palette** (**Categorical, Sequential,** and **Diverging**) to edit. You can select the colors by providing the **hex** code or selecting the color.

o You can also select edit all and provide the list of colors in hex code separated with a comma. For example, #FCCF41, #7CC8FA, #f56776, #10C871

o Click on **Create**. A new color collection will be added to the dropdown list.

o You can select the new color collection and click on **Update** to make it default. After that, for each visualization created in the **Explore** tab, the new color collection will be used. You will have an option to change this when you edit the visualization.

- **Email domain allow list for scheduled content**: If you want to limit the users to send the content (Looks, dashboards, or queries with visualizations) or alert notifications through emails, you can mention the domains in this setting. For example, if you would like to restrict sending the Looker content to only emails under your company (say, abccorp.com) domain, you can mention the domain: anccorp.com here, and update.

- **Labs**: This page includes some features that are still under development and not part of the actual application. Use caution while enabling these features.

This is divided into two categories:

o **Beta**: These are expected to remain in the product. Any errors found during the Beta phase will be resolved.

o **Experimental**: As the name suggests, these features may or may remain in the product. The purpose of these is to get the feedback from users.

- **Legacy features**: This page lists all the legacy features that are no longer available in the product. These can be enabled to avoid disruption in case your organization still uses these features. These features will be removed in future versions of Looker. You can disable these features test your code and content and fix the errors by either using a newer feature or a workaround.

- **Homepage**: This page shows different options to set the default home page for either, the entire organization or based on the group or user. We can set either the Looker's prebuilt homepage or any URL within Looker (a board or a dashboard) as the default home page.

- **Private label**: This page has settings that are useful if you want to customize the Looker portal to remove Looker logos and links and is disabled by default. You can ask Looker support to enable this if needed. This page has options to load custom logos and customize certain links to Looker.

- **Localization**: This page has options to set the default locale (language) and number format at the instance level. The default language is English. The locale and number format can also be set at the user or group level. Settings at the user or group level override the settings at the instance level.

- **Internal help resources**: This page if enabled will have the resources, links, and content that can be displayed in the Help drop-down. The text can be written in markup language.

- **Support access**: This page has the option to allow Google or Looker support personnel access to the Looker instance. You can choose the time that access will be given and provide the list of users that will access.

System activity

Looker has an internal application database that stores the system activity including user activity, historical query information instance performance statistics, etc. The system activity model explores connects to this database, and system activity dashboards use the explores to display the information that shows the activity and will be useful to monitor and diagnose any issues. Users who have **see_system_activity** permission can view these dashboards, who, by default, are Admins. Admins can grant this permission to other users or groups to allow them to see these dashboards, which we usually recommend for IT for administrative checks, or engineers seeking for performance optimizations.

System activity explores: There are different explorers, each for a specific purpose, and has information about a specific component of Looker, like:

- Content usage has data about Look and dashboard usage, frequency of views, favorites, schedules, and access to content through API calls.

- Dashboard explore has data about dashboards and their elements including queries, users, folders, etc.

- Users explore data about users, the access they have, and the queries the users run.

There are other explorers like folders, history, query performance metrics, SQL query scheduled plan, etc. each for a specific purpose.

System activity dashboards

Some prebuilt dashboards are using the preceding explores that include the visualizations showing usage and performance metrics. These dashboards can be used similarly to the other dashboards, including downloading, scheduling, creating alerts, drilling into the details, etc. Data in the system activity dashboards is updated and cached every 12 hours.

User activity

This shows different user metrics including the type of users and counts, time the users spent, number of queries they ran, the feature or component the users are using the most, top users for dashboards, top dashboard builders and developers, and users that are not using the system recently, etc.

This information is very helpful in understanding the way users are interacting with the system. Some sample questions that can be answered with this dashboard are as follows:

- Is there a need to purchase more licenses?
- If some users are not using the application, do they need some training, is there any improvement that you can do to the existing dashboards that can increase the usage?

Understand the usage trends and take necessary actions like increasing the performance, creating more meaningful content that can increase the adoption, etc.

Content activity

This dashboard has information about several dashboards, Looks, and schedules and out of those what is a split of used and unused content. Popular dashboards and explores unused content and the explore.

This helps clean up the environment by archiving the unused content so that the application performance gets better, and maintenance of the application will become easier. The daily scheduled jobs should be distributed so that the application and the database can perform better.

Database performance

This page shows the dashboard performance metrics. A few visualizations here include:

- **Percentage of queries run from the cache**: The more the queries run from the cache the better it is in terms of costs, especially for cloud data warehouses.
- **Query run times by user sources and system sources**: User sources include dashboards, drills, downloads `sql_runer` queries, etc. System sources include PDT Regenerator, scheduled tasks, and API calls for data downloads.
- **Top users by query count**: It shows the users who ran the most queries by day.
- **Top sources by query count**: It shows the query counts by source and day.
- **The concurrency timelines**: It shows how the queries are spread across the day by each hour. Use this chart to see if we can reduce the concurrent queries to improve the performance.
- **Performance details**: This section has details of the model or explore, dashboard, and Look. These will help in identifying and optimizing the content.
- **The PDT overview section**: It has details of PDT build activity details and average build time. You can check the frequently failed builds, diagnose the root cause, and fix the issue. These will help identify and optimize the slow-running PDTs.

Instance performance

Looker automatically generates visualizations that reports on the performance of various jobs, each of which can impact the speed of the instance. These jobs include scheduled content and memory-intensive dashboards.

This page has two sections, as follows:

- **Scheduler performance**: Scheduler performance has details of schedule distribution over the days, outlier scheduler days, and the number of scheduler jobs by explore.

- **Taxing content**: This section has visualizations that show the Looker components causing issues or deviating from best practice recommendations.

  For example:

  o Unlimited download of data should be enabled only if necessary.

  o It is the best practice recommendation that dashboards should not have more than 25 tiles. If any dashboard has more tiles, it shows up here and is a good candidate to think about breaking up into multiple dashboards.

Performance recommendations

In the preceding dashboards, Looker showed some issues that need to be investigated. After observing those, you will have to decide what to do. However, this dashboard has warnings and readily available recommendations at the dashboard and explore the level.

Some sample recommendations are:

- Reduce the number of query tiles or create a second dashboard.

- Reduce the number of merge result tiles.

- Increase or disable the auto-refresh interval setting to avoid overloading the database.

- Remove unnecessary views from the included parameter of the LookML model. Ensure that LookML production code is changed infrequently, ideally at times when users are not running many queries.

- Move custom fields and Table Calculations into LookML wherever possible.

- Avoid complex SQL logic such as window functions, CTEs, join conditions on date fields, or large join chains. Put complex SQL logic into PDTs to reduce query times. Use aggregate awareness when possible.

Errors and broken content

This dashboard shows the errors at different levels, including content (dashboards, Looks), schedules, and PDTs at query run time. If there are any errors in LookML and the dashboards or Looks that use the LookML fields, and the content validator (about which we will learn later).

Database

The database pages show Looker's interactions with database. This includes the configurations of databases connected to Looker, queries sent by Looker, tables materialized by Looker, and Looker's caching policy.

Connections

You can create, view, test, and edit the database connections and IP addresses that are needed to allow network traffic. The required configuration for a connection change based upon the selected database type (i.e. BigQuery will have slightly different requirements than Snowflake). Generally, each connection will require the database's name and location, so Looker can find it, and some form of credentials to the database, so Looker can access it.

For example, if we want to connect to the BigQuery database where the application data is stored, we need to create the dashboards through the following steps:

1. Click on **Add Connection** on this page. A new window opens, with the details, as shown in the following figure:

Edit your database connection

Fill out the connection details. The majority of these settings are common to most database dialects. Learn more

Name *
test_bq_connection

Connection Scope *

All Projects | Selected Project

Dialect *
Google BigQuery Standard SQL

Billing Project ID *
bi-eng-internal

Dataset *
ecommerce_sample

Authentication *

Service Account | OAuth

bi-eng-internal-97422fd1fd42.json | Upload File

Figure 6.4: Add connection details

2. Enter the name for this connection, for example `test_bq_connection.`

3. Select the **Dialect** of the database as Google BigQuery Standard SQL.

4. Enter the **project ID** and **dataset** name. (You can get these details from the BigQuery console, or your database admin can give you the details).

For **Authentication**, the Service Account gets the service account **JSON** file from BigQuery Admin and uploads it here or you can connect using OAuth.

5. To use **PDTs**, we need to create a temp database that can store the tables created by PDT. PDT can be enabled here by providing the database name, as follows:

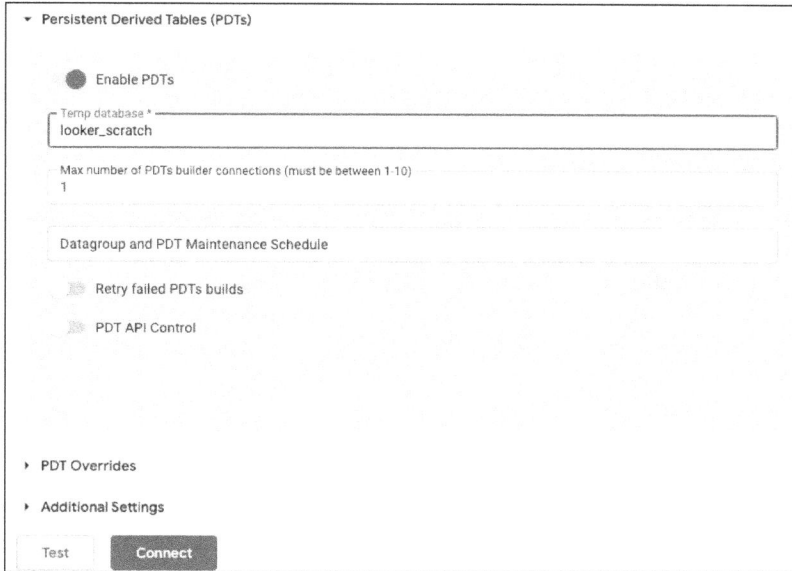

Figure 6.5: *Connection—PDT details*

6. Enter the time zone the database times are stored in and the **Query Time Zone**, the time zone from which the dashboards are run. This will enable the Looker to automatically convert time dimensions in the queries, as shown in *Figure 6.6*. You can check the SQL generated by the queries to see this conversion when a time dimension column is used.

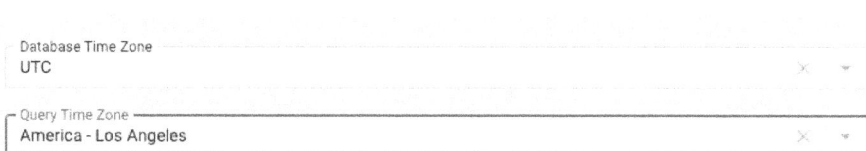

Figure 6.6: *Connection—PDT details*

7. Enable other additional settings like SSL, verify SSL, etc. if needed.

8. For BigQuery, cost estimate is always enabled. This is why you will not see a toggle. However, if you have other supported databases like Snowflake, redshift, PostgreSQL, etc., you will see a toggle for cost estimates. This will estimate the costs for queries run through Explore or SQL Runner interfaces.

9. If you click on **Test**, it will try to connect to the database and test.

A successful test message will look as follows:

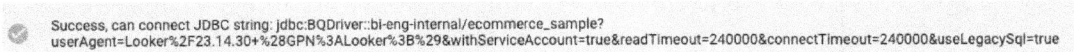

> Success, can connect JDBC string: jdbc:BQDriver::bi-eng-internal/ecommerce_sample?
> userAgent=Looker%2F23.14.30+%28GPN%3ALooker%3B%29&withServiceAccount=true&readTimeout=240000&connectTimeout=240000&useLegacySql=true

Figure 6.7: Connection—success message

10. Click on **Connect** to save the connection. It will be one of the connections listed in the **Databases** section. This is the same connection we use in the model file under the connection parameter.

Looker is using the database JDBC drivers internally to connect to your database. There is a list of dialects that Looker supports and are available in the dropdown list (of the database dialect) on the Add Connection page. You can simply provide the details specific to your database and add connections. You can see the major database dialects here. Snowflake, Redshift, Oracle, SQL Server, Teradata, PostgreSQL, MySQL, etc. are the dialects to name a few.

Queries

This page displays information on the last 50 queries submitted to the database. If you want to view more queries here, enable the *enhanced query admin* lab feature. It will show up to 500 queries. Users with **see_queries** permission can view the queries on this page.

Each query will have details like time, status (**running**, **queued**, **error**, **complete**, **cache**, etc.), connection, user, source, run time, and details button, as follows:

Time	Status	Connection	User	Source	Runtime		
5:43pm	✓ Complete	looker_partner_demo	Tanya Leung	Dashboard	Query #68761 – thelook_partner – events	3s	Details
5:43pm	✓ Complete	looker_partner_demo	Tanya Leung	Dashboard	Query #68768 – thelook_partner – order_items	2s	Details
5:43pm	✓ Complete	looker_partner_demo	Tanya Leung	Dashboard	Query #68766 – thelook_partner – events	2s	Details

Figure 6.8: Queries list

The details button has more details about the query including the **Start Time**, **End Time**, and **Runtime**, and the **SQL** tab will show the actual SQL that ran against the database, as shown:

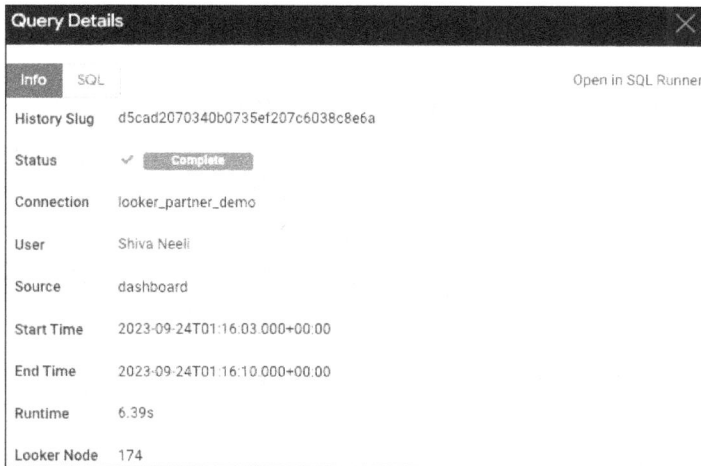

Figure 6.9: Query details

This information is useful to diagnose the issues. If any query runs for longer than expected, admins can stop the queries from this page by simply clicking on the stop button.

Persistent derived tables

This page displays the details about **persistent derived tables** (**PDT**). It shows a summary and details of the PDTs. This page is also customizable by selecting the connection, adding filters, and selecting the fields you want to display.

The summary includes the number of PDTs, build errors, currently building PDT count, expired, and the count of PDTs that are taking longer the 30 minutes.

Details include **PDT Name**, status as successful, failed, last attempt status, and last attempted time, persistence rule, connection, project, and model, as follows:

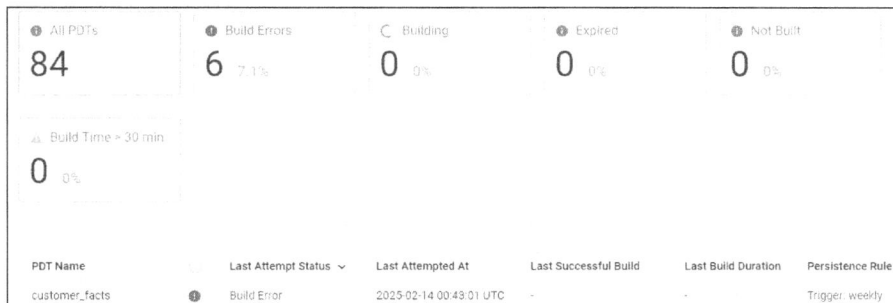

Figure 6.10: Persistent derived tables

On the details, there is a three dot menu at each line. It has further options to **Go to LookML, PDT Activity Dashboard**, and **PDT Details**, as follows:

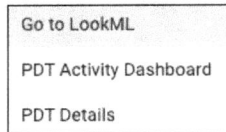

Figure 6.11: *PDT three dot menu*

The **PDT Activity Dashboard** opens a dashboard that has more details about the PDT, including the model, view, last build and average build times, failure details, and queries.

PDT Details have information about the PDT that helps diagnose the issues. Some information includes **Table Name**, **Model**, **Connection**, the status of the PDT, error details, etc., as follows:

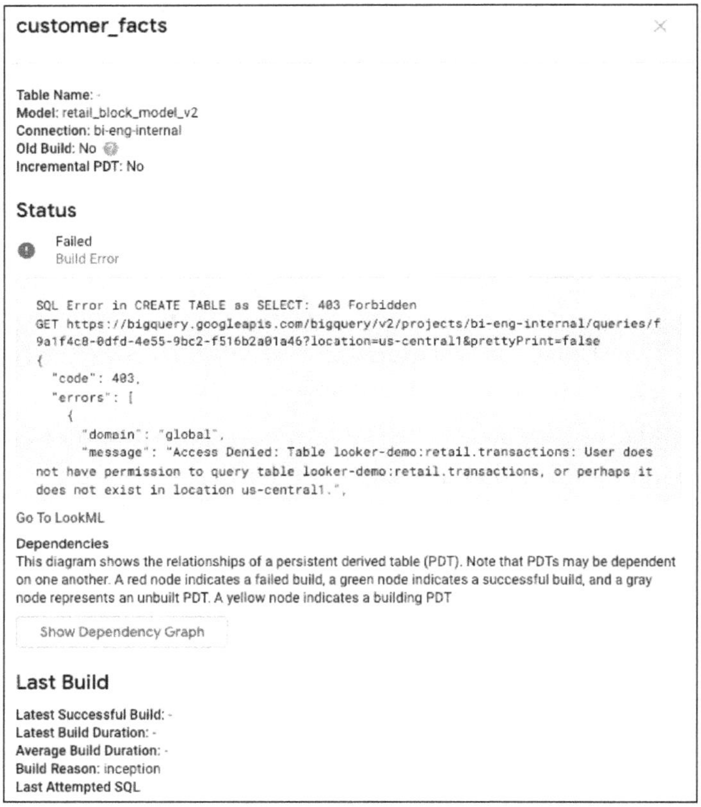

Figure 6.12: *PDT Details*

Datagroups

As we have discussed, datagroups are used to specify query caching policies and triggers for rebuilding PDTs. This page shows information about datagroups, reset their cache and you can also trigger rebuilds on this page.

It has a **Name**, **Label**, **Connection**, **Model**, **Type**, **Description**, and **Actions** you can take on the datagroup, as follows:

Name	Label	Connection	Model	Type	Description	Actions
● daily_group		auditlog-viz	block_gcp_audit_logs_v2	sql_trigger		LookML ⚙
● Status: error ● Trigger error: cannot compute sql_trigger for datagroup with oauth connection ● Trigger last checked: 3m ago						
● case_studies_demo_gt_default_datagroup		bi-eng-internal	case_studies_demo_gt			LookML ⚙
● billing_dev_default_datagroup		bi-eng-internal	cloud_billing			LookML ⚙

Figure 6.13: *Datagroup details*

There are three actions you can take on datagroup:

- Click on the **LookML** to go to the model file where the datagroup is defined.
- Reset cache will invalidate all the cached results of the explorers that are using the datagroup.
- Trigger datagroup will invalidate the cached results of the explorers that are using the datagroup and rebuild all PDTs using that datagroup. The schedules that use the datagroup as a trigger will be sent when the triggered datagroup reaches the ready state.

Alerts and schedules

Users can set alerts and create schedules on the dashboards. Admins can view and manage the alerts set by all users on these pages. Users need **see_alerts** permission to view this page and options.

Alerts

On this page, you can manage, view, edit, and delete the alerts.

If the number of alerts is more, you can use the filters to reduce the number of alerts shown on this page. There are three filter options, **Frequency**, **Condition Met**, and **Status**, as follows:

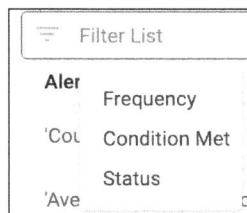

≡ Filter List	
Aler	Frequency
'Cou	Condition Met
	Status
'Ave	

Figure 6.14: *Manage alerts—filters*

You can select one or more of these filters and narrow the list. For example, **Frequency**: **Weekly**, **Condition Met**: **Yes**, as follows:

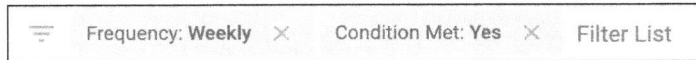

Figure 6.15: Manage alerts—filter selection

Another option to organize the alerts to view is to **Group By** on the top right section of the list, as follows:

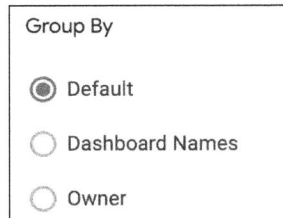

Figure 6.16: Manage alerts—filter selection

The list on this page has alert details like **Alert Name**, and **Dashboard Name** with a link to the **Dashboard, Owner, Avg Run Time, Condition Met, Frequency, Status**, and a link activity where the past activity related to the alert is shown, as follows:

Alert Name	Dashboard	Owner	Avg Run Time	Condition Met
'Average Spend per User' is less than 20	Sales Dashboard	Tanya Leung	3.40s	Yes
'Order Count' is less than 200	Brand Lookup	Tanya Leung	3.47s	Yes

Figure 6.17: Manage alerts list

The three dot menu on each alert has options to assign the alert ownership, view, edit, enable or disable, and delete the alert, as follows:

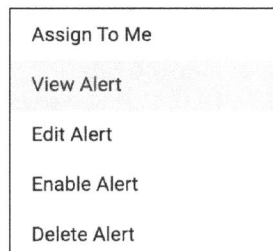

Figure 6.18: Manage alerts three dot menu

The alert history page has the history of all the alerts. The list of alerts includes the details: time, status, alert name, dashboard, owner, condition met, message, and run time.

If this list is big, you can also use the status filter that can narrow the list, as follows:

| All | Running | Complete | Failed |

Figure 6.19: Alert history—status filter

Schedules page

On this page, admins can view, reassign, and delete the schedules. Users with **see_ schedules** can also view this page.

The list has scheduled information including **Owner**, **Content Type**, **Name**, **Scheduled Times**, **History**, **Recipients**, and **Summary**, as shown in *Figure 6.20*. Each alert had options like reassign and delete:

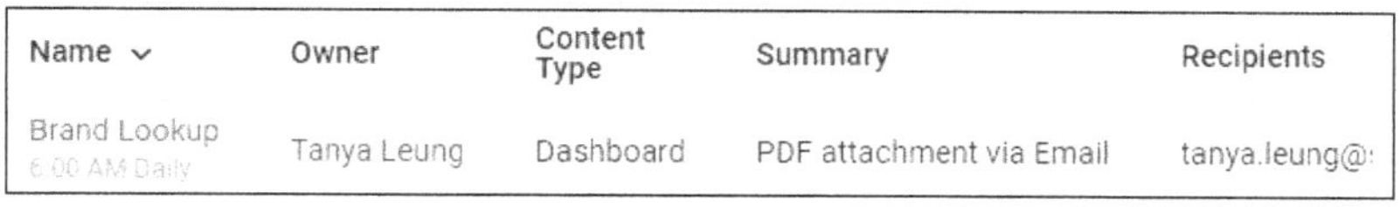

Name ⌄	Owner	Content Type	Summary	Recipients
Brand Lookup 6:00 AM Daily	Tanya Leung	Dashboard	PDF attachment via Email	tanya.leung@:

Figure 6.20: Manage schedules

Each of these schedules can be either reassigned or deleted using the buttons on the right.

Schedules history

On this page, admins can view the history of the schedules and troubleshoot in case of any issues. This page has information about schedules: time, test, status, stage, user, source, name, type, format, message, and runtime. The details will show additional details like start time, end time, error message, etc. The list of schedules can also be filtered based on the status: **running, successful**, and **failed**, as shown in *Figure 6.21*:

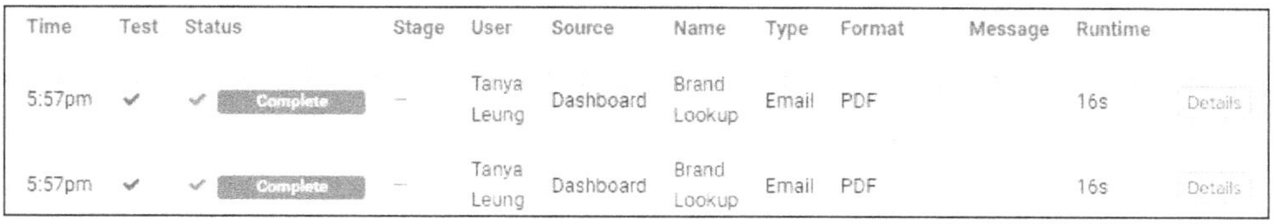

Time	Test	Status	Stage	User	Source	Name	Type	Format	Message	Runtime	
5:57pm	✓	✓ Complete	—	Tanya Leung	Dashboard	Brand Lookup	Email	PDF		16s	Details
5:57pm	✓	✓ Complete	—	Tanya Leung	Dashboard	Brand Lookup	Email	PDF		16s	Details

Figure 6.21: Schedules history

Scheduled emails page

This page has settings for data policy and external recipients that are receiving Look or dashboard results.

There are three options for sending the dashboard or results, as follows:

- **Send link only**: Emails will include only a link and will require a log-in to view the scheduled Look or dashboard. Recommended for sensitive data.

- **Send data only**: Allow data tables and visualizations to be attached or embedded in emails.

- **Send links and data**: With this option, users can decide whether to include links on an individual schedule, but data will always be included.

The external recipients' page lists the email addresses that are scheduled to receive Looks or dashboards but that are not associated with one of your Looker instance's user accounts.

Platform pages

This section lists the following feature settings that affect the entire platform. These pages include interface configurations to external entities, from Looker to external applications (like API, Embed) and external programs to Looker (Marketplace, Looker Studio Pro):

- **Actions**: On this page, there is a list of applications and services that can be integrated with Looker. You can enable or disable those services and give settings information to connect to those services. We already learned about delivering data through the action hub in the previous chapter.

- **Application programming interface (API)**: Looker provides a restful API and UI for exploring the supported API versions through API explorer. The API Host URL is shown here. Once the Looker API explorer extension is installed from the Looker Marketplace, it can be explored through the User API explorer link on this page. The documentation for the API and available functions can be explored through API explorer. The same is also available on Looker Developer's portal.

- **Business intelligence (BI) connectors**: BI connectors enable Looker users to send Looker data to non-Looker services. These can be enabled or disabled from this page. We learned about these in the previous chapter.

- **Embed**: On this page, you can configure the settings related to embedded content.

- **Extension framework**: On this page, you can enable or disable Looker extension framework options. If the extension framework is enabled, you can build and run Looker-hosted applications. You can also install and run extensions from Marketplace. For example: Data dictionary, API explorer, and LookML diagram.

  o **Marketplace**: We learned about the marketplace in the previous chapter. This page lets you configure settings for the Looker Marketplace. Marketplace option is enabled by default. If this option is disabled, users will not see the Marketplace icon on the Looker home page.

  o **Auto install**: This option allows for the auto install of a suite of fundamental Looker-built applications (for example, API Explorer). Looker will automatically install and update these applications.

  o **Auto update Looker applications**: Allows for the automatic update of Looker applications in Looker. Looker will automatically update these applications whenever a new version is published.

o **Auto update third party applications**: This option allows for the automatic update of third-party applications in Looker. Looker will automatically update these applications whenever a new version is published.

- **Themes**: This page has options to customize the appearance of embedded content from Looker. There is a default theme called Looker that is preloaded. From this, you can create a new theme, change settings like style, and color specifications, and save. The new theme can be set as a default on this page, or you can use the new theme in the embedded dashboard or explore the URL by adding **theme=<theme name>**.

  For example,

  https://example.cloud.looker.com/embed/dashboards/123?theme=themename

  Or,

  https://example.cloud.looker.com/embed/explore/model_name/explore_name??theme=red

- **Simple Mail Transfer Protocol (SMTP):** Looker instances send emails for many operations including new user notifications, password resets, and administrative notifications. Also, when delivering the content, the Looker can use emails. The SMTP page under Admin has configurations for email settings.

  For the Looker-hosted instance, there are two options, to either use default Looker-provided SMTP settings or use a custom SMTP server.

- **Visualizations**: This page shows all custom visualizations that are added to the environment. We learned how to add custom visualizations in the previous chapter.

Authentication pages

The pages under authentication are related to the configurations for logging into Looker. Please refer to *Chapter 7, Looker Security* for more details on these pages.

Server

This section contain pages related to the Looker server. Admins can see where users are accessing the Looker instance, as well as general usage, from here. If allowlist is enabled, admins can also strictly control which IP addresses Looker can be accessed from. Each page shows a different aspect of the Looker server.

IP allowlist

This page lets you specify a list of IP addresses that can access your Looker instance. If this is disabled, Looker can accept connections from any IP address. This is helpful in cases where Looker contains highly sensitive information, and users should only log in from specific locations (e.g. specific offices).

Log

This page shows the 50 most recent logs generated by the Looker instance. This is useful in diagnosing any system issues. The filter field is used to limit the logs containing a particular text.

There are logs for different services of the Looker and log level can be set to control the type of information stored in the logs. Available log levels are debug, verbose, info, warn, error, and fatal. Detailed descriptions of these levels can be found in the documentation link on this page. The default level is info. If needed, you can change the log levels of different services.

Usage

This is a Looker dashboard that shows the usage information like system activity dashboards. It has multiple tiles. Each tile's purpose is explained as follows:

- *Query by source tile* includes information about the number of queries run from different sources within Looker. Different sources in Looker include dashboard, explore, saved Look, scheduled tasks, SQL Runner, API, private embed, public embed, etc.
- *Active users* per day shows the number of active users by day for the selected date range.
- The *top users'* tile shows the top 10 users by usage minutes and query count.
- *Query run time performance* shows the top 10 explore list and for each explore it shows the number of queries and users by the query run time range buckets.
- *Scheduled plans performance* shows the schedule information.
- The list of *public Looks* shows the Looks that can be accessed by all Looker users.
- The list of *top Looks* shows the top 10 Looks by query count and average run time.
- *Commonly used fields* show the top 10 commonly used fields from different explorers.
- The list of *top dashboards* shows the top 10 dashboards by query count.

Conclusion

In this chapter, we discussed different features of the Looker administration, options available for settings, and how we can use those features to effectively manage the instance including, configuring the settings that affect the entire environment or, a few components or functions, monitoring the usage and diagnose the issues and enable external application interactions with Looker.

We will discuss *security* under admin in detail, in the next chapter.

CHAPTER 7
Looker Security

Introduction

Looker security and user management are essential concepts, required to provide secure access to the content and data in Looker. Looker provides features and flexibility to manage access to different components, including models, explores, reports/dashboards, row and individual column levels within the reports.

We will learn about all the security and access control features available in Looker, and how admins and developers use these features to create different layers of access. After this chapter, admins will be able to create custom experiences for all their users(different types).

Structure

In this chapter, we will go through the following topics:

- User pages
- Feature access
- Data access
- Content access
- Authentication

- Security best practices
- Access control examples

Objectives

In this chapter, we will discuss the concepts and key features of Looker security and how admins can use those to provide secure access to Looker users. Data can be restricted in Looker reports, using model and access parameters that control what data can be shown to the users. This chapter describes how to add users, groups, and roles and how those can be used to control access to the Looker reports, dashboards, and models.

Users pages

Under the admin menu, Looker admins can access the pages that control Looker security. Non-admin users require the **see_users** permission to view these pages.

The users' section is divided into the following pages:

- Users
- Groups
- Roles
- Content access
- User attributes
- Custom welcome email
- Login lockouts

We will discuss each of these pages in detail.

Users

Users and user permissions are managed through this tab. Admins can view every user currently on the instance, including their name, email, and permissions on this page.

This page lists all users on the Looker instance. There are two tabs for users:

- **Standard users**: Users who can login to Looker directly or through other authentication methods will be shown under this tab.
- **Embed users**: Signed Embed users who are authenticated through **single sign-on (SSO)** embed; often, a third-party app will be shown under this tab.

You can add, edit, manage, and delete users on this page as follows:

To add a new user, perform the following steps:

1. Click on **Add Users** button on the page.

2. A new window opens where you can enter the details.

   a. Enter an email ID or a list of email IDs separated by a comma.

   b. Select the **Group** and/or select a **Role**.

3. Click on **Save**, as shown in the following figure:

Adding a new user

Email Addresses *
shiva.neeli@abccorp.com

Separate with commas, semicolons, or new lines.

Send setup emails

Groups ⑦
Select...

Test_Group ✕

Roles ⑦
Select...

Developer ✕

Save   Cancel

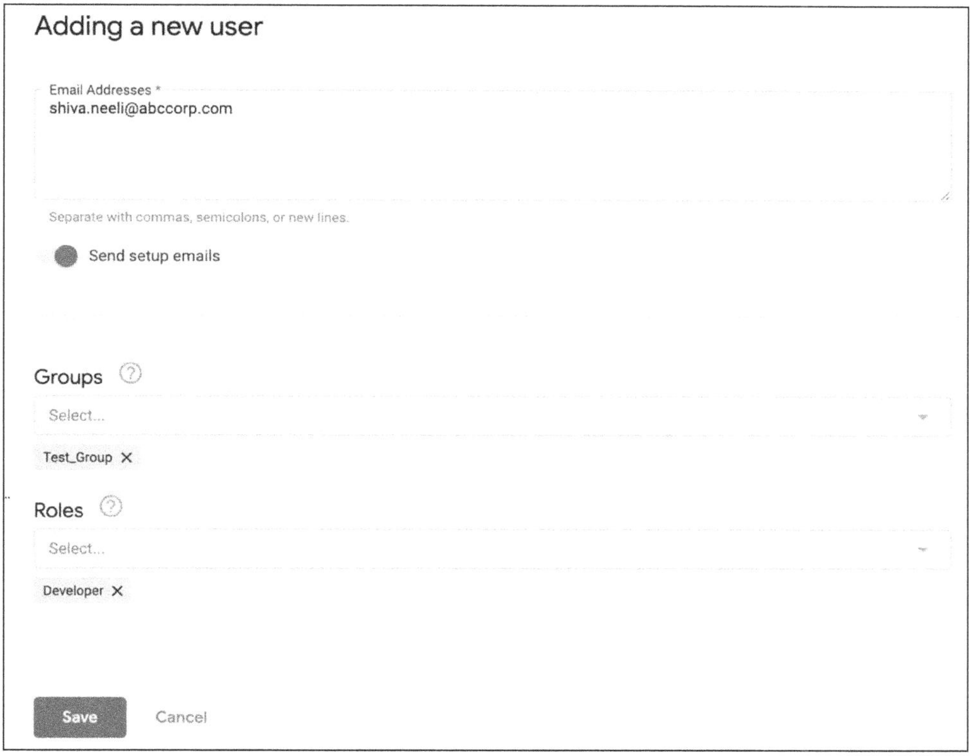

Figure 7.1: *Add a new user*

To edit the users, perform the following steps:

1. Click on the user row. A new window opens.

2. You can edit the details of the user: **First Name**, **Last Name**, **Email**, **Locale**, **Number Format**, and **Timezone** of the user.

3. You can also send a reset link and edit **API keys**. Other functions here include assigning **groups** and **roles**. The list of **user attributes** is also shown with the values, in the following figure:

First Name	Shiva
Last Name	Neeli
Email	shiva.neeli@sada.com

Localization

Locale
en ✕ ▾

Number format
1,234.56 ▾

Timezone
America - Los Angeles ⇕

Password	Send reset link
API Keys	Edit Keys
Groups	Select... ▾
	West ✕
	test3 ✕
Roles	Select... ▾
	Admin ✕

User Attributes	Name	Label	Value

Figure 7.2: *Edit user*

Admins can revoke user access using the following steps:

1. Disabling will prevent the user from logging into the system. User information, groups, and history will remain intact.

2. Deleting will remove the user permanently from the system. This is not reversible, so use caution when deleting a user.

   There are 3 options available in the three-dot menu of a user, as shown in the *Figure 7.3*:

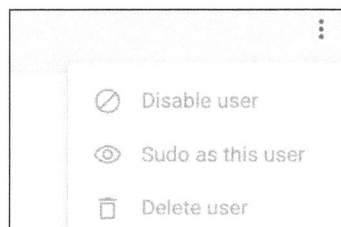

⋮

⊘ Disable user

👁 Sudo as this user

🗑 Delete user

Figure 7.3: *User options*

3. **Sudo as user** option lets you log in and navigate as if you were a different user. This is generally used to test the permissions of a user. This option is available to admins and to users who have **see_users** and **sudo** permissions. A red bar appears on the top menu that indicates that you are logged in as that user.

Groups

Groups are managed on the *Groups* page. Here, developers can create new groups and manage group membership. Instead of assigning permissions to individual users, groups can be used to assign roles, so that all users under in the group inherit the group's permissions.

Admins can perform the following actions:

- To add a new group, click on **Add Group**. A new window pops up where you can enter the name of the group.

- To add a member to the group, click on **Add Members**. A window pops up where you can search for the username. Select the user by selecting the check box next to the username and click on **Add Members**.

- To remove a user from a group, click on the group. A new page opens with the members. At each member line, you can click on the three-dot menu and select **Remove Member**.

Default groups

Looker creates one default group for all instances, that is **All Users**. This group contains every user on the instance, including embed users. It is continuously managed by Looker and cannot be edited. It is best used when you want to grant permission you would like to apply to everyone, for example, it is common for all users to have view access to the *shared folder*.

Managing access with groups

It is strongly recommended that user permissions be managed with groups. Managing permissions with groups allows permissions to be applied and changed en masse. It is not recommended to apply permissions on a per-user basis, as it can be difficult to manage and is simply not a scalable way to manage users.

Permissions can be assigned to groups through the *Roles* and *User attributes* page, as follows:

To add a user attribute to a group, take the following steps:

1. Navigate to the User Attributes page, select a specific attribute (for example, **landing_page**), and select the action *edit*. This will bring up the user attribute definition.

2. Next to the user attribute definition, there should be Group Values tab. Navigate to Group Values. This page will list any groups that already have an attribute value set. If multiple groups have a value set, this is where admins can reorganize the hierarchy to determine which user attribute should take precedence.

3. Select + **Add group**. This will bring up a dropdown menu where admins will select the group the value should apply due. Underneath, there is a text box where admins will insert the value for the select group.

4. User attributes are not additive. A user can only have one user attribute value for each attribute assigned at a given time. If multiple groups have a different value set for the same user attribute, make sure to correctly sort which groups' values should take precedence in the case that a user is assigned to multiple groups.

To add a role to a group, take the following steps:

1. Navigate to the **Roles** page and select a role that you would like to assign (for example, Viewer). Select the action edit for that role.

2. Scroll past *name, permission set,* and *model set*. Groups will be listed next. Check any groups that should have the selected role assigned.

3. Select **Update Role** at the very bottom of the page to save any selections.

Permissions are additive, meaning if someone is in multiple groups, they will inherit the combined set of permissions of all their groups. Admins can, by default, give all users Viewer permissions and then add users to specific groups to add additional permissions. Additive permissions allow admins to create groups for specific purposes and assign users to multiple groups to achieve the correct set of permissions.

Roles

A *role* is a combination of a model set and a permission set. Permission sets, model sets and roles are used to control what users (and groups) can do and what they can see. Users can have multiple roles assigned to them at once–if multiple roles are assigned, permissions are additive.

Each explore is configured to use a database connection, schemas, and tables or views. So, Data access control is at the model level and can be controlled with a *model set*. It defines which models a user or group can access.

A *model set* is a list of models to which a user or group should have access. It limits what data and LookML fields a user can see. Create a model set using the following steps:

1. To create a model set, on the **Roles** page, click on the **New Model Set**. In the new page, enter a name for the model set. Select the models that you want to include in this set.

2. Click the **New Model Set** button at the bottom. A new model set will appear on the roles page, as shown in the following figure:

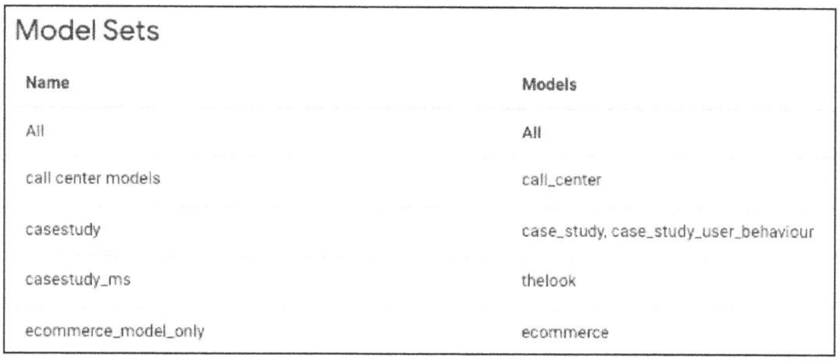

Model Sets

Name	Models
All	All
call center models	call_center
casestudy	case_study, case_study_user_behaviour
casestudy_ms	thelook
ecommerce_model_only	ecommerce

Figure 7.4: Model set

Note: **You can also edit or delete a model set from the same page.**

A *permission set* defines what a user or group can do. Looker has some default permission sets like, admin, developer, user, and viewer. Each permission set has a list of permissions for example: **`access_data`**, **`create_table_calculations`**, **`develop`** etc.

By default, Looker will create five permission sets for every instance: Admin, Developer, User, User who cannot view LookML, and Viewer. Admins have the option to create a custom permission set.

Features on Looker are broken down into several permissions, let us look at them in following are outlined in the table as follows:

Data access permissions

These permissions determine if Looker users can access explores, dashboards, and looks:

Permission name	Permission	Use case
access_data	Allows users to access/query data from Looker.	Required for any user that should be able to query data and/or view dashboards. Only gives the general ability to access data–the actual data available can be refined.
see_lookml_dashboards	Gives users access to dashboards created via LookML	Required for users who need the ability to see dashboards that have been codified into LookML. Best for users who need to be viewing static content.
see_looks	Gives users ability to view looks (does not include dashboards)	This is the minimum permission required to view any look, recommended for all users.
see_user_dashboards	Gives users ability to view dashboards (does not include looks or LookML dashboards)	This is the minimum permission required to view any dashboard, recommended for all users.

Permission name	Permission	Use case
explore	Allows users to access the Explore page and create visualizations.	Recommended permission for any user that should be allowed to create visualizations.
create_ table_ calculations	Allows users to view, edit, or add Table Calculations	This will allow users to create their own custom metrics. Table Calculations allow for much more advanced aggregations beyond what is available in Custom Dimensions or measures. Not recommended if you do not want users to define their own aggregations.
create_ custom_ fields	Allows users to view, edit, or add custom fields (includes both dimensions and measures)	Recommended for power users, as it will give them the flexibility to create their own metrics
can_create_ forecast	Enables the forecasting feature for users	Recommended for power users
can_ override_ vis_config	Allows users access to the chart config editor, a JSON-based method of editing visualizations	Recommended for power users familiar with JSON with special visualization requirements, otherwise can be confusing for regular users
see_drill_ overlay	Allows users to drill into a visualization, if a drill has been set up. Note that the explore permission will automatically enable this permission.	Recommended for all users that have access to visualizations.

Table 7.1: Features on Looker

External interactions permissions

These permissions determine the various ways a user can bring data outside of Looker:

Permission name	Permission	Use case
save_ content	Allows users to save and edit both looks and dashboards.	Base permission required to allow users to save and edit any visualizations that they have created. This should generally be enabled for anyone who has explore permissions.
create_ public_ looks	Allows users to make looks into public looks and generate URLs to the look to be viewable without any authentication.	Generally recommended to be reserved to a few select users, as this permission will let a user expose data outside of Looker.
download_ with_limit	Gives user permission to download data, but users must specify a row limit of <5,000	Recommended if the database has large tables that should not be queried without filters

Permission name	Permission	Use case
download_ without_ limit	Gives user permission to download data without any row restrictions	We recommend restricting this, if possible, so that users are not accidentally downloading large chunks of data
schedule_ look_ emails	Allows users to schedule deliveries of dashboards, looks, and queries to users on the Looker instance and any emails in the allowlist.	Generally recommended for all internal users
schedule_ external_ look_ emails	Allows users to schedule deliveries of dashboards, looks, and queries to anyone with a valid email.	Generally recommended to be limited to select users, as anyone with this permission can deliver data outside the instance to anyone.
create_ alerts	Allows users to create and edit alerts on top of dashboard tiles.	Generally recommended for all internal users
follow_ alerts	Allows users to view and follow alerts that have already been created.	Generally recommended for all internal users
send_to_s3	Allows users to send looks, dashboards, and queries to an Amazon S3 bucket.	Recommended for data engineer developers only
send_to_ sftp	Allows users to send looks, dashboards, and queries to a SFTP server.	Generally recommended for users of the SFTP server
send_ outgoing_ webhook	Allows users to send looks, dashboards, and queries to a webhook.	Generally recommended for users of the webhook
send_to_ integration	Allows users to send looks, dashboards, and queries to a third-party integration.	Generally recommended for users of the integration

Table 7.2: Features on Looker

Development permissions

These permissions are related to LookML development:

Permission name	Permission	Use case
see_sql	Gives users access to view the SQL tab in explores.	Recommended for any user with explore and develop permissions, as it allows users to troubleshoot SQL if an explore throws an error
see_lookml	Gives users read-only access to the LookML.	Recommended for power users and developers
develop	Allows the user to toggle on Development Mode and edit LookML.	Base permission required to allow development of the LookML.

Permission name	Permission	Use case
deploy	Allows users to deploy LookML to production	Deploy and develop are required to allow a user to make changes and make those changes available to the entire instance.
support_access_toggle	Gives users the permission to toggle support access. Support access gives admin permission to Looker support.	Recommended to developers in the case they do need to contact Looker support, they can provide access on demand.
manage_project_models	Allows users to add, edit, or delete a model configuration. Users with this permission can determine what connections a model has access to.	Recommended for all developers, unless specific developers should only have permissions to a specific dataset.
use_global_connections	Allow users to change accessible connections for a project.	Recommended for all developers, unless specific developers should only have permissions to a specific project.
manage_project_connections_restricted	Allows users to see the Connections page under the admin menu, but with restrictions (cannot edit connection additional settings of Persistent Derived Table settings).	Only required for non-admins if the user is setting up the database connection.
manage_project_connections	Allows users to see the Connections page under the admin menu without restrictions	Only required for non-admins if the user is setting up the database connection.
use_sql_runner	Enables the SQL Runner tab under Develop. Users with this permission can run their own SQL directly against the database and download any returned results (only from the SQL Runner).	Recommended for developers, as this can often be used for troubleshooting or for viewing the database tables without needing to provide access to the database directly.

Table 7.3: Features on Looker

Administration permissions

These permissions relate to mostly administrative tasks:

Permission name	Permission	Use case
clear_cache_refresh	Allows users to clear the cache of a visualization and re-run the data.	Generally recommended for all users so that they can refresh stale data
manage_spaces	Allows users to create, edit, and delete folders. Note that this is the base permission required to view any folder but will still need to also be applied on a per folder basis.	Recommended to any user that is responsible for dashboard and/or folder management.

Permission name	Permission	Use case
manage_ homepage	Allows users to edit sidebar content that appears on the pre-built homepage (/browse). Note this permission is not related to the ability to change the landing_page user attribute.	Recommended to any user that is managing the homepage links. This permission is not required if the Looker instance is using a custom homepage.
manage_ models	Allows users to create, edit, and delete projects.	Recommended to developers unless developers should only have access to specific projects or models.
login_ special_email	Allows the user to log in with email/ password credentials if alternate login mechanisms (Google, LDAP, SAML, etc) have been enabled.	Recommended for any user that should only have temporary access to an instance (e.g. consultant). It allows users access to Looker without having to add them to Google, Okta, etc.
embed_ browse_spaces	Enables content browsing for embed users	Only recommended if embed users have permission to save content
embed_saved_ shared_space	Enables access to the shared folder space for embed users	Only recommended if proper content permissions are in place so that the embed user has access to a specific set of dashboards. Embed users without this permission only have access to their own personal folder.
manage_ embed_ settings	Allows users to access the Embed page under Admin. This page is only available if embed has been enabled on the instance.	Recommended for admins only
manage_ themes	Allows users to access the Themes page under Admin. This page is only available if embed has been enabled on the instance.	Recommended for admins only
manage_ privatelabel	Allows users to access the Private Label page under Admin. This page is only available if embed has been enabled on the instance.	Recommended for admins only
manage_ groups	Gives users access to the Group page under the Admin tab. Allows users to create, edit, and delete groups.	Recommended to restrict this permission to admins.
sudo	Allows users the ability to sudo into other users.	Recommended to restrict this permission to admins.

Permission name	Permission	Use case
manage_roles	Allows users to create, edit, and delete any role except the Admin role. This does not give permissions to edit models or permissions sets.	Recommended to restrict this permission to admins.
manage_user_ attributes	Gives users access to the User Attributes under the Admin tab. Allows users to create, edit, or delete user attributes.	Recommended to restrict this permission to admins, as user attributes are often used for data access management.
manage_ groups	Gives users access to the Group page under the Admin tab. Allows users to create, edit, and delete groups.	Recommended to restrict this permission to admins.
manage_roles	Allows users to create, edit, and delete any role except the Admin role. This does not give permissions to edit models or permissions sets.	Recommended to restrict this permission to admins.
manage_user_ attributes	Gives users access to the User Attributes under the Admin tab. Allows users to create, edit, or delete user attributes.	Recommended to restrict this permission to admins, as user attributes are often used for data access management.
see_users	Gives users view access to the Users page under the Admin tab. Users can see user information, but cannot modify the user or any user privileges.	Recommended to restrict this permission to admins, as users can contain sensitive information.

Table 7.4: Features on Looker

Looker instance activity log permissions

These permissions relate to being able to view previous actions performed by the Looker instance, like caching, PDTs, run schedules, etc:

Permission name	Permission	Use case
see_ schedules	Allows users to see Schedule and Schedule History under the Admin tab. This permission does not give the ability to edit schedules.	This permission can be given to users to help them monitor if their schedules have successfully run, or if there is a duplicate schedule created.
see_pdts	Gives users access to the Persistent Derived Tables page under the Admin tab. Users will only see PDTs for connections they have access to.	Recommended for developers, as it will allow them to see if any PDTs they have defined were successfully built.

Permission name	Permission	Use case
see_datagroups	Gives users view access to the Datagroups page under the Admin tab.	Recommended for developers, as datagroups are defined in the LookML.
update_datagroups	Gives users access to the Datagroups page under the Admin tab. Users will have access to manually reset the cache or trigger a datagroup.	Recommended for developers, as the ability to trigger the datagroup will assist them in correctly defining datagroups in the LookML.
see_system_activity	Gives users access to the System Activity explores and the System Activity section under the Admin tab.	Recommended for any IT analyst to allow analysis of usage across the instance.
mobile_app_access	Allows users to sign into the Looker instance using the mobile app.	Recommended to anyone viewing dashboards.

Table 7.5: Features on Looker

Content access

The content access page is used to manage access to folders in one centralized place, as shown in the following figure:

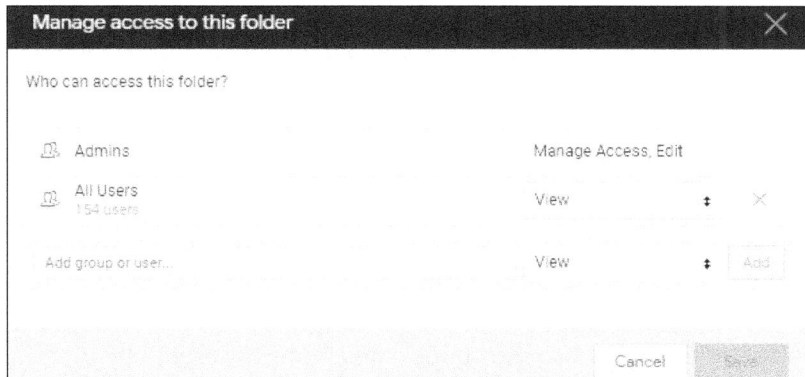

Figure 7.5: Folder access

Three different levels of permission can be granted to users on a folder:

- **Manage access and edit**: Users with this permission can create, edit, and move dashboards and looks that live in the folder. This permission extends to any folders within this folder.

- **View**: Users can only view the dashboards and folders within this folder.

- **No permission**: Users cannot see the folder at all. This permission is automatically granted if a user or group is not given view or manage permissions.

Looker does not have permissions at the dashboard or Look level, access is only determined at the folder level. Dashboards and looks that exist within a folder automatically inherit that folder's permissions. If a user has edit access to a folder, they will also have edit access to all the looks and dashboards in that folder.

User attributes

User attributes are values that Looker admins can apply to users and groups in order to create custom experiences. They are defined in key-value pairs, the *key* is the name of the user attribute and is constant for all users, while the *value* can be a custom value tailored to the user.

While Looker has a default set of user attributes, Admins can also create their own user attributes to attach to users. To create or edit user attributes, the user attributes are defined using the following fields:

- **Name**: This name is how the attribute will be referenced in LookML.

    Note: **Changing the name will require developers to also change how it is referenced in the LookML, so it is best to decide on the name carefully.**

- **Label**: This is the display name for the user attribute.
- **Data type**: This is the data type of the user attribute and determines how the attribute can be filtered and interacted with in the LookML.

    The different types are as follows:

    o **String**: Accepts one string value.

    o **Number**: Accepts one numerical value.

    o **Date or time**: Accepts a single date.

    o **Relative URL**: Accepts a URL relative to the Looker instance. Start each relative URL with a forward slash (/).

    o **String filter (advanced)**: Like string but is compatible with Looker's filter expressions (that is, compatible with wildcarding using %, accepts comma-separated lists, and exclusions using dashes).

    o **Number filter (advanced)**: Like number, but compatible with Looker's filter expressions (that is, compatible with greater than or less than, using NOT for exclusions, equal, not equals, etc.)

    o **Date or time filter (advanced)**: Like date or time, but compatible with Looker's filter expressions (that is, compatible with relative periods defined with a string such as *this month*)

- **User access**: This determines if users can view and or edit the attribute. For a user attribute to be used for access control, it will need to be set as *none* or *view*.

- **Hide values**: This determines if the value will be masked like a password. If set to Yes, once the value is set, it cannot be viewed. This is recommended if the user attribute contains a password, which may be the case if using, GitHub HTTPS or a webhook authentication.

- **Default value**: This can be used to set a value for users in the case they do not inherit a value from a group, or a value is not manually applied to them, as shown in the following figure:

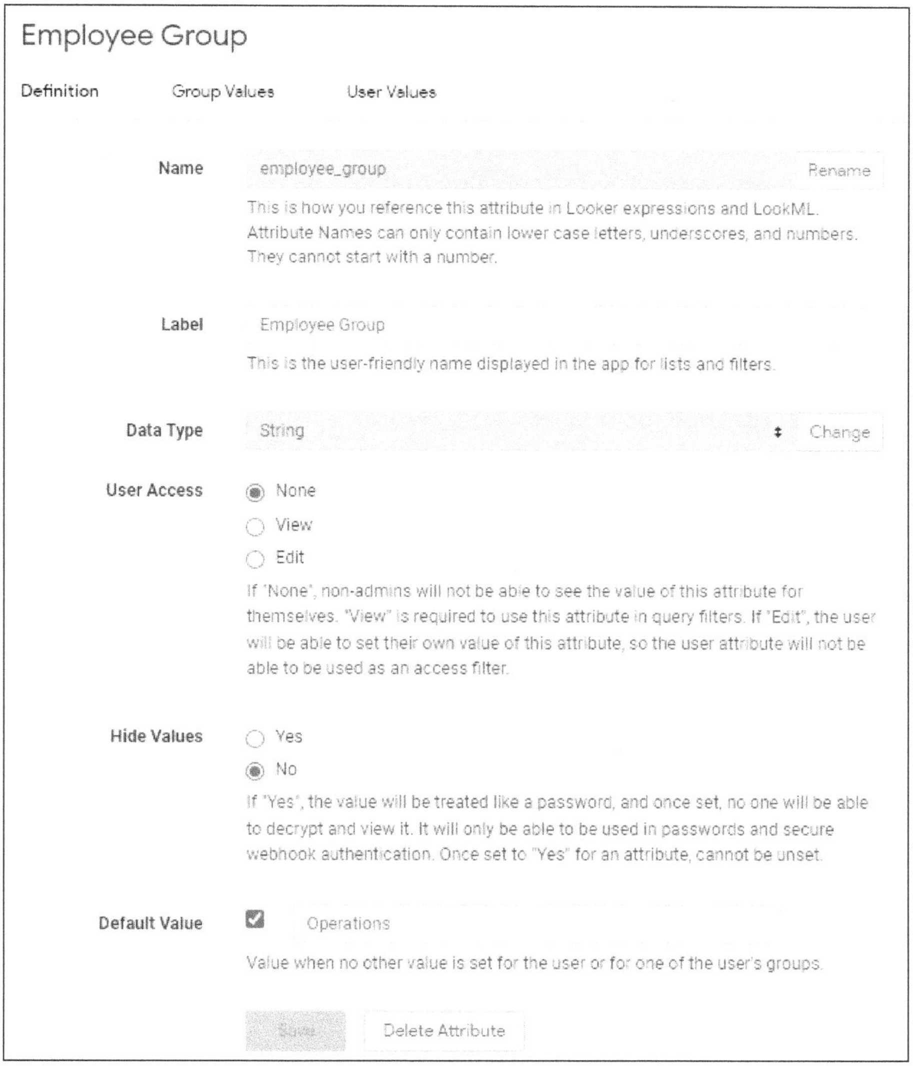

Figure 7.6: *Sample user attribute*

- **Assigning user attributes**: User attributes can be assigned at the user or group level. Select *edit* on any user attribute to assign it.

- **User attribute priority**: Multiple user attributes can be assigned to a single user through either a group or directly to the user. A user, however, can only have one value for the attribute at a time. Looker determines a single user attribute value using the following hierarchy:

  o **User value**: If a value has been applied directly to a user, this will always take precedence.

  o **Group value**: If a value has been inherited through a group, it will override the default value. Within groups, admins can determine which group values take priority. The priority is determined under *group values* for each user attribute. Groups listed first take precedence. The order of the groups can be changed by dragging groups in the list.

  o **Default value**: This is the value that can be assigned when a user attribute is configured. It has the least amount of precedence.

The common user attribute uses are as follows:

- **Git HTTPS**: If any LookML project is configured with a Git connection using multiple account HTTPS authentication, user attributes will need to be created to facilitate the connection. A user attribute must be created for a user's GitHub username (**github_username**) and a user's GitHub token (**github_token**). Developers will need to add the corresponding information to each attribute manually:

  o **github_username**: The developer's own GitHub username. This user will need read and write access to the repository attached to the LookML project.

  o **github_token**: A personal access token, generated with the username defined in **github_username**.

    ▪ It is highly recommended that this user attribute's Hide Values be set to Yes so that the personal access token is not publicly exposed.

- **Connections settings**: User attributes can be used to dynamically configure a connection. The fields configurable with user attributes vary by connection–any field that can be configured will have a user attribute button available to the right of it, as outlined in *Figure 7.7*:

Dialect *
Google BigQuery Standard SQL

Billing Project ID *
bigquery_project

Dataset *
dataset_name

Figure 7.7: Connection settings configured with user attributes

If selected, the setting will convert from a text field to a dropdown field. Admins will be given the option to select from an existing user attribute that the setting will use the value of. This setup can enable dynamic connection settings for each user.

- **Data access management**: Using LookML, user attribute values can be used to dynamically grant users access to specific explores, views, dimensions, measures, and even specific subsets of data. (See more in the *Data Access Management Using LookML* section.)

Custom welcome email

Here, admins can customize what Looker sends on the welcome email to users. The welcome email is sent to every user when they are first added to the instance. It redirects users to Looker to set up their account.

The welcome email can be customized using HTML and inline CSS. Scripts are not accepted.

Note: **Welcome emails are not sent to users who authenticate using SAML.**

Login lockouts

This page contains a list of users that are currently locked out. Users will be automatically locked out if they fail to enter valid credentials four times in a row from the same IP address. When a user is locked out, they will not be able to try to log in again for five minutes.

Admins can unlock any users listed here to remove the five-minute lockout.

Feature access

In this section, we will discuss the different ways to manage *the actions that a user can perform*. Feature access determines what Looker pages and features are available to a user. Should a user be able to create visualizations, edit LookML, or create schedules? These actions and more are determined using feature access.

Permission sets

Feature access for Looker users is maintained using the permissions sets. Each performable action on Looker, such as viewing dashboards, accessing explores, or editing LookML is a permission. Permission sets are a list of permissions that can then be attached to Roles; roles are then attached to users, which dictate what they have access to do. Admins can create roles by creating the permissions sets with specific permissions.

Looker's default permissions sets are a good starting point for a basic grouping of permissions. Let us see a summary of what each default role can do. The following are the default roles and recommendations:

- **Admin**: It includes every permission in its permission set, as well as additional permissions that are only available to admins, such as adding users, configuring Looker settings, etc. This is the only role that cannot be altered.

- **Developer**: It contains every permission needed to edit LookML and push changes to production. Developers also contain the permissions of Users.

- **User**: This role grants permissions required for users to be able to browse, create, and edit visualizations. Users do not have access to the Admin tab.

- **Users who cannot view LookML**: The same as the user who cannot view LookML. The *develop* tab will not appear as an option for these users.

- **Viewer**: This limits users to a read-only version of Looker. They can view dashboards, but they cannot edit or create visualizations. Viewers do not have access to the Explore, Develop, or Admin tab.

The following are some additional permission sets that could be set up:

- **Alternate login**: `login_special_email`

  o This permission set will allow users to log in with an email or password combo. We recommend this set if an external authentication application has been configured for Looker. Granting users this permission will allow them to bypass that authentication method, which helps set up temporary users (for example, consultants) who do not have an account on the authentication application.

  o It is recommended that alternate login only be provided to consultants and admins, since it may confuse normal users about which method they should use to login

- **Embed viewer**: `access_data`, `see_lookml_dashboards`, `clear_cache_refresh`, `see_drill_overlay`

  o This permission set gives the minimum number of permissions required for an embed user to be able to view LookML dashboards. Usually, embed users interact with visualizations outside of Looker, narrowing down the permissions guarantees they do not have access to anything else on Looker through the embed.

  o This permission set can be expanded to include **see_looks** and **see_user_dashboards** if non-LookML dashboards are included.

- Embed user: `access_data`, `see_lookml_dashboards`, `clear_cache_refresh`, `see_drill_overlay`, `see_looks`, `see_user_dashboards`, `explore`, `save_content`, `embed_browse_spaces`

  o This permission set contains the minimum required permissions for an embed user to create and save dashboards outside of the Looker instance.

  o Admins can also add **embed_saved_shared_space**, but with extreme caution as this will give embed users access to the shared space. Folder permissions will need to be properly set up. Embed users will always have access to their personal folder, in the case that **embed_saved_shared_space** is not granted.

Note: **Embed users have access set up dynamically upon creation, which will be covered in Chapter 9, Application Programming Interface, Software Development Kit and Embed.**

Data access

In this section, we will discuss the different ways to manage the data that a user can access. Should they be able to access the entire dataset, or should they only have access to select tables? Within those tables, should they be able to query anything, or should they only have access to specific rows? The availability of data to users is governed with data access.

Data access management using model sets

Access to entire models and their corresponding data and explores can be managed using model sets. The model set for default roles (Admin, Developer, User, Viewer) is All, meaning they have access to all models on the Looker instance.

Model sets can be used to restrict access to specific connections and, or explores.

Data access management using LookML

Granular access control is also possible in Looker using LookML. There are several parameters available to facilitate access at a more granular level than what is available using model sets. These LookML parameters can be categorized into three different categories: access, filters, and masking. We will discuss each one of these, as follows:

Access

`Access_grant` are parameters that can be used to restrict what is available to users on the explore. Access grants are like model sets in that they essentially turn the visibility of an object on or off for a user. They can be applied at a much more granular scale than model sets. Whereas model sets limit access to entire models, access grants can be used to control access to the following:

- **Entire model files**: Restricting at this level is like a model set restriction.

- **Individual explores within a model**: Restricting at this level will obscure the entire explore, including all joins.

- **Specific joins within explores**: Restricting at this level will only obscure the join. This is separate from access grants on views, and it will only apply to the join for the specific explore it is part of.

- **Views**: Restricting at this level will prevent users from seeing this view, even in all explores, including all the explores it is part of.

- **Dimensions and measures within views**: Restricting at this level will prevent users from seeing the dimension and measure, including all explores that it is part of.

Access grants are also distinct from model sets in that they rely on user attributes, whereas model sets are defined as part of a user role. Access grants look at a specific user's user attribute and grant access based on its value.

Setting up access grants

Developers can set up an access grant using the parameter **access_grant** and **required_access_grants**, and **user** attributes.

- The parameter **access_grant** is defined on the model file, ideally before explore definitions. **access_grant** is where an access grant policy is defined, it requires two parameters to be defined: **user_attribute** and **allowed_values**. User attribute is where developers define what user attribute Looker should be looking at; **allowed_values** are the values Looker will accept that will enable users to view the restricted object. Let us look at an example of an access grant, as shown in *Figure 7.8*:

```
access_grant: can_view_financial_data {
  user_attribute: department
  allowed_values: [ "financial", "executive" ]
}
```

Figure 7.8: Sample access grant policy

- This access policy states that users with their department set as financial or executive are allowed to view the object. This access policy can be applied to objects using the name **can_view_financial_data**.

  Access grant policies are attached to Looker objects using the parameter **required_access_grants**. Attaching this parameter to an object's definition will apply the access grant policy to that object. Let us look at an example of attaching access grants, shown in *Figure 7.9*:

```
23 ▾  explore: order_items {
24       label: "(1) Orders, Items and Users"
25       view_name: order_items
26
27       required_access_grants: [can_view_financial_data]
28
29 ▾     join: order_facts {
30         required_access_grants: [can_view_financial_data]
31         type: left_outer
32         view_label: "Orders"
33         relationship: many_to_one
34         sql_on: ${order_facts.order_id} = ${order_items.order_id} ;;
35       }
36  }
```

Figure 7.9: Sample access grant

The parameter **required_access_grants** is in two locations on the explore **order_items**:

o **Line 27**: If added here, it will limit access to the entire explore. Only users that meet the requirements of **can_view_financial_data** can see the **order_items** explore and all associated dashboards or looks.

o **Line 30**: If added here, it will limit access to only the **order_facts** join. Users will see the **order_items** explore under the explore tab, but when on the **order_items** explore, any dimensions and measures under **order_facts** will not be visible for users who do not have the user_attribute department set to either financial or executive for users who do not have the user_attribute department set to either financial or executive. Additionally, attempting to access it on visualizations that reference it will return an error.

- **Access grants allowed_values restrictions**: When defining acceptable values in access grant policies, the values must match user attribute values exactly. Even if a user attribute's data type is string filter (advanced), it will only match the exact text. For example, say a user's department is type string filter (advanced) and their value is set to *finance, sales*. In the access grant definition, **allowed_values** must be set to *finance, sales*" to allow that user access to the object. Something like just *finance or sales* will not work.

- **Access grants versus model sets**: When an access grant policy is attached to the model level, it functions very similarly to model sets. The major difference is the setup. Model sets are set up through roles, whereas access grants are implemented using user attributes.

- **Hidden**: The parameter **hidden** can be used to remove the visibility of dimensions and measures from an explore. Hidden only removes dimensions and measures from view but does not restrict the underlying access. It should only be used to clean up and explore. In *Figure 7.10*, we can see an example of when a hidden visualization may be useful:

```
dimension: total_orders_raw {
  type: number
  hidden: yes
  sql: ${TABLE}.total_orders ;;
}

measure: total_orders {
  type: sum
  sql: ${total_orders_raw} ;;
}
```

Figure 7.10: Sample of a hidden parameter

In our original table, we have a column called **total_orders**. However, we want to be able to aggregate the column, therefore, we create it as a measure. To reduce confusion for users, we hide the original dimension so that only one total orders appears on the explore. By hiding it, we clean up the explore for end-users, but we are still able to reference and use the dimension.

The hidden parameter is useful for any situation where we have a dimension or measure that is used as an intermediate variable, but we do not want to expose it to the end user.

Filtering

Looker has a variety of different filter parameters that can be used to restrict what data is available to users:

- **access_filters** dynamically restrict data according to a user's user attributes. Access filters are applied at the explore level. Defining an access filter, requires two parameters: **field**, which is the dimension that the filter should be applied to, and **user_attribute**, which is the attribute the access filter should be referencing.

  In *Figure 7.11*, we have a sample access filter defined, as follows:

```
explore: order_items {
  label: "(1) Orders, Items and Users"
  view_name: order_items

  access_filter: {
    field: distribution_centers.name
    user_attribute: region
  }

  join: distribution_centers {
    view_label: "Distribution Center"
    type: left_outer
    sql_on: ${distribution_centers.id} = ${inventory_items.product_distribution_center_id} ;;
    relationship: many_to_one
  }
}
```

Figure 7.11: Sample access filter

It will apply a filter to the dimension name from the view **distribution_centers** (observe that the field requires the format be view. dimension). The user attribute defined is a region.

Access filters will automatically add a **WHERE** statement to fulfill the **access_filter** definition–this filter cannot be edited or changed by users unless the user attribute value is changed. Say a user is interacting with the explore defined in *Figure 7.11,* and the user attribute region has been set to Midwest. Whenever they interact with the **explore: order_items**, they will always have the statement, **WHERE distribution_centers.name = "Midwest"** applied to every query they try to run.

Access filters will apply to all users, including admins. To give specific users unrestricted access to all data, set their user attribute value to %, *NULL* in case it is a type string, or <0, >=0, NULL if a type of number (does not include quotations).

Looker has another set of parameters, **sql_always_where**, and **sql_always_having**, that can apply filters to explores. In these parameters, developers can define simple to complex filters.

The parameters **sql_always_where** and **sql_always_having** are structured and function in the same way, except **sql_always_where** is used when applying a filter to a dimension, and **sql_always_having** is used when applying a filter to a measure. From this point forward, we will be referencing only **sql_always_where**, but the structure and setup are the same as for **sql_always_having**.

- **sql_always_where** is defined at the explore level, like **access_filters**. The parameter accepts SQL syntax. Anything defined will automatically be inserted after a **WHERE** statement. For example, *Figure 7.12*, will add the statement: **WHERE distribution_centers.name = "Denver, CO"** to every single query created in the explore.

```
sql_always_where: ${distribution_centers.name} = "Denver, CO" ;;
```

Figure 7.12: Sample SQL always where a filter

Note: **This filter will apply to all users, including admins, and cannot be changed on the explore UI.**

In its most basic use case, as seen in *Figure 7.12*, **sql_always_where** functions the same as an **access_filter**, except the value it filters on is statically defined (whereas **access_filters** change dynamically according to user attributes). Since this parameter accepts SQL syntax, developers can create far more complex filters than what is available using **access_filters**.

In *Figure 7.13*, **sql_always_where** is defined using logical liquid syntax, as follows:

```
sql_always_where:
  {% if _user_attributes['department'] == "sales" %}
    ${distribution_centers.name} = "{{ _user_attributes['region'] }}"
  {% else %}
    # Apply no filter
  {% endif %} ;;
```

Figure 7.13: Sample SQL always where filter, with liquid

In the example, it will apply a filter on the dimension name from the distribution center to match the user's region. The filter will apply to any user where their user attribute department equals sales. If they do not belong to sales, it will not apply a filter at all.

- **always_filter** is like the **sql_always_where**, in that, Looker will create a filter for every user interacting with the explore, but in always filters, users have the option of changing the value of the tiler.

Always filters are used to set a default filter, to limit the data a user can interact with. By default, Looker does not apply any filters to data. When a user first queries and explore, they are querying the entire table(s) if they do not always apply a filter. Adding an always filter can reduce querying costs by guaranteeing that users are always filtering the data, as shown in *Figure 7.14*:

```
always_filter: {
  filters: [order_items.created_date: "1 year"]
}
```

Figure 7.14: Sample always filter

Always filters are set up at the explore level. They are structured the same as filters applied to measures. Developers can add a comma-separated list of dimensions and measures they want filtered on. Each item on the list are key-value pairs, with the key being a dimension or measure and the value being the filter value. In *Figure 7.14*, we apply a filter to the dimension **created_date** from the view **order_items** to only show data within the past year.

In *Figure 7.15*, we can see how the **always_filter** appears on the explore. Unlike **access_filters** or **sql_always_where**, the **always_filter** will appear in the filter section of the explore, where the user can change it as needed:

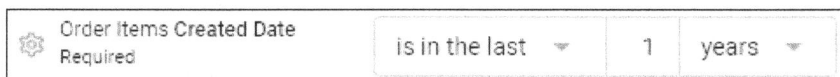

| ⚙ Order Items Created Date Required | is in the last ▾ | 1 | years ▾ |

Figure 7.15: Sample always filter as it appears on an explore

- Conditional filters are like always filters; however, a user can select between two different dimensions that they are required to filter on. The following is a sample of a conditional filter:

```
conditionally_filter: {
  filters: [distribution_centers.name: 'Houston TX']
  unless: [distribution_centers.location]
}
```

Figure 7.16: Sample conditional filter

Conditional filter setups are very similar to access filters. They are defined at the explore level and have a parameter called filters that accepts a comma-separated key-value list. Conditional filters require a second parameter called unless, which also accepts a comma-separated key-value list.

Figure 7.17 shows how the conditional filter created in *Figure 7.16* appears on the explore:

Figure 7.17: Sample conditional filter as it appears on an explore

Users are required to select a value for one of these filters. If a value has been filtered on the **Distribution Center Name**, users will be given the option to remove the **Distribution Center Location** and vice versa.

This type of filter is a great option if you would like users to always filter on a specific parameter, but that parameter can be interchanged, such as in the case of location, where they could select between a state or a more granular dimension like city, zip code, or coordinates.

Masking

Liquid can be used to obscure or alter the contents of a dimensions and measures according to user attributes. This is helpful in cases where admins may want to selectively alter, or completely obscure, columns of data for specific users.

There are several locations where the liquid is usable, including description, HTML, link, and filter parameters. Liquid can also be most notably utilized in any parameter that accepts SQL syntax (for example, SQL, **sql_on**, **sql_always_filter**, etc.).

We can utilize liquid in SQL to create conditional statements to mask dimensions. Let us look at *Figure 7.18* as an example:

```
dimension: ssn {
  label: "SSN"
  type: string
  sql:
    {% if _user_attributes["can_access_pii_data"] == "yes" %}
      ${ssn_raw}
    {% else %}
      CONCAT('XXX-XX-', RIGHT(${ssn_raw},4))
    {% endif %}
  ;;
}
```

Figure 7.18: Sample liquid example

In this example, users that have their user attribute **can_access_pii_data** set to yes can see the field SSN without any masking. If they do not have a yes set, they will see a masked version of the SSN. For example, users who can access the data will see 123-45-6789, whereas users with the data restriction will instead only see XXX-XX-6789.

Content access

In this section, we will show the different ways to manage the content that *a user can access*. Should a user from sales have access to see dashboards created by finance? Should a user be able to edit dashboards, or just view them? Content access goes over the access management of dashboards and Looks.

Dashboards and Looks access cannot be managed on a per dashboard or look basis. Instead, they automatically inherit the permissions of the folder they are in. If a user has manage permissions on a folder, they can edit all dashboards that exist within that folder. Alternatively, if they have view-only permissions to the folder, dashboards in the folder are read-only.

Specific permissions are required for users to even interact with any data on the instance. The permissions related to viewing content are **access_data**, **see_looks**, **see_user_dashboards**, and **see_lookml_dashboards**.

Looker automatically creates two types of folders on the Looker instance:

- The first, shared folders, is essentially the public space where dashboards can be viewed by all users.

- The second, personal folders, is a folder that is created for every single Looker user. This is their private folder, by default, only the user and admins can see what is in their folder.

Folders can be created within folders for organization and permission management. There is no limit to the amount of nesting and subfolders that can be created. Folders should be created within the Shared folder space that matches the access policies of a company.

Folder permission inheritance

Folder permissions are always inherited from parent folders. Meaning, that if a user is granted permission to a folder, that user will have the same permission for all subfolders. Permissions for subfolders can be elevated, but not removed.

For example, say a Looker instance has a folder called *Folder A,* and within Folder A there are two subfolders, *Folder Ax* and *Folder Ay*. The following scenarios are possible:

- If a user is given manage permission to Folder A, they will also have manage permission to Folder Ax and Folder Ay. Manage permission to Folder Ax and Ay cannot be removed at the Ax and Ay level.

- If a user is given view permission to Folder A, they will have view permission to Ax and Ay. If an admin grants user manage permission to Ax, they will have manage permission to Ax but only view permission to Ay.

- If a user is not given view or manage permission to Folder A, they will not be able to see Folder A at all.

Open and closed access systems

It is highly recommended that admins establish a folder system before onboarding any users. Folder systems should be carefully selected according to the level of access users should have to different dashboards. There are three main types of folder permission setups, from most open to most restrictive, as follows:

Open system

Open systems are the default Looker configuration. In this system, there are no folder restrictions in place, and all users can view and modify any content.

It is recommended for the following:

- Smaller companies with open policies for data
- No internal restrictions about who can access what data
- Users that are all internal

To set up an open system, set up the permissions on the top level of Shared Folders to match *Figure 7.19*:

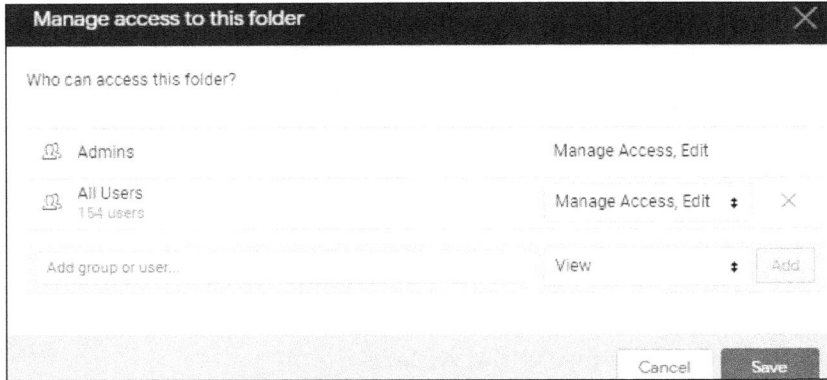

Figure 7.19: *Open system permission on shared folders*

All folders that are created within Shared folders will inherit these permissions, meaning that all users will have manage access to all dashboards in the Shared folder space.

Open system with restrictions

Open systems can be configured with additional restrictions. This is the most common setup for instances that are used exclusively by internal users.

It is recommended for the following:

- For medium companies with some data restrictions.
- Data reports that may be highly diversified and not relevant to everyone.
- Different levels of users, such as dashboard viewers and dashboard editors.
- Users that are all internal.

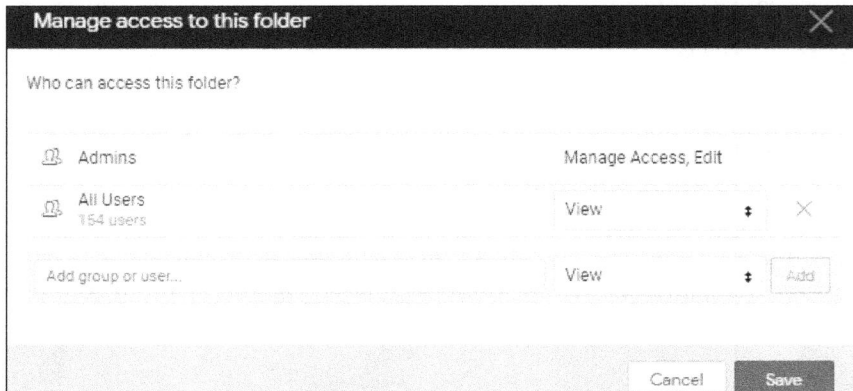

Figure 7.20: *Open system permission, with restrictions, on shared folders*

To set up an open system with restrictions, set up the permission on the top level of the Shared folders to match the permissions outlined in *Figure 7.20*. This will give more flexibility in permissions than can be assigned to subfolders within the Shared folder space. Subfolders will inherit the access policy View for All Users but, unlike in the case of open system where All Users have Manage, edit permissions, admins can remove this permission from the subfolder. This allows admins to adjust user and group permissions to each folder to match the desired level of access.

Closed system

Closed systems have content completely siloed away from each other. This type of system must be enabled by Looker Support to be used, as it changes many of Looker's default settings and behaviors to enforce and encourage better security, as follows:

- Removes the all-users group, thus disabling the ability to easily give folder access to All users. Groups must be established to match the security policy.

- Makes all personal folders private. By default, users can see another user's folders but cannot edit anything in another person's folder. Personal folder owners can still change their folder permissions to allow access again.

- Users cannot see other users unless they are in a shared group.

After a closed system has been enabled, further configuration is fairly like an Open System, with Restrictions. It is recommended that Admins give all groups View access to the top level of the Shared folder, as it is generally required for anyone to interact with dashboards on the shared space. From there, admins will need to plan out a folder structure and groups to satisfy content restraints. The constraints of a closed system will force admins to be more aware of group users and access.

It is recommended for the following:

- If your instance has external users (that is, users who are not part of the company) directly accessing the instance.

- The Looker instance connects to data from different clients whose access must be completely isolated.

Authentication

In this section, we go over the pages under the authentication section of the Admin tab. Here, admins can configure how users authenticate into the Looker instance.

Passwords

Admins can define the password requirements here. This will only affect users who log in with email, and password. Users who authenticate using an external authentication provider (for example, Google OAuth, Okta, OpenID, etc.) will not be affected by any of these settings.

Two-factor

Admins can enable two-factor authentication with mobile devices using the Google authenticator. The Google authenticator is a mobile app that automatically generates codes used for 2FA (instead of the conventional codes sent through SMS). Codes automatically expired 30 seconds after creation.

Note: **This will only take into effect non-SAML users who log in with the conventional username and password combo through Looker.**

Google

Admins can enable Google OAuth as a method of authentication for users. Instead of logging in with an email or password, users can authenticate with a Google account, as follows:

Log In

AUTHENTICATE WITH GOOGLE

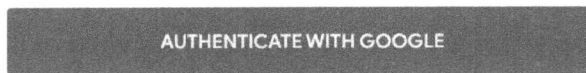

Alternate login page (email/password)

Figure 7.21: Login page when alternate login enabled

When enabled, users have the option to authenticate with a Google account. The option to log in with an **email/password** is removed unless it has been enabled.

The Google OAuth requires the following information in order to configure it:

- **Client ID and secret**: Looker must be enabled as an authorized domain on the Google OAuth side via the Google Cloud (GCP) console. Admins on GCP will need to create new OAuth credentials that will generate the client ID and secret.

- **Domains**: Enter your organization's Google account's domain name here. Multiple domains are accepted as comma separated.

The migration options are as follows:

- **Alternate login for admins and specified users**: It allows users to also log in with an email/password for admins. It will make the Alternate login page (from *Figure 7.19*) an available option for all admins. This is highly recommended to be enabled so that admins have a way of accessing the instance in cases where Google OAuth is unavailable.

- **Merge by email**: This option will automatically merge a user's account if their email already exists on the instance. This is recommended to reduce the chances of duplicate accounts.

- **Roles for new users**: The selected role will become the default role for every user when they first authenticate into the instance. This can be changed later for a user after their first login. We recommend giving all users at least Viewer permissions—if no role is assigned by default, new users will not be able to interact with anything.

External authentication

Admins can configure LDAP, OpenID, or SAML on their Looker instances to allow users to authenticate using an external authentication application. These features need to be enabled on the instance, so if it is not available underneath the Authentication section of the Admin tab, admins will need to contact Looker Support to enable it.

LDAP, OpenID, and SAML appear as different pages underneath the admin tab, but only one can be configured on an instance at a time—they exist as separate pages due to the different configuration requirements. Enabling one will require users to authenticate into the configured authentication application (for example, if Okta has been enabled, users will need to log in via Okta to access Looker).

Syncing with an external authorization application consolidates the management of users on one platform. Looker will continuously sync with the configured application, any users that are added and removed can be handled on the application instead of Looker.

When configuring an external authentication application, admins may be presented with the following optional configurations:

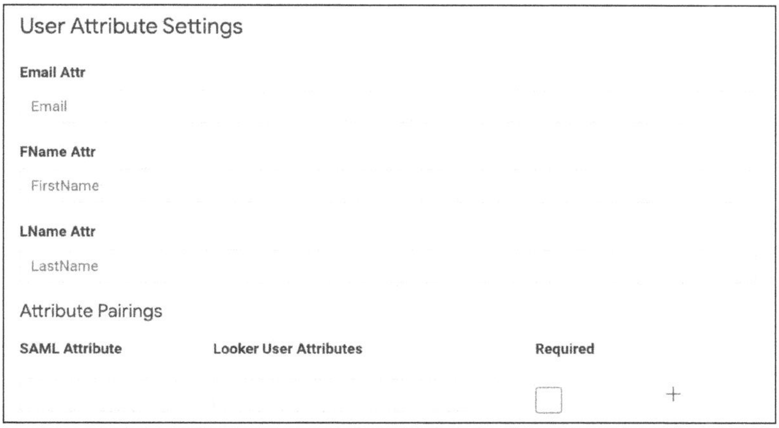

Figure 7.22: *Available User Attribute Settings for SAML applications*

Optionally, admins can mirror existing attributes and/or groups from their authentication applications to Looker. By mirroring, admins can maintain attributes and groups on just their authentication application, instead of maintaining it in both applications separately:

- **Attribute mirroring**: Although the setup for LDAP, OpenID, and SAML may be different, all configurations allow for attribute mirroring. Enabling attribute mirroring will pull whatever attributes exist on the authentication system and map them to a Looker attribute. The values applied to users on the authentication application will automatically apply to their corresponding Looker user. If enabled, these attributes can only be edited through the authentication application, not Looker.

- **Group mirroring**: Admins can also set up mirroring for groups. This can allow consolidation of group management into one application. The configuration for group mirroring can be seen in *Figure 7.23*:

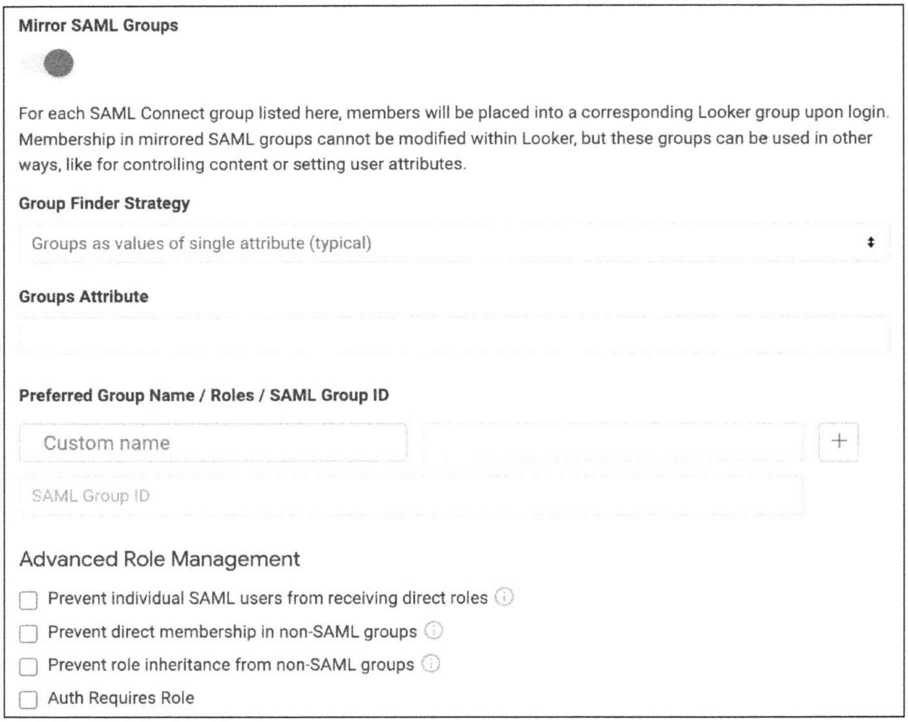

Mirror SAML Groups

For each SAML Connect group listed here, members will be placed into a corresponding Looker group upon login. Membership in mirrored SAML groups cannot be modified within Looker, but these groups can be used in other ways, like for controlling content or setting user attributes.

Group Finder Strategy

Groups as values of single attribute (typical)

Groups Attribute

Preferred Group Name / Roles / SAML Group ID

Custom name

SAML Group ID

Advanced Role Management

☐ Prevent individual SAML users from receiving direct roles ⓘ

☐ Prevent direct membership in non-SAML groups ⓘ

☐ Prevent role inheritance from non-SAML groups ⓘ

☐ Auth Requires Role

Figure 7.23: *Group mirroring configuration for SAML applications*

Like user attributes, the exact configuration to set up mirroring may differ according to the authorization application, but generally admins will need to provide Looker with how groups are defined in the application (Group Finder Strategy and Groups Attribute or Member Value) and how the different groups should be mirrored and named on Looker.

Under Advanced Role Management, admins can determine how strictly Looker groups and user configurations should match the authorization application configuration, as follows:

- o **Prevent individual SAML users from receiving direct roles**: This prevents admins from being able to directly assign specific roles to users.

o **Preventing direct membership in non-SAML groups**: This prevents users from being able to be part of Looker-only groups.

o **Prevent role inheritance from non-SAML groups**: The users can be part of Looker-only groups but this prevents users from inheriting any permissions from those groups.

o **Auth Requires Role**: It requires all users to have a role, otherwise they will not be able to access the Looker instance at all.

Selecting the first three options will prevent admins from being able to adjust permissions on Looker–permission and group management will have to be handled by the application.

If mirroring is toggled off, admins can instead assign default groups and roles for users. The group and/ or roles will be applied only to users when they first log in–if they already have an active account on the instance, it will not be applied.

- **Alternate email login**: Users can have multiple credential types active, meaning they can have multiple different ways of authenticating into Looker. If an authentication method besides email has been enabled, users by default can only authenticate using that method. However, if a user is granted special permission (`login_special_email`), they can configure an email and password alongside the configured authorization application. This permission is one of the permissions available in a permission set under *roles*.

It is highly recommended that admins maintain at least one email and password account or have an email authentication method set up alongside this. On the small chance that the connected external authorization application becomes unavailable, no one will be able to authenticate while the application is down. However, the email authentication method will always be available if the Looker instance is up–this method can be used as emergency access.

Sessions

Admins can manage the user's Looker session settings on this page. This section determines how long users can be idle for before they are automatically logged out or need to reauthenticate. It also determines if users can be logged into multiple devices at the same time if Looker is allowed to log the location of each log in. The different available configurations are explained in further detail:

- **Inactivity logout**: Admins can toggle an automatic inactivity logout for users. If enabled, users will automatically be logged out after a set duration, as defined in Session Duration. This cannot be enabled at the same time as *Persistent sessions*. All Looker users will be affected, including users authenticated using Private Embed. It does not, however, affect SSO Embed sessions (this is set when creating the SSO embed).

- **Persistent sessions**: Admins can toggle on persistent sessions. If users select *stay logged in* when logging into Looker, Looker will maintain the session on the device for a set duration, as defined in Session Duration. For the entire session duration, users will not need to log into Looker again. This cannot be enabled at the same time as Inactivity Logout.

- **Session duration**: The amount of time a session is valid for is defined here. This determines how long a user can be inactive before they are automatically logged out (if Inactivity Logout is enabled) or how long a user's session can last before a user is requested to log in again (if Persistent Sessions is enabled). The duration of time that can be set differs according to which session type has been selected.

- **Concurrent sessions**: Admins can enable users having active sessions on multiple devices at once. If enabled, users can access Looker on their laptops, mobile devices, etc. at the same time. If disabled, whenever users log into a new device, they are automatically logged out of their previous device.

- **Session location**: Enabling session location means the user's IP location will be tracked whenever they log in. This location information becomes available in the System Activity explores, which can be helpful for admins to track where the Looker instance is being accessed from. If disabled, Looker will not track the locations of user devices.

Security best practices

Looker has several different security features that it can be overwhelming to know which ones to use. In this section, we will go over different best practices we recommend implementing in order to improve general security:

- **General**:
  - Use hidden on any dimensions and measures that are not likely to be used by users. This will help keep the Explore clutter-free.

    When developing dashboards, have users first create dashboards in their folder. Once it is ready to be shared, let the user, or whoever must manage permission in the shared folder space, move the dashboard to essentially *publish* it for public viewing.

- **Authentication**:
  - Always maintain at least one admin account that can be authenticated with email and password in case the configured authorization services become unavailable.

    Set up SAML, Google OAuth, OpenID, or LDAP, if available to your company, instead of manually adding users. Manually adding or editing users can become difficult as users grow in numbers. Only admins should be manually added to the instance.

- **Permission management**:

  o It is highly recommended that permissions be managed using groups. It is not recommended to assign permissions to users individually.

  o Check if permissions are working as designed using the sudo function.

  o Separate model files based on data access.

  Change the default permission on the Shared Folder for the *All Users* group from *Manage, Access, Edit* to *View*. This prevents any user being able to edit anything on the shared workspace – editpermissions on shared folders should be granted purposefully. Implement a folder structure in the Shared Folder space before onboarding users

  o When applying **access_filters**, set the associated user attribute to be String/Number Filter advanced (instead of just String/Number). This allows developers to set multiple values for the filter.

  o When applying **access_filters**, set the user attribute value for admins to be *%, NULL* if a type string or *<0, >=0, NULL* if a type of number (do not include quotations). This will essentially remove the filter for admins so they can query the entire dataset unrestricted.

  o Utilize the **sudo** function for a variety of users to verify that their access is as planned/intended.

Access control examples

In this section, we will discuss some access control examples. The following are the scenarios for access control:

Securing sensitive data

All explores on the Looker instance are currently available to all users. However, there are specific dimensions that contain sensitive information, like customer phone numbers and email. You need to hide these fields from the average Looker user. Users with no PII access should see the last four numbers of a phone number, and users with PII access should see the entire phone number, unmasked. What is the best way to set up the Looker instance?

The steps for the solution are as follows:

1. Set up a user attribute to identify if a user should or should not have access to sensitive data. See a sample of how to define this user attribute in *Figure 7.24*:

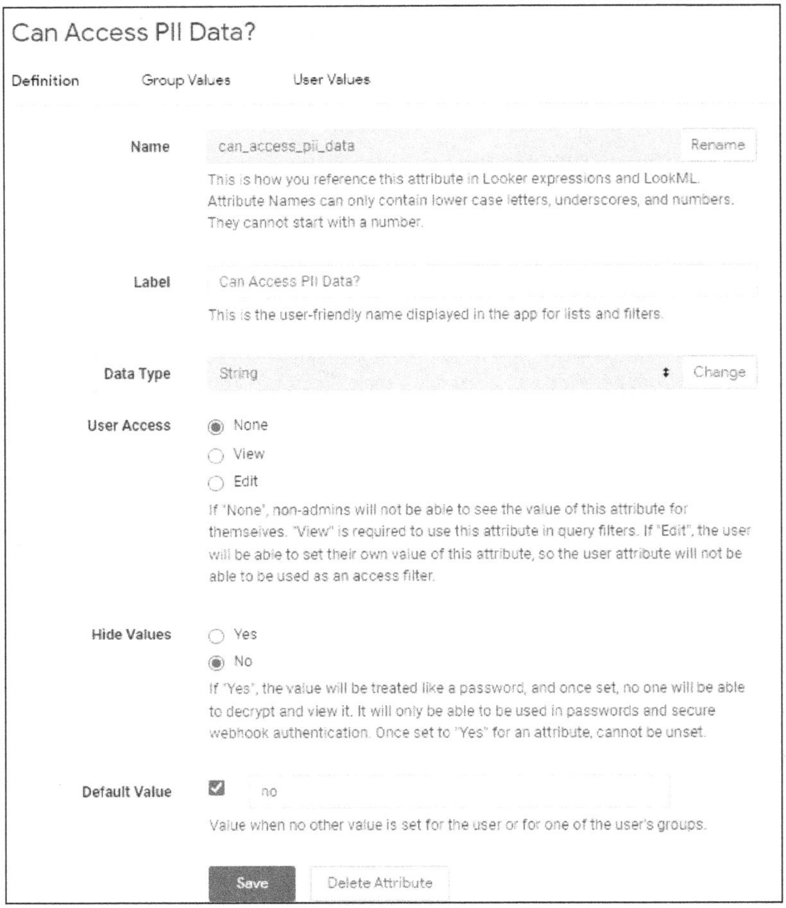

Figure 7.24: Sample user attribute to identify security level

Set user access to **None** so that users cannot view their security level (or set it to **View** if you would like that transparency). Do not set it to Edit, as editable user attributes cannot be used for access control.

For best security practices, set the default value to indicate they cannot access the sensitive data so that newly onboarded users or users that are not directly assigned are assumed to not have secure access.

2. Create an **access_grant** policy. See an example in *Figure 7.25* of how we utilize the user attribute created in *Figure 7.24* to create an access grant:

```
access_grant: sensitive_data {
  user_attribute: can_access_pii_data
  allowed_values: [ "yes" ]
}
```

Figure 7.25: Access grant example

Apply the access grant (using **required_access_grant**) to, in this case, the dimension email (see *Figure 7.26*). Only users with their **can_access_pii_data** set to **yes** will be able to query email, for everyone else they will not even be able to see the field listed in Explore:

```
dimension: email {
  required_access_grants: [sensitive_data]
  label: 'Email'
  sql: ${TABLE}.email ;;
}
```

Figure 7.26: *Example of applying an access grant to a dimension*

3. Utilize *liquid* to dynamically create a mask for the dimension phone number:

```
dimension: phone_number {
  type: string
  sql:
    {% if _user_attributes["can_access_pii_data"] == "yes" %}
      ${TABLE}.phone_number
    {% else %}
      CONCAT('XXX-XXX-', RIGHT(${TABLE}.phone_number,4))
    {% endif %}
}
```

Figure 7.27: *Example of dynamically masking dimension according to a user attribute*

Note: **The SQL in *Figure 7.27* was made compatible with BigQuery, the exact function may vary according to the database.**

4. Create a group to manage who should have secure access. By assigning permissions only via group inheritance, admins can easily keep track of who has their **can_access_pii_data** value set to *yes*.

Restricting data by zip code

You have a set of dashboards that are available to different regional managers of your company. However, you only want managers to see data for a specific zip code. What is the best way to set up the Looker instance?

The steps for the solution are as follows:

1. Set up a user attribute to identify which zip code a user belongs in:

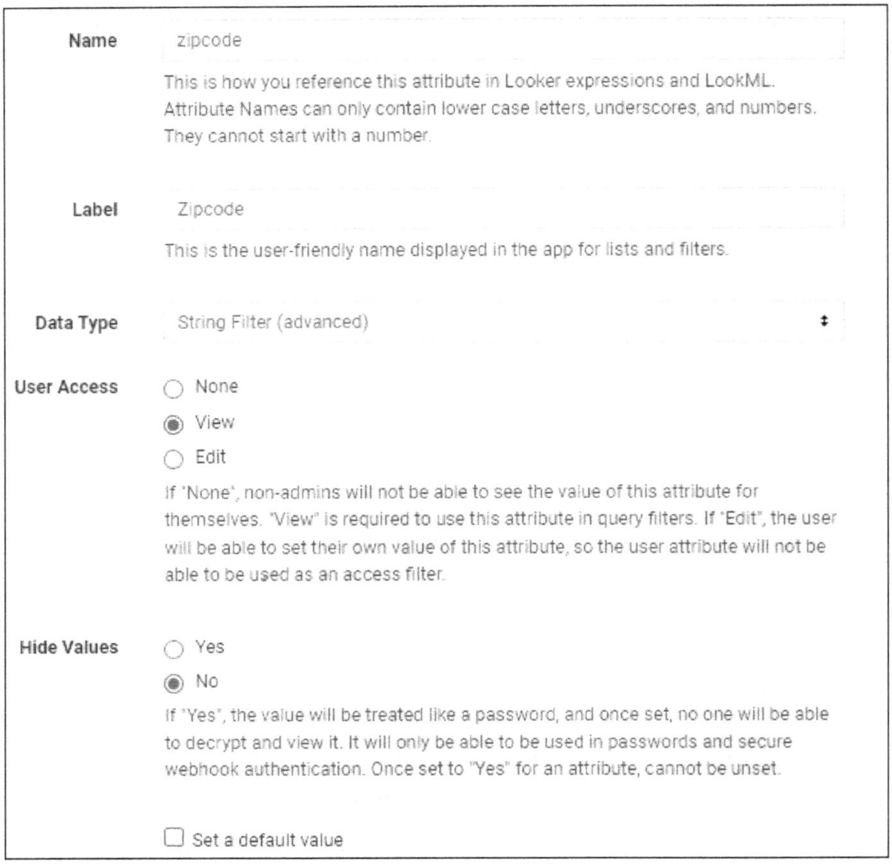

Figure 7.28: Sample attribute to identify zip code

Configure the data type to **String Filter (advanced)** if you would like a user to be able to view multiple zip codes at the same time. Even if a user should only see one zip code at a time, it is helpful to set the data type to this so that admins can be configured to see the data without any restrictions.

2. Create an **access_filter** in the explore definition that the filter should be applied to.

Note: **Access filters cannot be applied at the model level, they must be applied individually to each explore if admins want it to affect all explores.**

For example, in the access filter defined in *Figure 7.29*, the filter will only apply to the explore **order_items**:

```
explore: order_items {
  label: "(1) Orders, Items and Users"
  view_name: order_items

  access_filter: {
    field: users.zipcode
    user_attribute: zipcode
  }

  join: users {
    view_label: "Users"
    type: left_outer
    relationship: many_to_one
    sql_on: ${order_items.user_id} = ${users.id} ;;
  }
}
```

Figure 7.29: Access filter example

Access filter policies will be applied to all users. If no default value is set for the user attribute, users without an assigned value will not be able to see any data, as their region will essentially be set to NULL.

To grant users unrestricted access to regions, assign their value as %, **NULL**.

3. Create groups to manage which users belong to what regions. Assign the different groups the correct user attribute value to match the desired data restriction:

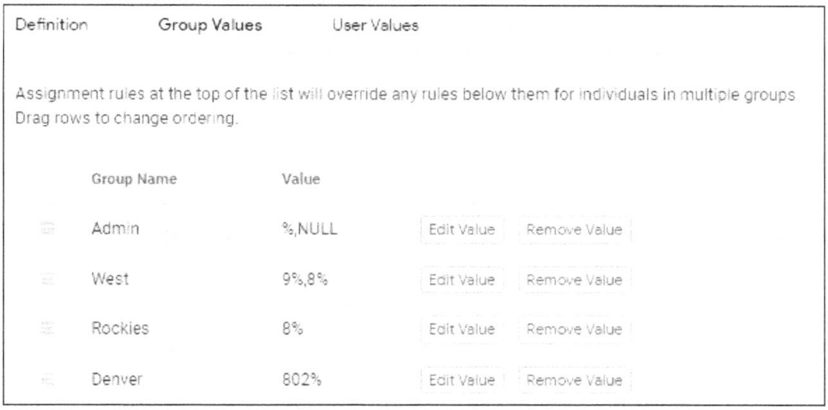

Definition	Group Values	User Values

Assignment rules at the top of the list will override any rules below them for individuals in multiple groups. Drag rows to change ordering.

Group Name	Value		
Admin	%,NULL	Edit Value	Remove Value
West	9%,8%	Edit Value	Remove Value
Rockies	8%	Edit Value	Remove Value
Denver	802%	Edit Value	Remove Value

Figure 7.30: Group assignments example

In *Figure 7.30* we can see an example of four different groups being assigned a different user attribute value. According to the hierarchy set in the example, the user attribute that takes precedence is from: **Admin** group, **West** group, **Rockies** group, and finally **Denver** group. If a user is in both the West group and the Denver group, their user's attribute will be set as **9%,8%**.

In *Figure 7.30*, we can also see an example of the advantage of using a type String filter (advanced). Looker will parse the string expression to allow multiple values to be matched.

Rockies, for example, will match all zip codes that start with an 8. West will match all zip codes that start with an 8 and 9.

Managing access for multiple departments

Several departments within your company want to utilize Looker to create various dashboards. You have multiple departments: sales, finance, and engineering. Users should only have access to dashboards that belong to their department. Within each department, you want your power users to have edit access and other users to have read-only access. What is the best way to set up the Looker instance?

The steps for the solution are as follows:

1. Create two groups for each department, for a total of six groups: Sales Power User, Sales User, Finance Power User, Finance User, Engineering Power User, Engineering User.

2. Set up an open system, with restrictions folder setup. Set up an open system, with restrictions folder setup corresponding to the groups. This will require a folder for each department. For example, for the Sales folder, the Sales Power User will have manage, edit access while the Sales User only has view access (see the different permissions options in *Figure 7.20*).

3. Migrate dashboards into the appropriate folders.

Managing external users

For example, your company is creating dashboards for a series of different clients. Some dashboards are general and can be accessed by all clients, but some dashboards should only be visible to specific clients. Additionally, to secure each client's data, we have their data in separate projects. The schemas for each project are the same. What is the best way to set up the Looker instance?

The steps for the solution are as follows:

1. Create a user attribute to indicate which project a user has access to (we will call this attribute Database in this example).

2. Configure the connection to be dynamic to the user attribute project:

Figure 7.31: Connection configuration example

Observe in *Figure 7.31* Billing Project ID has been configured to look at the user attribute called database. The value next to Database, **bigquery-project-id**, is the value of the user attribute for the admin that is setting up the connection. This will make it so that whenever a user sees a dashboard created from a model using this connection, it will automatically query from the database assigned to them.

Note: **This setup is only possible if the schema of each project is the same. Since each project will be using the same LookML project, any custom LookML added for a specific project will cause errors for different connections.**

3. Set the connection for the LookML project to be the connection created in *step 2*.

4. Set up a closed system for the instance's folders. Closed systems are generally recommended whenever users external to the Looker instance are granted direct access to Looker.

Conclusion

In this chapter, we learned to set up a variety of different access controls. Looker access management is divided into three categories: feature, data, and content. Each is integral to setting up the correct access management policy. Carefully plan out the different groups of users, their levels of content and data access, and the organization of dashboards before onboarding any users.

In the next chapter, we will learn how to optimize instance and query speeds on Looker and how to tackle common LookML issues developers may encounter.

Join our book's Discord space

Join the book's Discord Workspace for Latest updates, Offers, Tech happenings around the world, New Release and Sessions with the Authors:

https://discord.bpbonline.com

CHAPTER 8

Troubleshooting, Performance Tuning, and Best Practices

Introduction

In our exploration of various Looker components and LookML parameters, we inevitably encounter hurdles during development or utilization. This chapter discusses common development issues and their resolutions. We will also do performance tuning of an explore, which necessitates, a deep understanding of its underlying causes and effective tuning strategies for dashboards. We will discuss diagnostic approaches and potential remedies to enhance performance. Additionally, we will also cover the best practices for code, and dashboard development, aiming to ensure code maintainability and enhance overall system performance.

Structure

In this chapter, we will go through the following topics:

- Development issues
- User issues
- Performance tuning
- Looker development best practices

Objectives

This chapter will explore common challenges encountered by Looker developers, including LookML code, configuration, user concerns, and performance bottlenecks. We will discuss troubleshooting methodologies and provide practical examples to effectively resolve these issues. By leveraging the outlined resolutions and techniques, Looker developers and administrators can streamline their development processes. Additionally, adhering to the best practices outlined here can aid in preemptively avoiding many of these common pitfalls.

Development issues

In Looker, errors and warnings typically occur when there is a problem with your LookML code, SQL queries, Git configuration, or when interacting with the Looker UI. These errors and warnings can help developers identify issues in their models, explores, or dashboards. Understanding how to interpret and resolve these issues is crucial for maintaining a smooth development experience. We will look into some common errors in the next section.

Common LookML errors

The LookML validator does an excellent job of linting the code by highlighting of objects broken by code changes. However, sometimes its error messaging can be vague or incomplete.

In this section, we will be discussing the following common issues and their possible resolutions:

- Error: `Unknown view (?). View does not exist in the model (?)`
  - o **Issue**: If a view is referenced in an explore, Looker is unable to locate the view, and it will throw this error.
  - o **Resolution:**
    - First check for typing errors and missing include statements.
    - Check that the included statement is referencing the correct file.

      When Looker can find a file that matches the include value, an (i) will appear next to the include parameter. Developers can hover over the (i), to see what files are being included in the statement. (See Figure 8.1 to understand better):

Figure 8.1: *Files included*

If the file is being properly referenced, check whether the name of the view that the explore is referencing, is correct as shown in *Figure 8.1*. For example, in *Figure 8.2*, the name of the view is **order_items**, but the name of the view file is **01_order_items**. Whenever this view is used in an explore, it needs to be using the name **order_items**, not the **01_order_items** view:

```
01_order_items.view   ▾

i   1 ▾   view: order_items {
    2         sql_table_name: dataset.order_items
    3         view_label: "Order Items"
```

Figure 8.2: File name versus view name

Note: Explores need to reference the name of the view object, not the view file.

- **Error:** `Measures with Looker aggregations (sum, average, min, max, list types) may not reference other measures`.

  o **Issue:** Whenever a developer tries to make a measure of type sum, average, min, max, and list types that reference another measure in its SQL definition, Looker will throw this error. Most SQL dialects are unable to perform nested aggregations (e.g., **AVERAGE(SUM(column))**), and so double-aggregated measures cannot be defined this way.

    The only notable exception to this is if the measure is of type number. Arithmetic is allowed between measures and will not throw an error (see *Figure 8.3*):

```
measure: average_sales_price {
    type: average
    sql: ${total_sale_price}
}

measure: average_spend_per_user {
    label: "Average Spend per User"
    type: number
    value_format_name: usd
    sql: 1.0 * ${total_sale_price} / nullif(${users.count},0)
    drill_fields: [detail*]
}
```

Figure 8.3: Invalid and valid reference of measures within measures

  o **Resolution:** There are two ways to resolve this error:

    ▪ The first method takes advantage of the fact that measures of type can still reference other measures. Aggregations like averages can be explicitly defined (like in *Figure 8.3*) to bypass the nested aggregation limitation.

    ▪ The second method uses a derived table. If it is not possible to represent the desired aggregation using a formula, developers will need to create a derived table to essentially *dimensionalize* a measure. From there, developers can then create a measure from the *dimensionalized* measure as shown in *Figure 8.4:*

```
view: dimensionalized_sales_price {
  derived_table: {
    sql:  SELECT SUM(order_items.sale_price) AS total_sale_price
      FROM dataset.order_items  AS order_items ;;
  }

  dimension: total_sale_price {
    type: number
    sql: ${TABLE}.total_sale_price ;;
  }

  measure: average_sale_price {
    type: average
    sql: ${total_sale_price} ;;
  }
}
```

Figure 8.4: Dimensionalizing a measure

In SQL terms, the preceding code effectively creates the original measure as a subquery, that Looker can then use to perform the aggregation:

- **Error**: `An explore named (?) has been defined multiple times`.

  o **Issue**: Looker will throw this error when multiple explores have been defined with the same name. Since explore names are defined by a view, this can occur when a developer tries to make multiple explores using the same base view.

  o **Resolution**: Whenever multiple explores need to use the same view as the base view, developers can use the parameter **from**, so that the explore can be defined using a different name but the same view:

```
explore: users {
  join: order_items {
    sql_on: ${users.id} = ${order_items.user_id} ;;
  }
}

explore: customers {
  from: users

  join: order_items {
    sql_on: ${customers.id} = ${order_items.user_id} ;;
  }
}
```

Figure 8.5: Explores using the same view as their base view

Note: If from is utilized, all references to the base view must use the explore name, and not the name of the base view the explore is derived from.

(See Figure 8.5 as an example of this setup)

- **Error**: `Measures of type count do not use the SQL parameter`.

  Use **count_distinct** to count by something other than the primary key, or remove the SQL parameter.

  o **Issue**: Looker throws this error when there is a measure of type count that also has the SQL field included in the measure definition. Looker will always auto-generate a measure of type count for every view (if the file was auto-generated). Type count is exclusively reserved to enable users to perform **COUNT(*)** on tables, therefore no SQL should be defined for the measure.

  o **Resolution**: If a developer wants to create a count on a specific dimension, use **count_distinct** instead of count.

  (See *Figure 8.6*, to see the acceptable ways to use type count and type **count_distinct**)

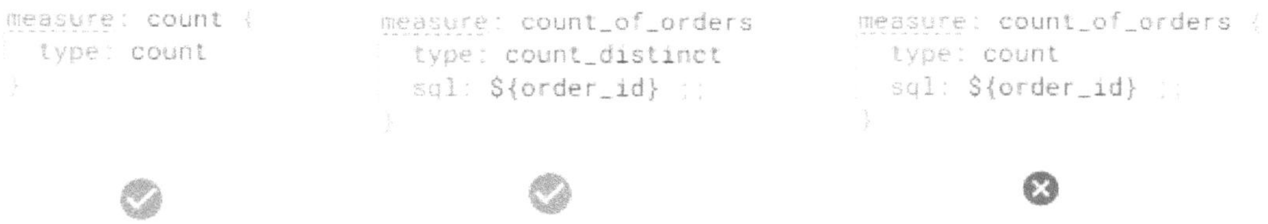

```
measure: count {          measure: count_of_orders      measure: count_of_orders {
  type: count               type: count_distinct          type: count
}                           sql: ${order_id} ::            sql: ${order_id} ::
                          }                               }
```

Figure 8.6: Valid and invalid uses of count and count_distinct

- **Error**: `Cannot construct persistent derived table (?), temporary schema for (?) is unset`.

  o **Issue**: Looker is unable to create the persistent derived table underlying the visualization. Whenever developers add a **datagroup_trigger** to a derived table, Looker will automatically try to materialize the derived table, into an actual table on the database. If Looker does not have a designated schema (or dataset) to place the table, it will throw this error.

  o **Resolution**: This commonly occurs when admins do not define a temporary schema for a connection. To check the persistent derived table configuration, navigate from **Admin | Connections** and select the connection underlying the visualization as shown in *Figure 8.7*. The availability and location of this configuration setting vary by database type:

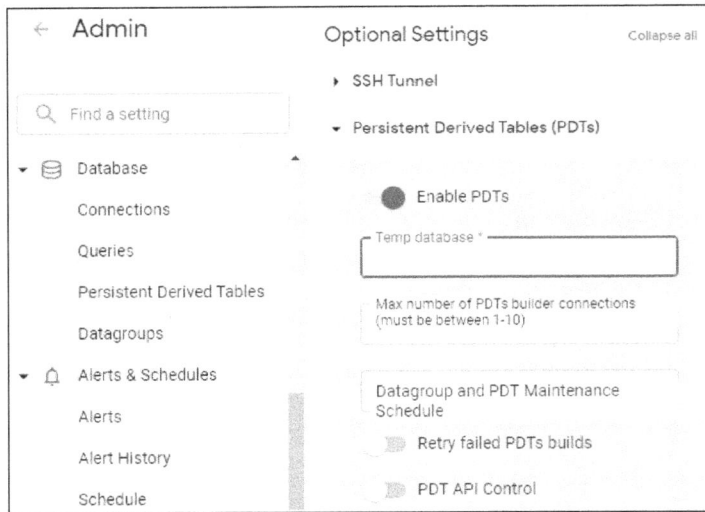

Figure 8.7: Persistent derived table settings

In the connection **Optional Settings** section, there will be a subsection dedicated to **Persistent Derived Tables** (if you do not see this section, your database does not support **PDTs**). When the **Temp database** is left blank or contains a schema name that the connection service account or user account does not have access to, it will throw this error. Resolve the error by defining a schema, where Looker can create tables.

- **Error**: `Unknown or inaccessible field (?) referenced in (?).`

  o **Issue**: Looker is unable to resolve a reference to a view or dimension in a LookML file. This issue usually has three common causes:

    - The field does not exist.

    - The field referenced is part of a dimension group.

    - The field references another field that lives in a separate view. When external view references are created, these two views must always be joined together at the explore level; otherwise, Looker will throw this error.

  o **Resolution**: It is simple, but resolving this error means removing the field.

However, if the field is required, developers can take the following steps to ensure that the field is properly set up through the following steps:

1. **Check if the field exists**: The specific field and the view that Looker expects it to be in will be stated in the error message, as shown in the following figure. If the field does not exist, developers will need to create the field or change the field reference, to a field that exists:

```
Inaccessible view 'users' referenced in
'order_items.days_since_signup'. 'users'
is not accessible in explore
'inventory_items'. Check for missing           ❓
joins in explore 'inventory_items'.
Learn more.

01_order_items.view:6
thelook_partner:inventory_items
```

Figure 8.8: *Sample error*

In *Figure 8.8*, we can see that an error is being thrown for the dimension **days_since_signup** from the view **order_items** stating that it is referencing something from an external view, **users**. In this example, developers should first check to make sure that the dimension **days_since_signup** exists within **order_items**.

2. **Check if the field is being referenced correctly**: If the field is part of a dimension group (often the case for date dimensions), then the timeframe needs to be specified. An example is shown in *Figure 8.9*:

```
dimension: days_since_signup {
  type: number
  sql: CAST(TIMESTAMP_DIFF(${created}, ${users.created}, DAY) AS INT64)



dimension: days_since_signup {
  type: number
  sql: CAST(TIMESTAMP_DIFF(${created_date}, ${users.created_date}, DAY) AS INT64)
}
```

Figure 8.9: *Example of fixing missing timeframe*

In *Figure 8.9*, we have an incorrectly defined dimension. We reference the dimension created from **order_items** and **users**, both of which are originally part of a date dimension group. Developers cannot reference an entire dimension group, otherwise, Looker will not know which level of granularity (day, month, year, etc.) to use. Resolve the error by specifying a specific timeframe such as **created_date** for date granularity, as shown in the example above.

3. **Check if the field is properly being joined into the explore**: If a developer references an external view, that external view must always be joined onto the original view. If you do not want to include another view in the explore, developers also have the option to exclude the field from the explore:

```
explore: inventory_items {
  join: order_items {
    sql_on: ${inventory_items.id} = ${order_items.inventory_item_id}
  }
  join: users {
    sql_on: ${order_items.user_id} = ${users.id}
  }
}
```

Figure 8.10: *Sample resolution to the error in Figure 8.8*

In *Figure 8.10*, we have an example of what joins are required to make the dimension in *Figure 8.9* viable. The view **order_items** is joined onto **inventory_items**, however since **order_items** has a dimension that references users, the view users must be joined as well:

```
explore: inventory_items {
  fields: [ALL_FIELDS*, -order_items.days_since_signup]
  join: order_items {
    sql_on: ${inventory_items.id} = ${order_items.inventory_item_id} ;;
  }
}
```

Figure 8.11: Alternate resolution to the error in Figure 8.8

If developers do not want to join an entire view onto the explore, such as to avoid clutter in the explore, they can instead use field exclusions on the explore. Developers can exclude the field with the external reference, as shown in *Figure 8.11*:

```
explore: inventory_items {
  join: order_items {
    sql_on: ${inventory_items.id} = ${order_items.inventory_item_id} ;;
  }
  join: users {
    fields: []
    sql_on: ${order_items.user_id} = ${users.id} ;;
  }
}
```

Figure 8.12: Second alternate resolution to the error in Figure 8.8

Alternatively, they can bring in the required external view, but omit all fields from the view, as in *Figure 8.12*, so that the view does not show up in the explore but resolves the external reference in **order_items**.

Project and model configuration errors

This section outlines potential errors in a project's model configuration. Configuration settings for a model can be found for each individual project under **Develop | Manage LookML Projects**.

By default, the page is available to developers for viewing. However, configuration settings can only be managed by admins.

Here are some common errors, causes, and resolutions:

- Error: **Configuration required for use**
  - o **Issue**: Developers will usually run into this error when they create a new project or a new model file. Every model is required to be configured to have access to connections.

o **Resolution**: Admins will need to configure each on the Projects page, located in the Develop tab model. For best practices, models should only have access to one connection, since model files themselves can only be defined with a single connection.

- Error: `Model already exists`

    o **Issue**: If two models exist with the same name, Looker will throw this error. There can never be two models with the same name, even if those models exist in different projects. Model names are used as references in several places, like dashboards or explore URLs. Therefore, no model can have the same name, as Looker will not know which model to refer to.

    o **Resolution**: Developers will need to rename one of the model files. To minimize the impact of any model name change, utilize the content validator to check if any content is broken.

- Error: `The LookML model file does not exist yet`

    o **Issue**: This can happen when a model that used to exist for a project is deleted. Even though the file is deleted, Looker does not automatically delete the model configuration.

    o **Resolution**: If the model file is meant to be permanently deleted, admins will need to delete the model configuration. The option to delete is available through the, **Manage LookML Projects** | **Configure** for the specific model. Navigate to the very bottom of the page, and the option to delete the model is available.

If the model is not meant to be deleted, developers will simply need to recreate the model file using the same name.

- Error: `Connection '?' does not exist`

    o **Issue**: Whenever a connection is deleted, but has already been used in a model configuration, this error will appear.

    o **Resolution**: Admins will need to reconfigure the model to have access to a connection that currently exists on the instance.

- Error: `Model '?' is not allowed to use connection '?'`

    o **Issue**: When a model tries to reference a connection in the connection parameter that it is not configured to have access to, Looker will throw this error. This is a feature working as intended, as admins can use model configuration settings to guarantee that developers are not accidentally or maliciously trying to access a different database than what is intended.

    o **Resolution**: There are two ways of resolving this error:

        ▪ Admins will need to reconfigure the model to allow access to the on the Projects page connection.

        ▪ Developers will need to change the connection parameter value.

Git errors

Looker utilizes Git for version control and change management. Each LookML project corresponds to a Git repository. Git integration options are visible in Development mode. Developers may encounter Git-related errors during check-ins, merges, or pulls from the production branch. This section outlines common errors, their causes, and potential resolutions.

- **Error: `Pull production failed`**
  - o **Issue**: Developers may encounter this error when they try to *Pull from Remote* to sync their development branch with the master. If, for whatever reason, git is not able to cleanly sync the branches, it will throw this error:

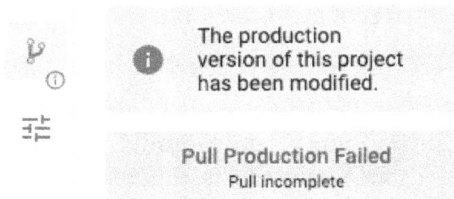

Figure 8.13: Pull production failed error message

  - o **Resolutions**: There are two possible ways to resolve this issue.
    - ▪ If developers do not have direct access to the underlying repository, they will need to *revert to production* and discard any committed changes, then *pull from production* to force a sync back with the master branch.

      Note: **Developers will lose all their changes from the development branch when undergoing this sync. If the changes are crucial, and not easily repeatable, resort to the other option.**

    - ▪ If the previously mentioned resolution is not successful, developers will need a user who has direct access to the Git repository. Either through the console or through the UI (if applicable), manually merge the master into the branch experiencing difficulties:

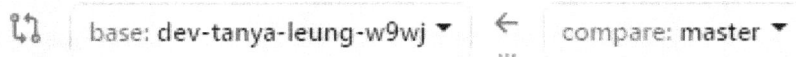

Figure 8.14: Direction of merge when resyncing personal branch with master

After this, return to the Looker development UI and select **Revert to…**, and select **Revert to shared state of branch**. If this option is unavailable to the developer, have them instead attempt to **Pull from Production** again.

- **Error: Merge conflicts**

  o **Issue**: Developers may encounter this error when they try to push their code to production. When going through the deployment process, developers need to merge their branches into production. If the master branch has changed, and conflicts with the developer's changes, a merge conflict will arise. Conflicts are more likely to occur if other developers are working on the same files at the same time.

  o **Resolution**: Developers will need to take the following steps to resolve a merge conflict.

    1. **Looker will highlight every file with a merge conflict in red**: Developers will need to select every file with a merge conflict and manually fix the conflict. In *Figure 8.15*, **case_study** is highlighted in red and therefore contains a merge conflict. The model **user_behavior** is not marked in red and can be ignored:

       ```
       ▾ models
           ⓐ case_study.model
           ⓐ user_behavior model
       ```

       Figure 8.15: Sample of merge conflict files

    2. For every occurrence of a merge conflict, git will apply markers to show your local state versus master state, as seen in *Figure 8.16*.

  The content between **HEAD** and the equal signs represents how the file looks on your branch. The content after the *equal signs* to **branch** is how the file appears on the master.

  ```
    join: inventory_items (
  <<<<<<< HEAD
      view_label: 'Inventory'
  =======
      view_label: 'Inventory Items'
  >>>>>>> branch 'master' of git@github.com:ORG/REPO_NAME.git
  ```

  Figure 8.16: Sample of merge conflict git markers

    3. **Resolve the conflict by selecting the version you wish to proceed with:** Remove all merge conflict markers. *Figure 8.17* represents the developer selecting the master branch version:

       ```
         join: inventory_items {
           view_label: 'Inventory Items'
       ```

       Figure 8.17: Resolved version of code from Figure 8.11

4. When all merge conflicts have been resolved, the button on the top right will change from *do not resolve* to *commit and resolve conflict*. Commit your changes and follow the standard branch merge flow.

- **Error: `Rolling back committed changes`**

  o **Issue**: Sometimes developers may push code changes, that inadvertently break dashboards or look across the instance. Developers may want to roll back their changes so that users can continue to work on an older, stable version of the code, while developers create a fix for the problem.

  o **Resolution**: Developers can deploy specific versions of production using **Advanced Deploy**. If advanced deployment has not already been enabled, developers can toggle it on through **Product Settings | Configuration | Deployment** for a specific project.

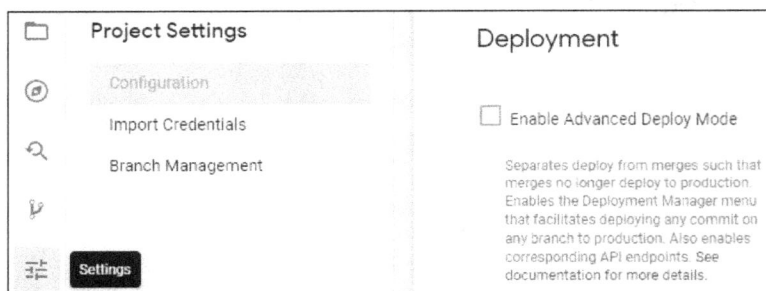

Figure 8.18: Location of advanced deploy mode in settings

After **Advanced Deploy** is enabled, a sixth tab underneath **Settings** will appear. Select the **Deploy** tab and from there, specific commits can be deployed to production.

Note: This will only deploy an older version of production, it will not update the production branch. If developers wish to make production revert, back to a previous state (that is, remove the new changes entirely), they will need to have direct access to the git repository.

User issues

This section outlines common problems that business users may come across while developing or viewing a visualization. The underlying issues of these problems may not necessarily be fixable by basic users; they will often require a fix from a developer or an admin.

Explore

Here are common user issues and their resolutions within the Explore interface of Looker:

- **Error: `Measures do not show up in the explore`**

o **Issue**: Measures do not appear in an explore even though they are part of a view included in the explore. This can occur when the base view or joined view does not have a primary key defined, and they are joined on a *many-to-many* or *one-to-many* relationship. Looker knows it needs to perform symmetric aggregation to accurately aggregate, but it cannot because the base requirement for symmetric aggregation (a defined primary key) is not being met. Since Looker knows these measures may not be inaccurately summing or counting, it will not display it to explore users.

o **Resolution**: Designate a primary key for every view using the field **primary_key**, as shown in *Figure 8.19*. If there is no native column that can be used as a primary key, developers can create their, own primary key by concatenating multiple columns together:

```
dimension: primary_key {
  type: string
  primary_key: yes
  sql: CONCAT(${id}, ${inventory_item_id}, ${created_date} ;;
}
```

Figure 8.19: Primary key example using derived columns

- **Error: Non-Unique value or primary key (or sql_distinct_key), value overflow or collision when computing sum**

  o **Issue**: When explore users attempt to run a measure, they may encounter this problem. This occurs when a primary key has been set and Looker attempts to perform symmetric aggregation to prevent fanout. When the designated primary key column contains non-unique values, Looker is unable to properly perform the aggregation and will throw this error.

  o **Resolution**: Developers will need to change the designated primary key to another dimension that is unique. If no dimension is natively unique, consider concatenating, as seen in *Figure 8.19*.

Dashboards and Looks

Here are common user issues and their resolutions that users and developers commonly face with Dashboards and Looks:

- **Error: The page does not exist, or you do not have permission to view it**

  o **Issue**: Users will receive this error when they load pages that do not exist, or they do not have permission to view. Most of the content on Looker can be accessed using a link, which can allow users to inadvertently hit dashboards they would otherwise not be able to view in the dashboard folders. However, Looker will still know if a user should or should not have access to dashboards and so if they do try to access one using a link, they will see this error instead.

o **Resolution**: If a user should be able to see a dashboard but is met with this error instead, admins will need to check the permissions of both the user and the folder the dashboard/look lives in. Dashboards inherit the permissions of the folder they reside in, and folder permissions are granted on a user or group basis:

  ▪ Check the folder permissions and identify what users and groups have permission to the folder.

  ▪ If folder permissions are assigned to groups, check what groups the user belongs to. Admins can do so by navigating to **Admin | Users** and selecting the user with the access issue.

  ▪ Either add the user directly to the folder (not recommended) or, add the user to a group that does have access to the folder.

  ▪ Check that the user has access to the page by sudoing into their account.

- **Error: `Trouble loading data`**

  o **Issue**: When there is an issue loading a dashboard dependency, Looker will throw this umbrella error. This error can have a myriad of causes, but it can usually be attributed to either a permission issue or an underlying dashboard object (model, explore, view, dimension, etc.) not existing.

  o **Resolution**: Developers can try to verify two of the following resolutions:

    ▪ Check the dashboard using elevated permissions (ideally an admin account). If the dashboard loads for another user, it is very likely a permission issue.

    ▪ Open the visualization into the explore view by selecting the three dots at the top right of every visualization and selecting *explore from here*. Looker will display the error preventing the visualization from loading.

    ▪ If no error is explicitly given, developers can narrow down what to check LookML side based on the URL. Explore URLs are always in the following format:

    `instance_name.looker.com/explore/MODEL_NAME/EXPLORE_NAME`

    ▪ Based on this, developers can inspect the specific model and, explore what may be potentially causing issues. Usually, this is a result of an object being renamed or deleted. Developers will need to resolve this dependency issue using the Content Validator, to replace the dashboard reference, or restore the renamed or removed object.

- **Error: LookML error**

    o **Issue**: Anytime a dashboard errors out, due to a LookML-related issue, it will throw this error. Any user or developer can click on the tile with the error to see the specific error causing the tile to fail to load.

    o **Resolution**: These errors are usually picked up by the LookML validator, so it is recommended that developers validate the underlying project.

- **Error: Query error**

    o **Issue**: If the SQL query Looker constructs and sends to the database returns an error, Looker will throw this error. Looker's validation only validates LookML code; it ignores everything defined in a SQL block (this includes any parameter that starts with SQL, including **sql_on**, **sql_always_where**, etc.). Since SQL dialects can vary between databases, Looker cannot support validating SQL logic defined in these blocks. Therefore, these errors sometimes only surface when users attempt to use the explores to hit the database. Clicking on the error will display the error the database returned, as shown in *Figure 8.20*.

    o **Resolution**: Developers will need to re-examine SQL statements that are defined in the LookML.

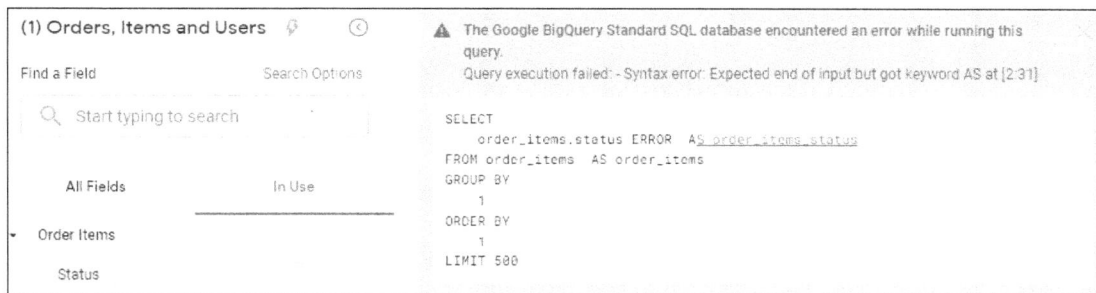

Figure 8.20: Sample query error

Developers can take the following steps to identify which field has the problematic SQL:

1. Check fields based on the dimensions and measures that the user selected that originally caused the error. In the example shown in *Figure 8.20*, all the fields part of the explore can be viewed by selecting **In Use**.

    Based on the dimension in use alone, developers can trace the objects that make up the query. We can see that Status was selected, so the SQL error may be coming from the dimension Status, or the view that it belongs in **Order Items**.

If Order Items is not the base view, developers should also check if the base view's SQL table name or, derived table definition is also correct.

2. On the explore itself, Looker will also highlight the line on the query that caused the error, which can further narrow down the source of the error.

   In the example shown in *Figure 8.20*, it is highlighting **order_items. status**. From this, we can conclude that there is something wrong with the definition of the Status dimension.

3. Once an object has been identified as potentially problematic, developers will need to navigate to the parameter definition and troubleshoot the SQL:

```
dimension: status {
  label: "Status"
  sql: ${TABLE}.status ERROR ;;
}
```

Figure 8.21: *Sample query error in SQL*

In this case, for the error in *Figure 8.20*, we navigate to the dimension status and see, the definition shown in *Figure 8.21*. We can see on closer look that there was an additional word (**ERROR**) added that made the SQL query invalid.

- **Error: No Results**
  - o **Issue**: A dashboard visualization or look will sometimes show no results instead of the original visualization type.
  - o **Resolution**: The Developer can check the following things to identify what is causing this:
    - ▪ Check the dashboard or Look filters. Sometimes specific filter values or combinations can inadvertently cause no data to return.
    - ▪ Check if there is any data in the database. The easiest way to do this from an explore is by selecting a dimension that is expected to be populated, like the primary key or an ID field.
    - ▪ Run the SQL query Looker generates directly against the database and check if it is returning any data.

Performance tuning

You will come across scenarios where the dashboards begin to run slow. This might lead to many issues including user attrition, delayed reports, and increased costs in the case of cloud data warehouses. So, as a developer, you need to make sure you are designing and creating Looker objects like the explores and dashboards that are perfomant. Other factors like server capacity, database, and # Looker objects also need to be considered, as they will play an important role in the performance.

Diagnosing and fixing performance issues

To effectively deal with performance issues, it is essential to understand the overall Looker architecture and functionality. As we discussed before, multiple components are involved in the process, such as the User Browser, Looker Server, database, and network between the Looker server and the database.

The process of Looker dashboard rendering will involve the aforementioned components and the flow can be described, as follows:

- User logs in navigates to a particular dashboard or Look, and runs the dashboard.
- The Looker server generates the SQLs queries for the dashboard and sends the query to the underlying database.
- The database runs the query and sends the results to the Looker Server, through the network, between the database and the Looker Server.
- The Looker server sends the data it received from the database to the users' browser.
- The user browser renders the dashboard and displays the visualizations.

In this process, the issue could be in any of the following components: the Database, Looker Server, or the network. First, we need to diagnose and identify where the issue could lie:

- **Looker server**: If the Looker navigation is slow, it means the instance is under heavy load. Increasing the server capacity, staggering the schedules, and using cache are some common remedies for this issue.

- **Network latency**: If all the dashboards from a database are slow, this could be because the network latency between the database and the Looker server may be causing this issue. Work with your network admin to resolve this issue. The location or region of the database and the Looker server also play a role here. So, work with Looker support and make sure your Looker instance is close to the database location.

- **Browser**: Dashboards that display large amounts of data often cause the browser to crash or render slowly.

- **Database**: The database processes the SQL query and sends the results. So, the load of the database equals the # of queries we are sending from a single dashboard, # of queries running, # of queries waiting in the queue, # of rows the query is scanning, etc. are the causes for database slowness.

   Looker provides some ready-made diagnosis dashboards under the system activity and database sections in Admin.

Note: **Please refer to Chapter 6, Looker Administration for a detailed explanation on each page under these sections.**

- **System activity dashboards:**

  o **Performance recommendations:** This dashboard shows the issues or causes of slowness and recommendations, both at the dashboard level as well as the explore level.

  o **Dashboard diagnostics:** This shows the usage statistics and Query metrics and shows recommendations for an individual dashboard.

  o **Database performance:** This dashboard shows information about the performance of the queries and the PDTs.

  o **Instance performance:** It shows the performance of the Looker instance including the scheduler and other content that is causing the load.

  o **Database queries**: Under the Database section, you can monitor the queries and, identify the ones that are running slow or in case of too many queries, running at the same time from a single dashboard or multiple users. You will observe that many queries are waiting for their turn.

If an individual query is taking too long to complete, that is a candidate for further tuning. You can identify the dashboard and model through the SQL tuning techniques that we will discuss later.

At the time of development, you can implement some best practices both at the model level and the dashboard level to make sure you will not encounter performance issues later.

The following are the LookML model-building best practices for optimum performance:

- In the explores, start with the most granular table and use many_to_one joins as much as possible.

- Avoid joining on the concatenated primary keys defined in the Looker view file. Instead, join on the base fields.

- Join on the indexed or partitioned columns. Use partitioned columns as filters either within the model or user input filters on the dashboards or Looks.

- Implement caching using datagroups and **persist_with** and sync the caching with the database refresh policies. This reduces the number of queries sent to the database and improves the performance of the dashboards.

- Use PDTs instead of derived tables. The derived table is like a view in the database, and it runs on-demand. Whereas a PDT is stored in the database and gives faster results.

Use Incremental PDTs if possible. This reduces the amount of time and resources Looker, and the database spend.

- Limit the amount of data that is returned from an explore, using filters or joins. You can use filters in many places in the model, for example, `sql_always_where`, `always_filter`, `conditionally_filter`, or templated filters in derived tables. If the database has five years of data, but users always need only two years of data, you can use the `sql_always_where` in the model to show only two years of data.

- For better performance during the development of LookML, include only the required view files in the, included statements in the model file.

- Use aggregate awareness to create summary tables that can increase performance.

- If the table has too many rows and aggregating is taking a long time for reports (especially, in row-based databases like MySQL, SQL server, Oracle, or Postgres) consider creating aggregate tables in the database and using those in Looker.

The following are the dashboard building best practices for Optimal performance:

- If the amount of data (number of rows or columns) displayed in the single visualization is too much, it causes browser issues and may also cause resource issues. So, limit the amount of data displayed in the dashboard. Use dashboard filters or Look filters to limit the rows. Use drill-downs to avoid showing all columns at once or split the reports.

- Limit the number of elements or tiles in a dashboard. The recommended limit is 25 tiles.

- Using merge results, Table Calculations or custom fields will consume more memory. So, use these with caution and limit the usage. Look for opportunities to move the Table Calculations logic to the LookML model wherever possible.

- Use the dashboard refresh option carefully. Try not to run the dashboard when there is no fresh data. In other words, sync the dashboard refresh with the **extract, transform and load** (**ETL**) refresh interval.

- Use required filters in the dashboards to avoid running the dashboard queries without the filter selections.

- Pivoting columns within visualizations will also, utilize more memory. So, use this feature with caution.

- Avoid using Looker as a data extraction tool for users, as much as possible. Limit the use of all the result options, in downloading the results or delivering the data (in schedules), especially when the result rows are too many.

- In case of multiple, single-value visualizations using the same clause, try using the same query, including all fields in a single query, across multiple tiles, and use the hide columns option. This will reduce the number of queries sent to the database and use the same query to power multiple tiles on the dashboard. An alternative to consider is multiple value visualization in the Looker marketplace.

The following are some common performance issues and measures that we can take to diagnose and resolve them:

- **A Dashboard is running slow**: There could be multiple reasons for a dashboard to run slowly. To diagnose, undertake the following steps:

  1. Check the *dashboard diagnostics* under system activity and filter for the dashboard ID that is in question:

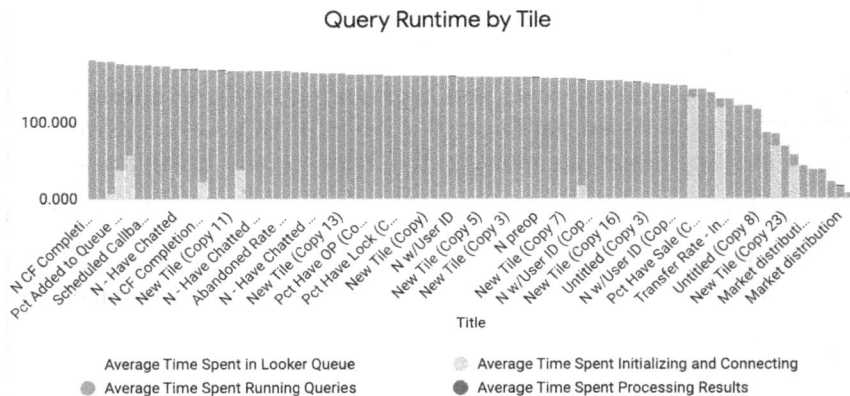

Figure 8.22: Query runtime by tile

  a. In **Query Runtime by Tile**, if there are tiles that have **Average Time spent Running Queries** more than the desired time(in seconds), it means the database is taking a long time, and queries for those tiles need to be tuned. Apply the database query tuning techniques like creating indexes, and clusters, using partitions, changing filters, etc.

  b. If the **Average Time Spent in Queue** is long, check if the max connections per node setting under connections can be changed, to fix this behavior.

  c. If the **Average Time Spent Processing Results** is taking too long merge, the results, Table Calculations, or downloads will need to be investigated.

  2. Check the recommendations on the Dashboard Diagnostics and or *performance recommendations dashboard*. If there are recommendations about the dashboard and the explore in question, try to implement those.

  3. Other options to tune the dashboards include caching, using PDTs, aggregate awareness, etc.

- **If running the dashboard individually does not cause performance issues or performance issues are intermittent**:

- o Check the hourly schedules under dashboard performance and see if any scheduled queries are concentrated during a particular time of the day.

- o Another issue could be the database refresh or ETL jobs load on the database.

- **If overall performance and navigation are slow**:

    - o Check the instance performance dashboard and see what is causing this issue. If any schedules and dashboard refreshes are running unnecessarily, you can disable them.

    - o Another reason could be that the number of users, and dashboards are beyond the server's capacity. Your organization may have overgrown the capacity provided initially. Work with Looker support to tune or add more capacity.

- **If Validation of LookML is taking too long**:

    - o Instances can also become slow when projects become big and monolithic. The majority of objects on Looker are a direct rendering of LookML files, so when there is a significant amount to process, it can slow down the instance. See the next bullet point about potential resolutions, as these two issues are often interconnected.

    - o The first thing to check is to include statements in the LookML view files. Include only necessary files and avoid using all files or *. Looker validates all the code in the files that are part of the includes.

    - o Archive or delete unused fields, join, and explore.

    - o Split the big project into multiple projects, separating the files.

Looker development best practices

In the previous chapters, we discussed about different components and features of Looker and how to use those features. Like any software development, Looker code and development also need to be clear, organized, efficient, and scalable. At the same time, it must satisfy the requirements, including security. So, it is essential to have some standards and learn about best practices in looker coding, which will make the code maintainable, speed up development, and ensure consistency across the projects.

The following are some of the best practices that work for most situations (use your discretion while using some of these):

- **General**:

    - o Write comments throughout blocks of LookML code. Intent, the purpose of the code, explanation of the calculations, derived logic, etc. are some of the examples of comments.

- o Use lowercase letters while naming LookML object names and file names. Do not use any special characters other than underscore.

- o Maintain proper indentation across LookML code. It will make the code easy to read and understand. You can use the format file shortcut (*Command-Shift-F* or *Control-Shift-F*) to do this automatically.

- **Git**:
    - o As much as possible, avoid using bare repo. The bare repo will not include all features of the git repository.

    - o Validate the LookML code frequently and commit small chunks of code.

    - o Use feature branches or shared branches to make changes for specific features.

    - o Set up the workflow to use *pull requests* and have a senior or lead developer review the code before merging.

- **Views**:
    - o Name the views to match the name of the table. Also, keep the file name the same as the view name as much as possible.

    - o Add the description of the view and its relevance at the beginning. Additionally, include any pertinent external documentation by providing the corresponding link (if it exists).

    - o Avoid writing multiple view definitions and explore in a single view file.

    - o In a view file, add dimensions at the top and measures at the bottom. Within the dimensions or measures section, order the fields alphabetically.

- **Fields**:
    - o Define a primary key in each view file.

    - o Each field in the database should be an untransformed dimension first. Then, build derived dimensions and measures using those base dimensions. This provides an additional layer of abstraction over the database and makes it easy to change the LookML if the database columns are renamed.

    - o Substitution operators (`${dimension_name}`) should be used throughout. Do not use measures that access columns (`${TABLE}. database_fieldname`) directly.

    - o Name the fields and ensure clarity:
        - For `yesno` field types, use `is_over_threshold` instead of `over_threshold`

        - Name ratios descriptively. For example, *orders per purchasing customer* is clearer than *Orders Percent*

- Do not use the word, *date,* or *time* in the time dimension group. Looker automatically adds this word.

- Name the measures with aggregate functions. For example, **total_sales** for sum measure, **avg_sale_price** for average measure, etc.

- Hide fields that are not useful to the end users. Examples include ID fields or database update dates.

- Use the label parameter to apply friendly names to fields and filters for end users. Make sure the labels are unique within the view.

- Use the description parameter on dimensions and measures to provide additional information to end users about the logic or calculations used within the model. This is particularly important for dimensions and measures that use complex logic or calculations.

- Use the **group_label** parameter to consolidate dimensions and measures, from individual or multiple related views as shown in the example in *Figure 8.23*.

  o Grouping all geographic information into a geography group will pull all address and location information together within the field selector, rather than having it all listed in alphabetical order. The group label function is shown *Figure 8.23*:

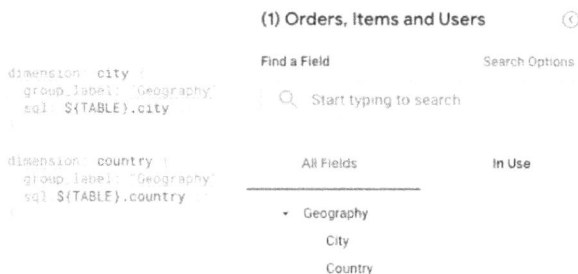

Figure 8.23: Group label

  o Group dimensions by the business entity. Common groups used are Product Dimensions, Customer Dimensions, and Order Dimensions.

  o Group measures by their related KPI. Some standard measure groups are *Revenue Measures, Order Measures, and Customer Measures.*

- Use **value_format** or **value_format_name** for applying formatting such as currency symbols, percentages, and decimal precision to numeric fields, to help make everything readable

- For custom formatting, use the manifest file to create custom formatting code in liquid, and use it across the views.

- Add **drill_fields** to all relevant measures. Drill fields enable users to click into aggregate values to access detailed data.

- Add **drill_fields** to all hierarchical dimensions. For example, adding a **drill_field** for city into a state dimension will enable users to select a state and then drill deeper into the cities within that state.

  Note: **This hierarchical drilling will automatically be applied within time dimension groups.**

- Always use the **NULLIF** function (or the equivalent in your database SQL) when creating a measure that involves division, to ensure it returns **NULL** if the divisor is zero. This will prevent a SQL error from being thrown for rows that are zero.

- **Explores**:
    - Use the from parameter to create an alias for the view in the explore join. Later, if there is a need to change the table, you can do so without breaking the code.

    - Use the label parameter to have a business-friendly name for the table in the explore.

    - Add a short description to each explore to specify the purpose and audience using the description parameter.

    - Describe what questions each explore can answer in the Documentation section, using one or many markdown LookML documents within each project

    - Use the fields parameter within explores or joins to limit the number of fields available to users. Included fields should be only those relevant to the explore. This reduces bloat and provides a better experience for end-users. Unlike the hidden parameter, this enables fields to be included or excluded, on an explore-by-explore basis.

    - Avoid exposing too much to users upon an initial Looker roll-out. Start small, and then expand the options. You do not have to expose all the tables or dimensions and measures at once. You can expose the most important fields, and then continue to build more functionality, as business users become more confident with data exploration.

    - Hide any explores that exist solely for populating specific Looks, dashboard tiles, or filters using the hidden parameter for explores. Explores that are not meant for exploration by end-users should be hidden.

    - Add labels to the model and/or explores so that they are ordered in the dropdown menu according to what is most important.

    o If you label a model *1. My Important Model*, that model, and all its explores will appear at the top of the explore menu. If you label an explore as *1. My Cool Explore*, that explore will appear at the top of the group of explores within a model

- **Joins**:

    o Define the relationship parameter for all joins. This will ensure that symmetric aggregates are calculated properly in Looker. Many-to-one join provides the best query performance.

    o Use the **view_label** parameter instead of the from parameter, for renaming views within an explore.

    o The **from** parameter should primarily be used when joining the same table multiple times (Polymorphic joins), self-joins, or re-scoping an extended view back to its original view name.

    o Do not use formatted timestamps within joins. It will impact the performance negatively.

- **Models**:

    o Use the fewest number of explores possible, which will allow users to easily get access to the answers they need. Consider splitting out into different models for different audiences. The optimal number of explores is different for every business, however too many explores tend to be confusing for the end user.

    o Organize explores across multiple models to help the end-user find the correct explore as easily as possible.

- **Dashboard development**:

    o Try to limit the number of Table Calculations. If there are Table Calculations useful for multiple reports or dashboards, move those to LookML so that the field is readily available for explores.

    o Use the simplest visualization possible to communicate a message. Overcomplicated visualizations are difficult to understand quickly and are easy to misinterpret.

    o Label axes and measures with user-friendly names wherever necessary. Do not include full field names in any chart, table, or visualization. It makes it repetitive and confusing to the user.

    o Use consistent colors (like a built-in color palette or implement a custom color palette, to implement consistent coloration).

o   Choose visualizations like column and bar charts over pie and donut charts whenever possible, as differences in angles and circular areas can be difficult for the brain to detect.

o   When used, include fewer than five categories in the pie or donut chart whenever possible

o   Avoid using stacked charts to visualize measures that should not accumulate, like averages.

o   When using dual-axis charts, consider combining different visualization types, (such as a line and a bar) to clearly illustrate each measure, especially when measures are significantly different magnitudes, like percents versus total amounts.

o   Linking from one dashboard to another is a good tactic to use, when clients have dashboards with many (>15) reports. The general design pattern is to create one dashboard with high-level KPIs and then a drill-down dashboard, that is filterable by product, client, region, etc. Set up links that enable users to easily navigate and pass filters to other Looker dashboards, systems, or platforms external to Looker.

Conclusion

In the preceding chapters, we delved into Looker components and features. This chapter focuses on practical issues and strategies for troubleshooting and resolution. Best practices represent proactive measures at the development stage, aimed at simplifying and maintaining code. By adhering to these practices, we can preemptively address potential issues that may arise in production. While generally applicable, there may be instances where implementation is not feasible. Exercise caution when applying best practices in such cases.

So far, up to this chapter, we have learned how to interact with Looker using the native user interface. In the next chapter, we will learn how to interact with Looker programmatically using APIs and SDKs. Looker APIs provide programmatic access to Looker's data, reports, and user management features, enabling automation and integration with other tools. Looker SDKs are pre-built libraries that simplify interacting with the APIs, allowing developers to easily build custom applications, manage resources, and automate tasks. Looker Embed enables developers to integrate Looker visualizations and dashboards into external applications or websites, offering seamless access to Looker's insights within custom environments.

CHAPTER 9

Application Programming Interface, Software Development Kit and Embed

Introduction

In previous chapters, we have explored different ways Looker can be interacted with and set up, all through the Looker interface. The functionality and visualizations are not limited by the interface. Looker also offer a variety of ways developers can interface with the instance programmatically. Anything performed on the instance can be procedurally done by integrating with Looker's **application programming interface** (**API**), enabling developers to script what could otherwise be tedious work. Additionally, with Looker's embed feature, developers can also integrate visualizations outside of Looker into their own applications, allowing users to easily create shareable metrics with users beyond the Looker platform.

Structure

In this chapter, we will go through the following topics:

- Application programming interface
- Embeds overview
- Public embed
- Private embed
- Single sign-on embed

- Practical applications
- Best practices

Objectives

In this chapter, we will review the various methods that developers can use to interface with the Looker's API: using the HTTP protocol and the **software development kit** (**SDK**). We will see various methods of authenticating into the API and ways to utilize API endpoints to programmatically perform various actions.

Afterwards, we will see the different ways Looker allows admins and developers to embed content outside of the instance. We will cover the three types of embeds available that are public, private, and **single-sign on** (**SSO**), and the implications for each.

Application programming interface

Looker offers developers the ability to perform any action available through the Looker application through an API. Using the API, developers can programmatically script any action, such as user management, schedule creation, or dashboard editing. This section will outline how developers can connect and utilize the Looker API for their own instances.

Note: Throughout this section, code block examples will be in Python, but the Looker API can be accessed through any programmatic language capable of handling HTTP requests.

Generating API key

Admins will need to generate a client access key and secret to send requests to the Looker API. Keys can be generated in the Admin panel, under Users, as seen in *Figure 9.1*. Keys are generated based on users:

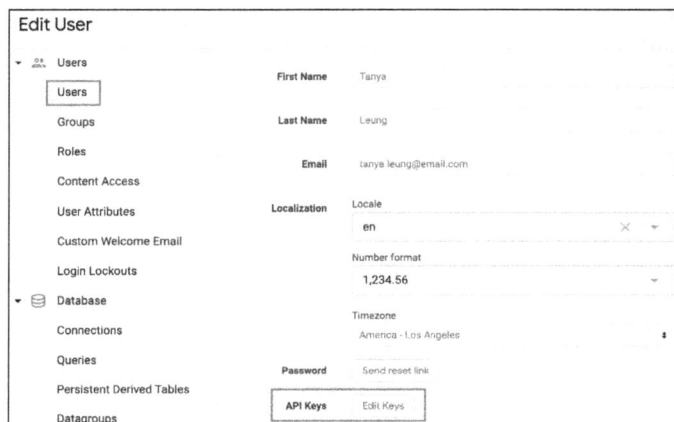

Figure 9.1: Location of API key generation

A user's client access and secret key can be accessed at any time after creation. If a key is accidentally leaked or compromised in any way, admins can delete the at any time to invalidate them.

API key permissions

The actions available and the data returned from the Looker API are determined by the API key user. Thus, the keys can only be used to perform actions that the user can do themselves. For example, if the API key was generated from a user who only has view permissions, they could hit endpoints like get dashboard, but not endpoints that perform traditional admin actions like update user.

API Explorer

Looker's API documentation is available through the API Explorer. There is a public version of the API Explorer available online, but the API Explorer accessed via the Looker instance is the recommended way of access for Looker developers because it enables developers to test the endpoints without needing to write any code.

The API Explorer is an optional add-on that admins can install from the Looker marketplace. It is located under applications and can be installed at no additional cost. After it has been installed, it can be accessed from the main menu, underneath the section applications.

The Explorer provides all the information developers need to use the Looker API. *Figure 9.2* provides a visual breakdown of the Explorer:

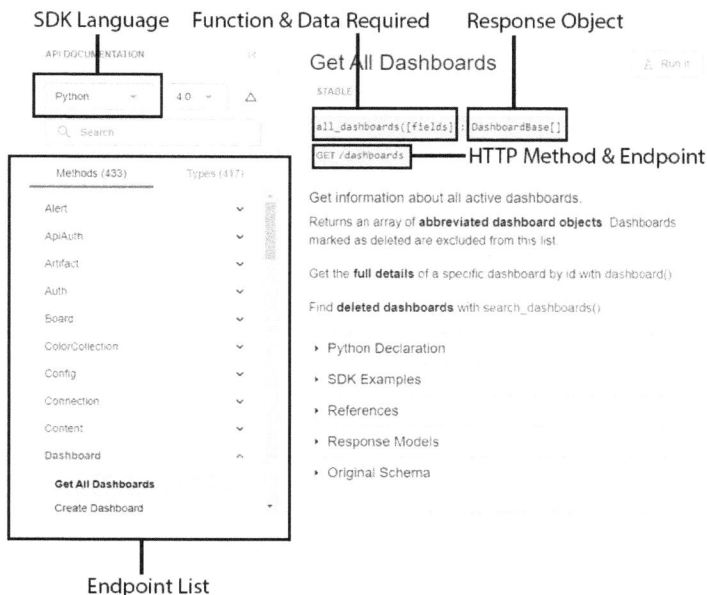

Figure 9.2: *Sections of the API Explorer*

Sections of the API Explorer can be broken down into the following:

- **SDK language**: Developers can choose the default programmatic language the Explorer displays when they select different endpoints. The selection will change the section declarations to whatever language is selected (e.g., Python Declaration).

- **Function and data required**: The Explorer lists the endpoint's equivalent function and a basic list of the function's required parameters. If the function lists **[fields]** as a parameter, it generally means developers do not need to pass anything into the function.

- **Response object**: The object type that the function returns. The object is listed in greater detail underneath the **Response Models** section.

- **HTTP method and endpoint**: The endpoint's HTTP request type, which can either be GET, POST, PATCH, or DELETE, and the actual endpoint itself that developers will need to hit to perform the action described directly below it.

- **Endpoint list:** This is a comprehensive list of all endpoints available to developers, organized by the type of action.

- **Declarations**: This section contains the SDK function equivalent of the endpoint, as well as the function's required parameters. It will display the function compatible with the programmatic language selected from the SDK language. If developers select All, every supported language (Python, TypeScript, Kotlin, C#, Swift, and Go) will appear under declarations, in their own tab.

- **SDK examples:** SDK examples are provided by Looker and organized by language.

- **Request body:** This section only appears for POST endpoints. The request body outlines the structure of the data body that developers will need to send to the endpoint. For all Looker POST requests, the body type expected is JavaScript Object Notation, commonly known as just JSON.

- **References**: It lists every object referenced throughout the endpoint and redirects to the specific object that lists the object's structure and it is used everywhere throughout the API.

- **Response models**: This outlines every response developers may receive when requesting a specific endpoint. Any response that returns a 400s code indicates a failure of some kind. If the error code returned is in the 200s, then the request was a success. 200 responses always return with information about the request—the structure of the request is outlined in this section of the API explorer.

- **Run it**: Looker gives developers the option to test the endpoint's functionality without having to worry about formulating the actual HTTP request. Using run it, developers can test to make sure that the endpoint they are constructing or the body of data they are sending to the endpoint is valid.

Note: Running it can cause actual changes on the Looker instance.

Run It is broken down into three sections, they are as follows:

o **Request**: Developers can insert their own input to the endpoint here.

o **Response**: Looker's output is the response to the API call constructed in the request tab.

o **SDK call**: This displays the corresponding SDK function for the endpoint. The language displayed is determined by the user's selection from SDK language. The function is also automatically pre-populated with values from request, if the user has provided them.

API requests

This section outlines one way to formulate an HTTP request to the Looker API. The code example uses Python and the library requests to simplify the HTTP request process, but developers can apply the general concept to any programmatic language.

Connecting to the API

Before developers can access any API endpoint, they must first generate an access token. Tokens can be generated by passing in a client ID and client secret (from the *Generating the API Key* section) to the endpoint **/login**.

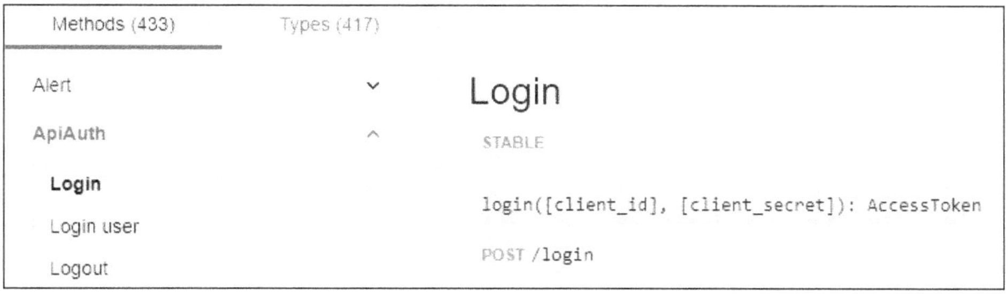

Figure 9.3: Endpoint to generate the authorization token

The **/login** endpoint requires simple **POST** requests where developers will need to pass in their client ID and client secret in a JSON body.

Let us take a look at a code snippet that uses this endpoint:

```
1   import requests
2   import json
3
4   BASE_URL = "https://mylookerinstance.looker.com:443"
5   ID = "qzYN6DzCbrdW9nVkHkjdJsa"
6   SECRET = "oRvxDgp5B7gSpD2WkPnj8nxT"
7
8   DATA = {'client_id':ID, 'client_secret': SECRET}
9
10  URL = BASE_URL + "/api/4.0/login"
11  r = requests.post(url = URL, data = DATA, verify=True)
12
13  data = r.json()
14  token = data['access_token']
```

Using the preceding code snippet, we can break down the basic process of generating the access token using the following login endpoint:

- **Lines 1 to 2**: Import the requests library to facilitate the HTTP request, and the JSON library to parse the JSON object that will be returned by the endpoint.

- **Lines 4 to 6**: Formulates the request body as required by the endpoint. The login endpoint is looking for the body to be in form **{'client_id':ID, 'client_secret': SECRET}**.

- **Lines 10 to 11**: Construct the URL to which the request should be made out to. This will always be in the form: base URL (of your Looker instance) **+ /api/4.0 +** endpoint. Send the request with the type defined by the endpoint (in this case POST) with the body made in 4-6.

- **Lines 13 to 14**: The returned response will always be a JSON object. Developers will need to parse the object in order to get the access token. Here, we use the Python library JSON to easily refer to the **access_token** attribute.

The access token enables developers to send requests to other endpoints and reduces the number of times the client ID or secret is sent over the network. Tokens are only valid for one hour, after that, developers will need to generate a new token.

Sending requests to the API

Sending requests to other API endpoints uses a very similar process to the login endpoint, but developers will also need to pass a header that includes the token created in the previous section into every request sent.

The Looker API requires an authorization header in the following form:

Authorization: <type> <credentials>

Looker accepts bearer tokens, so the type must be **Bearer**. Headers should be structure like the following:

```
headers = {'Authorization': "Bearer " + token}
```

Requests can be sent to the Looker API using the following steps:

1. **Structure the URL with the desired endpoint**: The URL is always a string in the following form:

   `https://name_of_looker_instance.looker.com:PORT/api/4.0 + endpoint`

   a. GET, DELETE, and PATCH requests may require developers to pass additional information into the endpoint. Whenever an endpoint contains a field enclosed in curly brackets, the API requests developers to replace it with a value.

   b. For example, for the GET endpoint **/dashboards/{dashboard_id}**, developers will need to replace **{dashboard_id}** with the ID of the dashboard they would like information on e.g. **/dashboards/11**.

2. **Send the request to the URL**: POST and PATCH requests usually always require developers to pass in a body of JSON-structured data. If applicable, the body's required fields will always be outlined in the request body section of the endpoint.

3. **Process the response returned by the API**: The response will always be a JSON object. The different JSON parameters are outlined in the API Explorer under the response model.

Let us take a look at an example of sending an HTTP request that requires data to be sent through the endpoint URL and through a JSON body.

For our example, let us take a look at the endpoint **Update Dashboard**:

Update Dashboard

STABLE   rate_limited

update_dashboard(dashboard_id, body): Dashboard

PATCH /dashboards/{dashboard_id}

Figure 9.4: Update Dashboard endpoint details

The API function **Update Dashboard** requires a **PATCH** request and requires users to pass in the following two things:

- The ID of the dashboard to be updated (via an endpoint)
- The updates to be performed on the dashboard (via body)

Let us say that we want to rename one of our dashboards to **My Dashboard**. These are the following steps we would take using the update dashboard endpoint:

1. **Structuring the endpoint**: The endpoint requires the dashboard ID to be passed in as part of the request URL. We can grab the dashboard ID from the dashboard's URL:

   a. In order to get the ID, navigate to the dashboard URL:

   https://my_looker_instance.looker.com/dashboards/157

   The ID for the dashboard is 157.

   b. **Constructing the endpoint with the ID**: The endpoint in this case is **/dashboards/{dashboard_id}**. Since we want to update dashboard 157, our endpoint becomes **/dashboards/157**.

   c. Add the endpoint to our base URL:

   https://my_looker_instance.looker.com:443/api/4.0/dashboards/157

2. **Send the request to Looker to perform the update:**

   a. As part of the request, we must send a body of data containing the updates we want to push to dashboard 157. Underneath the request body outlined in the Explorer, there are several things we can update, such as the description, model, folder, etc. Since we only want to update the title, we can send a body that only contains the parameter title, as shown in the following:

   ```
   body = {
     "folder": {},
     "title": "My Dashboard"
   }
   ```

   We can leave other optional fields blank (like we did with the folder) or omit them entirely (as we did with all other optional fields).

   b. Send a PATCH request to our constructed endpoint alongside the header containing our token (from the previous section) and the data constructed in the preceding code:

   ```
   response = requests.patch(
   url = https://my_looker_instance.looker.com:443/api/4.0/
   dashboards/157,
   headers = {'Authorization': "Bearer " + token},
   data = body, verify=True)
   ```

3. **Process the response returned by the API**: This specific endpoint returns a JSON representation of the edited dashboard. If the API returned anything other than code 200, an error has occurred.

There are a couple of ways we can process the API response:

a. Using the Python requests library, we can easily see the status code returned by the request. The function **requests.patch()** from 2b returns back a response object. The following will display the results of our request:

```
print(response.status_code)
```

In this example, we specifically tested the update dashboard endpoint. This process, however, can be generally applied to any endpoint.

Troubleshooting the API requests

It is inevitable to run into errors when coding. Here are some common troubleshooting methods developers can go through when diagnosing code:

- Test the endpoint directly through the API Explorer using **Run It**. Developers can check to see if their passed-in value and (if applicable) their constructed data body is accurate. This enables developers to test the structure of their request, separate from HTTP protocol. If the developer's tested values are successful, they may need to re-examine the token generation or HTTP request part of the code.

- If the API returns a 400s error code response, then the HTTP request was correctly formulated, but the token or data sent is incorrect. The API Explorer documents potential 400s errors that it may return, but generally, the cause for each error code is as follows (note that the potential problem and solution described are not all inclusive):

  o **400 Bad Request**: The Looker server received your request, but the request was not formed correctly.

  o **401 unauthorized**: The token sent in the request may be incorrectly formulated or expired. Look to regenerate the token and make sure the credentials provided to create the token are correct.

  o **403 Forbidden**: It usually indicates that the credentials used to make the request does not actually have permissions to perform the action. This may occur, for example, if the client ID and secret were generated from an account that only has viewer permissions but is used to perform an admin action, e.g., edit user. Double-check the credentials of the client ID and secret.

  o **404 not found**: It indicates that the page the developer is trying to access is not found. Check to make sure that the endpoint has been correctly structured.

  o **405 method not allowed**: The developer sent the wrong request type to the endpoint e.g., used a **POST** request, but the endpoint requires a **PATCH** request.

o **422 unprocessable entity**: The API will throw this error when the data body sent in the request is incorrectly formatted. Double-check the syntax and semantics of the data body, checking that fields are spelled correctly and that no fields are missing.

o **429 too many requests**: This request and its contents are correct, but the developer has sent the API too many requests and must wait before sending another.

Software development kit

The Looker SDK is a set of developer tools that offers a different way of accessing the Looker API. The SDK streamlines the HTTP request process so that the only thing developers need to worry about is the script's functionality.

The SDK abstracts away the HTTP request process entirely from the developer, meaning they will not have to worry about generating the token, creating the HTTP header, structuring the endpoint, or sending the request. The SDK also parses the response so that developers do not need to worry about parsing or converting the returned JSON object. In this section, we will be going over how to interact with the SDK, and how the SDK compares to the HTTP method of accessing the API.

Software development kit compatibility

SDK is essentially a set of tools bundled in one installable package. Looker has created an SDK for its API for multiple programmatic languages, which include:

- Python
- TypeScript
- Ruby
- Kotlin (community)
- Go (community)
- R (community)
- C# (community)

Looker only officially supports the Python, TypeScript, and Ruby SDKs; all the other languages are maintained by the Looker community.

For our code examples, we will be using the Python SDK but note that all functionality is also possible with any of the languages listed in the preceding list.

Configuring credentials

The credentials required to utilize the Looker SDK are the same as those used to access the Looker API user's client key and secret key. The SDK does require credentials to be formatted in an **ini** file, using the following structure:

```
[Looker]
base_url=https://INSTANCE.looker.com:PORT
client_id=CLIENT_ID
client_secret=CLIENT_SECRET
verify_ssl=True/False
```

The **ini** file requires the following values:

- **Base URL**: The **base_url** may require the port to be added at the end of the URL, depending on how and when your instance was provisioned.

  - o If the Looker instance was provisioned before 07/07/2020, the port is 1999.

  - o If the instance was provisioned on or after 07/07/2020 and is hosted on AWS, the port is 443.

  - o In all other cases, the port does not need to be specified and can be omitted.

- **Client ID**: A user's API client ID, see the previous section *Generating API Key*.

- **Client secret**: A user's API client secret, see the previous section *Generating API Key*.

- **Verify SSL**: This true or false value determines whether SSL certification verification should be required when establishing the connection to the API. It is generally set to true unless the developer is testing against a local, customer-hosted instance.

  The following is a sample of the contents of an **ini** file:

```
[Looker]
base_url=https://mylookerinstance.looker.com:443
client_id=qzYN6DzCbrdW9nVkHkjdJs
client_secret=oRvxDgp5B7gSpD2WkPnj8nxT
verify_ssl=True
```

In the subsequent sections, we will use these dummy values in our examples.

Initializing the software development kit

The developers, before initializing the SDK, will need to make the SDK available for the script or application being built. The steps to do this vary by language, but generally, developers will need to perform the following steps:

1. **Download the Looker SDK library**: For Python, this can be as basic as running **pip install looker-sdk**. For other languages that do not have a package manager or do not have the Looker SDK available in their package manager, developers will need to install the library files directly from Looker's official GitHub.

2. **Include the library in your program**: This involves adding to the top of the file **import looker_sdk**, or your language's equivalent.

Once the Looker SDK library is available to your program, you can initialize a Looker SDK object, enabling developers to hit any API endpoint as a function from the SDK.

Initializing the Looker SDK requires passing in the **.ini** credential file outlined in the previous section. By initializing with the credentials, developers are doing the equivalent of formulating the token headers required for the API HTTP request.

Let us take a look at how a request might be set up using the SDK versus the API:

SDK	API
``import looker_sdk

sdk = looker_sdk.init40("looker.ini")``` | ```import requests
import json

BASE_URL = "https://mylookerinstance.looker.com:443"
ID = "qzYN6DzCbrdW9nVkHkjdJs"
SECRET = "oRvxDgp5B7gSpD2WkPnj8nxT"

PARAMS = {'client_id':ID, 'client_secret': SECRET}

URL = BASE_URL + "/api/4.0/login"
r = requests.post(url = URL, params = PARAMS, verify=True)
data = r.json()

token = data['access_token']``` |

Table 9.1: Comparison between authentication using the SDK versus the API

The SDK's init40 function accepts the path to your **.ini** file, relative to the script's location. The function automatically performs the authentication process on behalf of the user. Additionally, users will not have to worry about refreshing the access token, as is required when interfacing directly with the API.

Once the Looker SDK has been initialized, developers can hit any endpoint using its corresponding SDK function.

Looker API Explorer

Looker's API Explorer provides the corresponding SDK function for every available endpoint. The API Explorer provides all the information developers need to access the SDK's function equivalent to an endpoint. *In Figure 9.5*, we can see a breakdown of SDK-related information from the API Explorer:

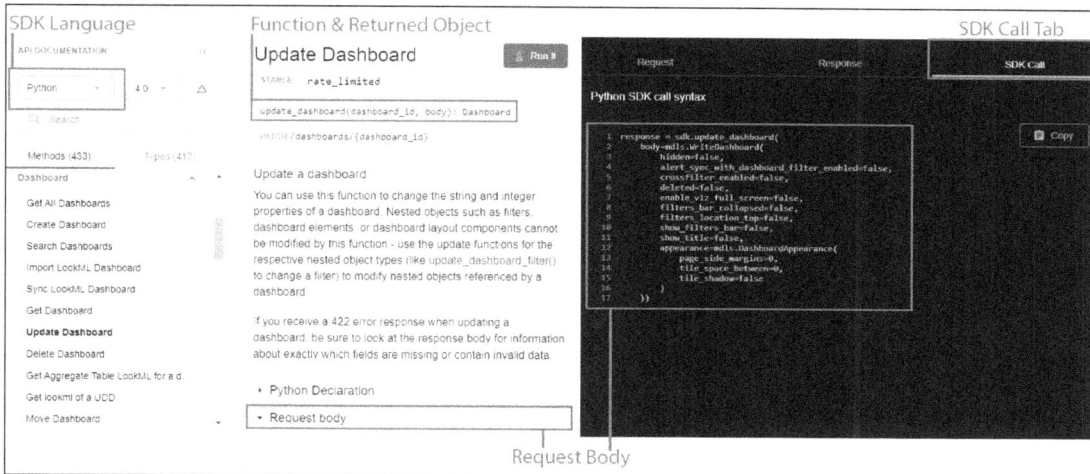

Figure 9.5: API Explorer Breakdown (SDK)

The most notable sections to keep in mind:

- **SDK language**: Determines what language the SDK call tab will be in.

- **Function and returned object**: This is the SDK function developers can call in their code. If there are parameters listed within parentheses, then the SDK function is expecting those parameters to be passed in when the function is called.

  If one of the parameters listed is **body**, it will be expecting data in a specific form, as listed in request body.

- **Request body**: Only appears if the endpoint is of type POST or PATCH. This outlines the structure of the object the SDK expects the developer to pass into the function when the function requests **body**.

- **SDK call tab**: It provides the function equivalent of the endpoint, dynamic to user input inserted in the request tab.

  It is recommended that the developers copy code from the SDK call tab (*Figure 9.5*) to their script, as it contains the exact parameters the function is expected.

Using the software development kit

The developers can implement any API endpoint as a function call instead. Using any function in the SDK can be broken down into the following three steps:

1. **Initialize the Looker SDK**: The SDK only needs to be initialized once in the script.

2. **Invoke the function**: Call the function using the initialized SDK object, providing any required function parameters (if applicable). Function parameters are generally two types. They are as follows:

- **Basic variable values**: These are usually of type string, number, or Boolean. Usually, any parameter that is passed as part of the endpoint in the original API method will exist as its own parameter in the function.

- **Structured object**: These take the place of the body in a **POST** or **PATCH** request. The Looker SDK creates a custom model for every data body. Developers will need to reference the API Explorer to see the model required for a function.

3. **Process the response**: This step is optional depending on the endpoint. The SDK will return a language-compatible class, meaning developers do not need to parse the API's response; they can directly reference the different attributes of the returned response.

   If the function is incomplete for whatever reason, the Looker SDK will immediately throw an error at runtime (versus users needing to parse and read through the API response to know if their request was successful).

Let us take a look at an example of calling an SDK function. For this example, we will be hitting the same endpoint from the API example, update dashboard.

As in the API example, we will use the update dashboard endpoint to update our dashboard's title to **My Dashboard**. We will be referencing the information from *Figure 9.4* to construct our script:

```
1   import looker_sdk
2   from looker_sdk import models40 as mdls
3
4   sdk = looker_sdk.init40("looker.ini")
5   response = sdk.update_dashboard(
6       dashboard_id="157",
7       body=mdls.WriteDashboard(
8           title="My Dashboard",
9           folder={} ))
10  print(response.title)
```
<box>

The script can be broken down into the following three steps as outlined previously:

1. **Initialize the Looker SDK**: In *Lines 1* to *4*, we import the Looker SDK library into the script. We also specifically import the **models40** module from the library and re-alias it as **mdls** so that it is compatible with the code snippet generated by the SDK call tab.

2. **Call the function**: In *Lines 5 to 9*, we call the function with the structure as outlined by the API Explorer. The function has two passed in objects:

   - **Dashboard ID**: It is a basic string that contains the ID of the dashboard we want to updated.

- **Body**: It is defined as a dashboard object for this endpoint. In this example, we use the function write dashboard from `mdls` in order to create the object. Similarly, to the original API example, we can choose to leave fields we do not want to change blank (as we did with folders), or we can omit them entirely. In this case, we only want to update the title, so the only attribute of the dashboard object populated is the title.

3. **Process the response**: In *line 10*, we are simply printing the title of the returned object, which is the dashboard we updated, to double-check that our update was successful.

In comparison to the API, this example shows how the SDK is able to abstract away the technical details surrounding how to communicate with the API so that developers focus on writing cleaner and more concise codes.

Embeds overview

Oftentimes, Looker is used to create dashboards for a company that owns internal analytics. However, it can also be used to create visualizations that can be shared externally outside of Looker. Looker has implemented a robust way of embedding visualizations outside of Looker, allowing users to interact with dashboards without having to interface with Looker at all. There are three types of embeds Looker offers: public, private, and **single-sign on** (SSO). The following is an overview of the differences between the three:

	Public	**Private**	**SSO**
Embeddable content	Looks	Dashboards, Looks	Dashboards, Looks, Explores, Applications
Implementation difficulty	Easy - URL is generated through the UI	Easy - URL is generated through the UI	Hard - Requires development time and intermediate coding abilities
Level of customization	Low - all end users see the same visualization	Medium - allows for the same amount of customization admins would apply to any Looker user	High - users for SSO embeds are created on the fly and the URL is dynamic, allowing for dynamic content
security	Medium - End users cannot access the Looker instance, but they will always be able to see the visualization, extra security must come from the application it is embedded into	High - End users must log in with the same method they use to log into the actual Looker instance	High - Developers create a placeholder user every time content is rendered, and the URL generated is single-use with an automatic timeout

Table 9.2: Comparison of the different embed methods

In the following sections, we will explore in depth the different embed methods, and ways developers can customize an end user's embed experience.

HTML iframes

All Looker embeds can be displayed using the HTML component **<iframe>**. Adding the generated embed URL to an **iframe** as the source will load that URL as a webpage within a webpage. The following is an example of adding an embed URL to the **iframe** tag:

```
<iframe src='https://my_looker_instance.looker.com/embed/public/
DCMbzXWTGJXr7V8yBzPjnk8' width='600' height='338' frameborder='0'></
iframe>
```

This is the method by which all embeds (public, private, and SSO) are displayed. The developers can also test their iframes by directly pasting their SSO embed URL into a web browser (recommended that developers use an incognito tab so that their own credentials are not used/replaced).

Public embed

Users can embed any look outside of Looker using Looker's public embed method. Embeds created using this method mean that anyone can view the Look as it appears on the Looker instance, without any data restrictions of personal customization.

Note: **Only Looks can be publicly embedded, not dashboards.**

Enabling public embeds

Before any user is able to create a Look as a public embed, admins must fulfill the following two requirements:

- Admins need to enable the feature, for instance. Underneath general settings, admins can enable or disable public URLs.
- Admins need to grant users the **create_public_looks** permission.

Once both conditions have been met, users with the correct permissions will have the option to convert Looks into public Looks.

Creating public embeds

Once public embeds have been enabled, admins (or anyone with the appropriate permissions) will need to enable public access on a per Look basis. Looks can be made public by toggling the Public Access tab, as seen in the following figure:

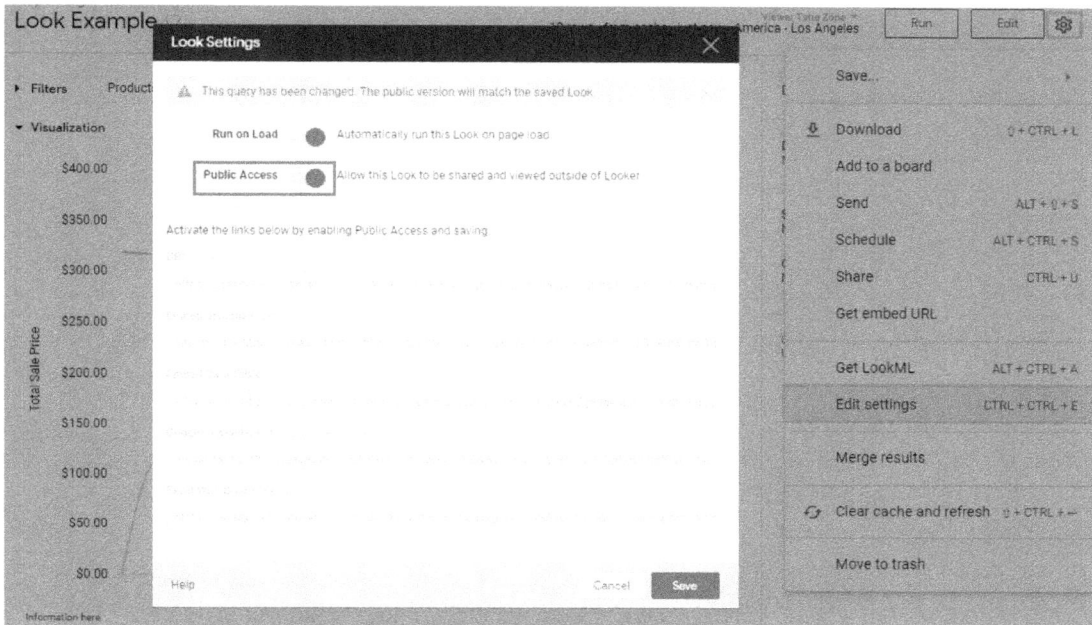

Figure 9.6: Toggling on public access for a Look

In *Figure 9.6*, the steps to enable a public access are demonstrated:

- Navigate to the Look to be embedded.
- Selecting edit settings from the cog menu.
- Toggle on **Public Access.**

After the initial toggle, admins will need to save these settings. Re-opening the settings menu will enable admins to copy the **iframe** compatible URL.

Private embed

Any look or dashboard can be privately embedded outside of Looker. When content is privately embedded, viewers will need to log into the Looker instance through the **iframe** in order to view the visualization(s).

Creating private embeds

In order to generate the private embed URL for a dashboard or look, users simply need to select the **Get embed URL** option from the desired visualization's settings, as shown in *Figure 9.7*:

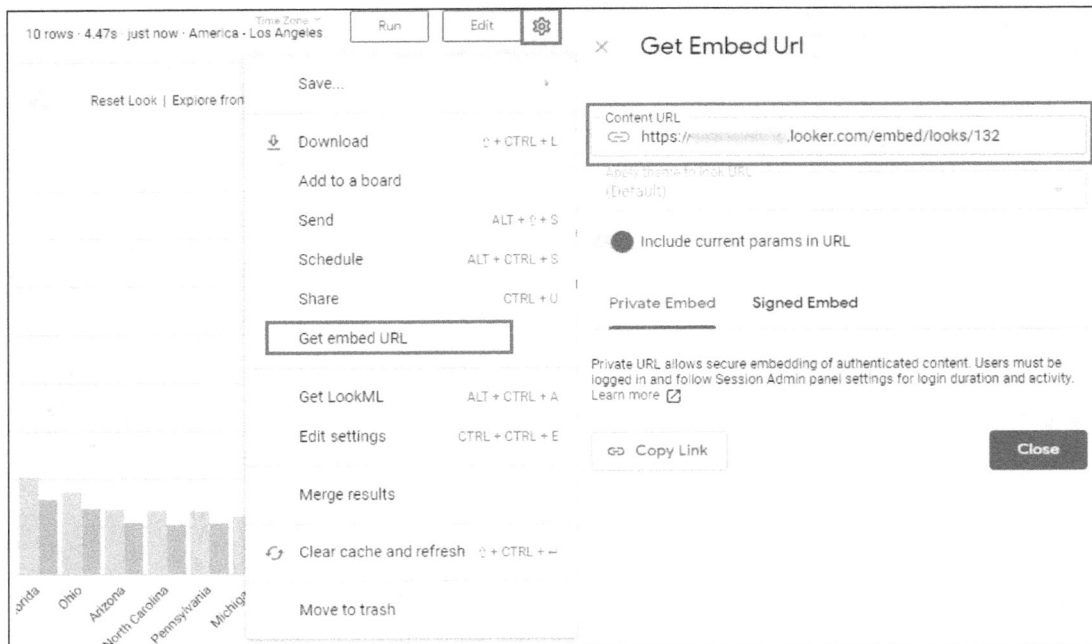

Figure 9.7: Generating a private embed URL

Looker will open up a separate menu for the embed URL. Users can copy the provided URL into an **iframe** to load the visualization outside of Looker.

Parameters

Developers can add parameters to the end of their embed URL to temporarily customize how the visualization is displayed without actually changing the base visualization. Parameters are added at the end of the embed URL after **?**. The general structure of the URL will look like this: **https://instance.looker.com/embed/dashboards/4?theme=red&Date=14+day**

Here, each section is as follows:

- **Hostname**: **https://instance.looker.com**
- **Path**: **/embed/dashboards/4**
- **Parameters**: **?theme=red&Date=14+day**

  Parameters must come after the path, with **?** added after the path. Each parameter field must be separated with a **&.**

  There are several parameters that developers can add to the end of the URL, all of which can be added in any order:

- **allow_login_screen**: Determines if the embed displays the Looker login screen to embed users. This parameter is only applicable for private embeds.

- o If set to false, the embed will return a 401, and users will need to log into the Looker instance directly to establish credential cookies.

- o If set to true, users can directly log into Looker through the `iframe`.

- **Theme**: Set the theme to change the background color, text size, font, etc., of the entire explore or dashboard. Admins can see pre-existing themes and create new themes by selecting the themes section under admin.

  - o This parameter is only available for dashboards and explores.

  - o The themes feature is only available for specific Looker instances. If admins do not see themes under the admin tab, contact Looker support.

- **_themes**: Set individual theme elements. This differs from theme, which is a set of pre-created theme elements admins have already created. Developers can use **_theme** to change specific elements.

  - o Accepts values in form `{"<property>":value}`.

  - o Properties include `show_filters_bar`, `text_tile_text_color`, and `title_color`

- **filter_name**: Set the default value of dashboard filters. Looker adds dashboard filters to the end of any URL, and the values of the filters dynamically change according to the user's selection. Developers can manually edit or copy a specific filter combination and add that to the end of the embed URL to override the default filter values.

- **hide_filter**: It removes a dashboard filter from the dashboard. The default value of the dashboard will still apply, but embed viewers will not be able to see or change the value. **hide_filter** can be defined multiple times to hide multiple filters.

  The following example hides the filters Date and State from view:

  https://instance.looker.com/embed/dashboards/4?hide_filter=Date&hide_filter=State

Parameter additions to the URL can be added at any time to public and private embed URLs. If adding to an SSO embed URL, the addition must occur before the URL is signed and encoded.

Single sign-on embed

SSO embeds is like private embedding, but instead of a user logging into Looker through the iframe, admins dynamically create a user during dashboard load. The permissions of the user created at execution are used to determine how the dashboard looks when loaded. Both Looks and dashboards can be embedded using the SSO embed method.

Note: SSO embeds are not available on all Looker platforms. They are an additional feature that must be negotiated as part of a company's Looker contract. If the embed tab is not available underneath Admin | Platform, it has not been enabled on your instance and you will need to contact Looker support about adding the feature.

Generating the embed secret

The credentials required to create an SSO embed are entirely separate from API keys. Looker maintains a single embed secret for every instance. The secret is accessible through the Embed tab under the **Admin** panel, as shown in the following figure:

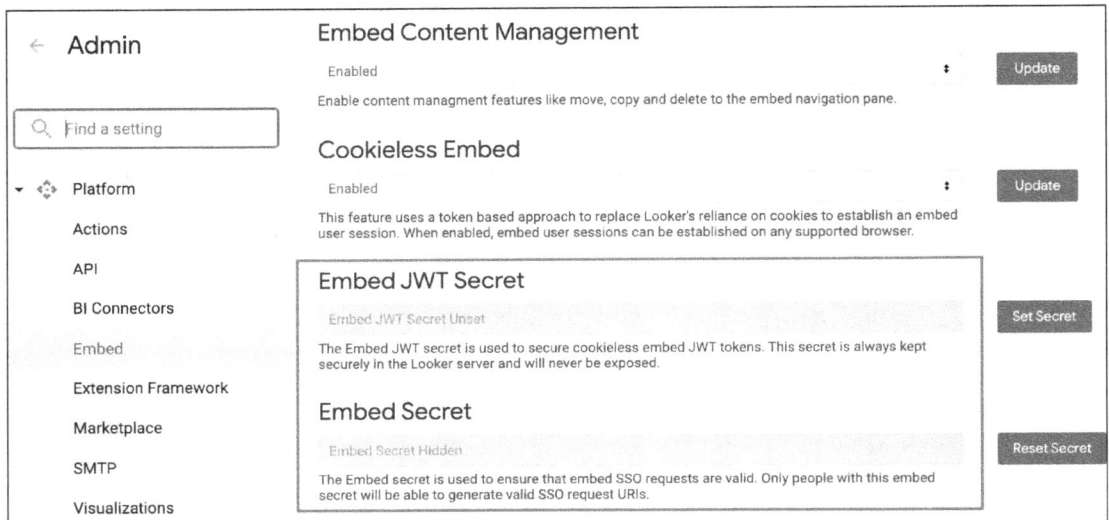

Figure 9.8: Location of the embed secret

If an embed secret has not been created yet, admins will have the option to set secret. If one already exists, admins will have the option to reset secret. Regardless of the option available, both options perform the same action that is generating an embed secret.

When creating or resetting a secret, Looker will then display the embed secret. This secret will only be shown once, afterwards, admins will not be able to view it again so make sure to have the secret securely stored somewhere immediately after creation.

Embed users

Whenever developers generate an SSO embed URL, they are also defining the user that is viewing the content. This placeholder user, or embed user, is used to tell Looker who is viewing the dashboards so that the right permissions and restrictions can be applied. An embed user is created every time, and information about the created embed user can be examined anytime in the **Admin** panel under **Users**.

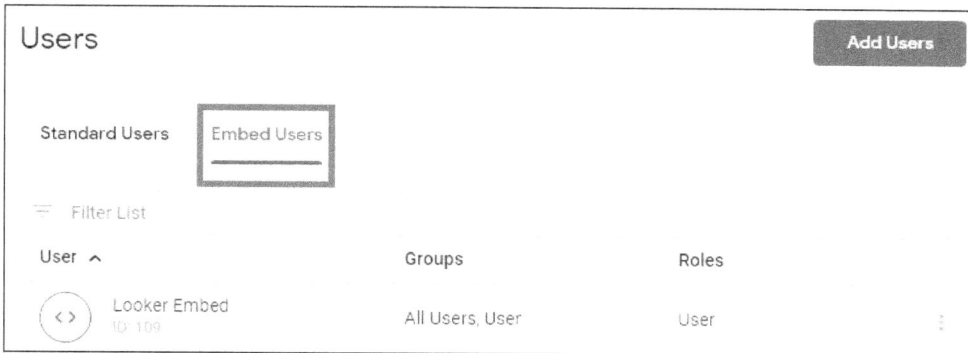

Figure 9.9: The Embed Users tab

Embed Users are the same as standard users in that they can belong to groups, be assigned roles, and have their own user attributes. Admins can also sudo into embed users at any time in case they want to check how that user's permissions would affect specific dashboards.

Standard and embed users have two majors differences:

- Embed users do not have their own set of credentials, meaning that they cannot log into the Looker instance. The only way to be an embed user on the Looker instance is through sudo.

- Embed users cannot be edited through the Looker console, they can only be changed by creating a new SSO embed URL.

Creating SSO embeds

SSO embeds are, in short, URLs that are placed into iframes, which display as a dashboard to the end user. Developers determine what is displayed to the user by configuring that SSO embed URL. In this section, we will go over how to create these URLs.

SSO embed URL structure

SSO Embeds have the following structure:

Figure 9.10: Embed URL Structure

- **Host**: The name of your Looker instance e.g. **https://mylooker.looker.com**

- **Embed URL**: The relative path to the content you would like displayed, including **/embed** before the path. The path can be extracted from the content's URL:

```
https://my_looker.looker.com/looks/123
https://my_looker.looker.com/dashboards/456
https://my_looker.looker.com/dashboards/my_model::my_dashboard
https://my_looker.looker.com/explore/my_model/my_view
https://my_looker.looker.com/extensions/my_project::my_app/
```

Figure 9.11: Different examples of relatives paths in Looker

Extract the relative path, then include **/embed** before it. The final URL will have **/embed//embed**—this is expected:

```
/embed/looks/123
/embed/dashboards/456
/embed/dashboards/my_model::my_dashboard
/embed/explore/my_model/my_view
/embed/extensions/my_project::my_app/
```

Figure 9.12: Examples of embed endpoints with different relative paths

- **Parameters**: Here is where the developer passes information into the URL to determine who is viewing the visualization, and how long the visualization session should be available for. The parameters available to be passed into the URL are as follows:

Parameter	Default Value	Description	Data Type
nonce	Value Required	Short for *number used once*, nonce is a randomly generated string that is used to prevent malicious parties from re-submitting the same URL. Nonce can be any random generation of letters and numbers, as long as it is less than 255 characters and has not been used in the last hour.	string
time	Value Required	The current time as a UNIX timestamp (number of seconds since Unix epoch).	integer
session_length	Value Required	The number of seconds the embed user should remain logged into Looker. After the set amount of time has passed, embed users are auto logged out and will need to have their embed URL regenerated.	integer

Parameter	Default Value	Description	Data Type
external_ user_id	""	The unique ID that can be given to a user. Looker will map this ID to the actual embed user on Looker. Once granted, developers can reference this ID to retrieve embed users, and all of their associated permissions. It is recommended developers use external_user_id to map the Looker embed user with their own application's user, instead of the autogenerated id Looker grants, because developers can set external_user_id, but they cannot set id.	string
permissions	Value Required	The list of permissions that the embed user should have. Reference the previous chapter for all possible permissions, but baseline embed users will need the permissions *access_data* and *see_user_ dashboards* or *see_looks* depending on the content the embed is trying to display.	array of strings
models	Value Required	The names of models the embed user has access to. Developers need to include the name of the model the visualization displayed is using.	array of strings
group_ids	[]	The list of group IDs (not group names) that the embed user should be added to. This can be used to assign permissions and user attributes.	array of strings
external_ group_ids	""	Group identifier developers can assign to the user. Looker will automatically create a folder for every embed group ID, and users with the matching ID are automatically granted access to the folder.	string
user_ attributes	{}	The list of user attributes that should be applied to the user. Developers can use this to customize dashboards/Looks to the embed user.	JSON
access_filters	Value Required	Empty placeholder value that was removed with Looker 3.10 but is still required in the URL.	Empty JSON
first_name	""	The first name of the embed user. Used solely for identification purposes for admins Looker-side.	string
last_name	""	The last name of the embed user. Used solely for identification purposes for admins Looker-side.	string

Parameter	Default Value	Description	Data Type
user_ timezone	*""*	The timezone of the embed user. Only useful is User Specific Time Zones have been enabled on the instance. Developers will also need to add: ?query_timezone=user_timezone right after the embed URL to make the dashboard dynamic to the value set here.	string
force_ logout_login	Value Required	If a user who is already logged into Looker views embedded content, developers can determine which set of credentials should take precedence. If true: the user will be logged out of Looker and will use the credentials generated as defined in parameters false: the user will use their own credentials. It is recommended, especially when testing, to set it as true.	boolean

Table 9.3: *Embed URL parameters*

o   Each parameter should be separated with an ampersand (&) in the URL.

o   Whenever **Value Required** is noted under default value, developers need to add the parameter and their own value for the parameter to the URL. It cannot be left blank. All other parameters can be omitted from the URL.

- **Signature**: A cryptographic hash added to the end of the URL based on the SSO URL's embed URL, parameters, etc. The signature is added for security reasons to check that URL parameters have not been tampered with during transit to the Looker server.

Generating single-sign on embed URL

In order to generate SSO embed URL, developers need to take the following steps:

1.   **Assemble the base URL**: This is your instance URL with **/login/embed/** appended to the end of it. The base URL will always be appended to when generating any SSO embed URLs.

https://instance.looker.com/login/embed/

2.   **Point the URL to content**: Add the relative URL of the content to be displayed to the end of the base URL.

https://instance.looker.com/login/embed//embed/dashboards/115?

3. **Create the parameters and add it to the end of the URL**: Determine the session and permissions of the embed user viewing the URL. Each parameter must be separated with an "&".

Here is an example of what your URL might look like at this point:

```
https://instance.looker.com/login/embed//embed/dashboards/115?
nonce="8j6h1z4e2r0q3a5t9w7u2y1i"&
time=1715240304&
session_length=3600&
external_user_id="ClientA_User_1"&
permissions=["access_data","see_user_dashboards"]&
models=["client_a"]&
group_ids=[1,2]&
external_group_id="ClientA"&
user_attributes={"pii_access":"false","country":"USA"}&
access_filters={}&
first_name="Jane"&
last_name="Doe"&
force_logout_login=true
```

4. **Generate the signature and add it to the end of the URL**: To generate the signature, structure the following parameters from *step 3* into a string, with each parameter separated with a newline (**\n**). The required parameters are as follows:

   a. Host URL

   b. Embed URL

   c. Nonce

   d. Current time

   e. Session length

   f. External user ID

   g. Permissions

   h. Models

   i. Group IDs

   j. External group ID

   k. User attributes

   l. Access filters (value must always set to {})

See an example of the string required to generate the following signature:

```
instance.looker.com/login/embed/
/embed/dashboards/115
"8j6h1z4e2r0q3a5t9w7u2y1i"
1715240304
3600
ClientA_User_1
["see_lookml_dashboards", "access_data"]
["client_a"]
"1,2"
null
{"pii_access":"false","country":"USA"}
{}
```

Use HMAC to create a hash using the embed secret as the key, the preceding JSON string as the Message and the hash function sha1. Whatever method is used to create the hash will return a string. Format the output as **signature=OUTPUT** and add it to the end of the URL as if it were another parameter:

```
https://instance.looker.com/login/embed//embed/dashboards/115?
nonce="8j6h1z4e2r0q3a5t9w7u2y1i"&
time=1715240304&
session_length=3600&
external_user_id="ClientA_User_1"&
permissions=["access_data","see_user_dashboards"]&
models=["client_a"]&
group_ids=[1,2]&
external_group_id="ClientA"&
user_attributes={"pii_access":"false","country":"USA"}&
access_filters={}&
first_name="Jane"&
last_name="Doe"&
force_logout_login=true&
signature=E8D4GFIHK1A396257LJBC
```

5. **Encode the URL**: Encode characters using percent-encoding. Developers will need to convert characters into a format that is compatible with servers. URL encoding includes:

   a. Replacing reserved **American Standard Code for Information Interchange (ASCII)** characters (special symbols like : and &) into the corresponding percent-encoded characters (e.g., & is converted into %26).

   b. Replacing spaces with a +.

We highly recommend using an encoding function compatible with your language of choice. For Python, for example, this is simply the encode('UTF-8') function:

```
Here is what the same URL looks like encoded:
https://instance.looker.com/login/embed//embed/
dashboards/115?
nonce=%228j6h1z4e2r0q3a5t9w7u2y1i%22&
time=1715240304&
session_length=3600&
external_user_id=%22ClientA_User_1%22&
permissions=%5B%22access_data%22,%22see_user_
dashboards%22%5D&
models=%5B%22client_a%22%5D&
group_ids=%5B1,2%5D&
external_group_id=%22ClientA%22&
user_attributes=%7B%22pii_
access%22:%22false%22,%22country%22:%22USA%22%7D&
access_filters={}&
first_name=%22Jane%22&
last_name=%22Doe%22&
force_logout_login=true&
signature=E8D4GFIHK1A396257LJBC
```
<box>

6. **Load the URL**: Insert the final URL into an **iframe** tag, like such:

```
<iframe src="SSO_EMBED_URL"></iframe>
```

Remember the URL is valid only once and will need to be regenerated every load. It is highly recommended developers create a script to generate the embed URL.

Access control

Access control for embed users is very similar to standard users. Although embed users cannot be directly assigned roles, developers can functionally assign permission sets using the permissions parameters and model sets using the model parameters. Embed users can be assigned to groups just like standard users and will inherit all permissions and user attributes associated with the role.

The primary difference between embed and standard access control is that embed permissions cannot be changed through the Looker UI. Permissions can only be set through the creation of the SSO embed URL.

Cookie policy

Developers will also need to determine a cookie policy for their SSO embeds, as the incorrect policy can result in the embed URL failing to load for end users.

Cookie-based embedding

Looker, by default, will create a session cookie for whoever is interfacing with Looker. The cookie is sent along with any requests the user makes to Looker (e.g., accessing Looker directly or viewing embedded Looker content). When implementing SSO embeds, the embed uses the same cookies to access Looker content, which leads to the following implications:

- When a user is testing embeds, it will automatically replace your current Looker cookies whenever the URL parameter **force_logout_login** is set to true. If you were previously signed into your Looker instance, the session will be replaced with the SSO embed session. The next time developers try to log into the actual instance after running an SSO embed URL, they will likely not be able to view the Looker page because it is using the embed user's credentials. Developers will need to take the following steps to use their own credentials again:

  o To re-authenticate as yourself, change the URL endpoint to **/login**, like the following: **https://your_instance.looker.com/login**.

  o Developers can avoid cookie replacement entirely by testing or using the SSO embed URL in an entirely different browser, or in incognito mode.

- If a user's browser blocks third party cookies, SSO embeds will not be able to load. Blocking third-party cookies will prevent the load of any content on a web page from a domain different from the current domain the user is on. Since SSO embeds loads data from your Looker instance, it will naturally be different from the web app it is embedded into.

  Admins can bypass this by adding a custom URL to the Looker instance so that it matches the web app it is embedded into. Admins will need to contact Looker support to change the domain name.

Cookieless embedding

Developers can look to implement cookieless embedding if they cannot change their Looker domain and/or their client's browsers will not allow third party cookies. This requires significantly more development to enable this, as developers will need to maintain a token as part of the request instead. The instance, the application client, and the application server must be updated to enable this. To see an example of implementation, please refer to *Looker's cookieless embedding guide*.

Troubleshooting single-sign on embeds

Looker provides the URL validator to assist developers with troubleshooting, which is available through the admin panel under **Platform** | **Embed**. Developers simply need to insert their generated URL into the text box, and Looker will validate it. Here are common errors that developers may face when validating, they are as follows:

- **Signature param failed to authenticate**: This error can be caused by a variety of things, but it generally means that the signature is invalid. There are a couple of things that can go wrong with the signature:

  o The signature was created off of an old URL. Any changes to the URL (host, embed URL, parameters, etc.) require the signature to be regenerated.

  o The signature was created using an invalid URL, double-check that every required parameter is included and the URL is properly structured.

  o The URL was manually changed after the signature had been created and/ or the URL had already been encoded.

  o The embed secret key used is no longer valid.

- **Nonce param already used this hour**: This error occurs when developers try to validate a URL that has already been used in an iframe. URLs are only valid for one use and afterwards, attempting to reload the same URL will result in this error. Developers will need to regenerate another URL.

- **Time param is not within 5 minutes of the server's system time**: This error is caused when developers try to validate an old URL. If the URL has been generated but not used within an iframe, it will automatically become invalid after 5 minutes.

Once the validator returns that the **Embed URI is valid**, then the developer's URL generation process is successful and is ready to be inserted into an iframe.

Practical applications

Using the Looker API or SDK and embedding unlocks a whole new world of development for users. Repetitive actions can be scripted to improve performance and security. In this section, we will provide some ideas of ways the API or SDK and embed can be utilized and the endpoints required for implementation.

Let us take a look at some ways the Looker API/SDK can be utilized to reduce repetitive work:

- **User creation and permission assignment**: Creating users and assigning groups, roles, and user attributes on a per-user basis can be tedious work. Developers can utilize the API to reduce a significant amount of manual work and reduce the chances of incorrect assignment.

  Developers can use the following endpoints to accomplish this:

  o **Create user (POST /users)**: Developers can use this endpoint to spin up a user with all of the desired group and user assignments. This is for creation only and not for update.

Note: **For best security practices, we recommend setting up a Security Assertion Markup Language (SAML) or SSO login integration to create users (see more information about this in *Chapter 7, Looker Security*). Create User will create a basic email and password user, which does not allow 2 factor authorization.**

o **Update user (PATCH /users/{user_id}):** The developers can programmatically assign groups and user attributes using this endpoint, reducing the amount of manual assignment being done. Although the endpoint only updates one user at a time, developers can use a for loop to feed in multiple user IDs to apply groups and user attributes en masse.

- **Sync user-defined dashboard with LookML dashboards**: In this scenario, where a user makes an edit to a **User-Defined Dashboard** (UDD) but wants to re-sync back to the LookML dashboard version of it, they can use this endpoint. Since UDDs do not maintain a version history of itself, its corresponding LookML dashboard is the next best thing. If a user saves changes to a dashboard, but wants to revert, developers can run this endpoint to resync the two dashboards:

Note: **This will only revert to the most recent version of the LookML dashboard, if a UDD has one.**

o **Sync LookML dashboard (PATCH /dashboards/{lookml_dashboard_id}/ sync):** Developers just need to pass in the `lookml_dashboard_id`, and any UDD that is linked to it will be automatically updated.

o **Update dashboard (PATCH /dashboards/{dashboard_id}):** Developers can use this endpoint to link a UDD and a LookML dashboard by updating the UDD's parameter `lookml_link_id` to the LookML's ID.

- **Automatically organize dashboards into folders**: Developers can use the API to organize dashboards into the correct folders. This is especially helpful in the case where there are many LookML dashboards being generated on the instance, as LookML dashboards always land in the LookML dashboards folder and need to be manually sorted into the correct place. endpoint(s) required.

The following URLs can be used to perform the organization:

o **Get all dashboards (GET /dashboards):** Developers can get a list of all dashboards in order to grab a specific grouping of dashboards they want to move, e.g., they can parse the returned response to get a list of all the dashboard IDs that belong to a specific model. This is useful for the next endpoint.

o **Move dashboard (PATCH /dashboards/{dashboard_id}/move):** Developers can implement a simple for loop that moves all dashboards in a list into a specific folder. The exact mapping of what dashboards belong into which folders will have to be managed by the developer, but we recommend this over manually managing dashboard location since the mapping can be easily viewed, updated, and reapplied (versus no mapping, where admins need to check every folder that it has the correct contents, and manually move every dashboard).

- **Dynamic SSO embed URL creation**: The API or SDK can also be used to generate the SSO embed URL easily. The following endpoint(s) is required:

    o **Create signed embed URL (POST /embed/sso_url)**: This generates the SSO embed URL. Developers only need to worry about passing in the content's relative URL and parameters. The endpoint will handle the signature and the encoding. The endpoint will return the SSO embed URL.

- **Downloadable custom SQL reports**: Developers can create, on the fly, custom SQL queries, that they can have Looker send to the database. Developers can then determine how they want the data returned back: JSON, CSV, HTML, md, txt, XLSX, and SQL are a couple of result format options. The following are the endpoint(s) required:

    o **Create SQL runner query (POST /sql_queries)**: Creates a query with the connection or model of the developer's choice. It also returns information about the query that the developers will need the slug (identifier of the SQL query) from the response.

    o **Run SQL runner query (POST /sql_queries/{slug}/run/{result_format})**: Executes the query (identified by its slug). Developers can determine how they want the data returned back to them here as well.

Best practices

In this section, we will go over our recommended practices to enhance the security pertaining to API, SDK, and embeds.

API/SDK

The following are the best practices API/SDK:

- Developers should handle API keys with care, as API keys allow anyone to perform the actions of the user they are derived from. Never hard code API credentials in your scripts, use a secret manager.

- Create a service account for Looker with custom permissions to generate the API keys.

- We recommend not creating API keys from an admin account, if possible. Practice providing the least amount of required permissions for scripts, so that in case the API key gets leaked, it does not have a full range of functionality.

Embed

Similar to API keys, embed secrets can be used by malicious parties to access data they otherwise would not have access to. Embed secrets require great care, as an instance only ever has one embed secret active at a time, and enable anyone with the secret to access any data available on the Looker instance.

- Never hard code the embed secret in your embed generation code, use a secret manager.

- Public and private embedded URLs never expire, so make sure to properly vet if the data being exposed is not a data risk. Users can forcibly expire the URL by making a copy and deleting the original visualization.

- Use groups to assign permissions and user attributes to embed users.

- If using SSO embeds to expose Looker content to external users, we highly recommend enabling a closed system.

- Enable secure authentication (SAML, 2FA, SSO) for your internal users if your instance is embedding content outside of Looker. Since embedded contents reveal the hostname of your Looker instance, we recommend making sure authentication into the instance has improved security beyond Looker's standard email and password login.

Conclusion

Throughout the chapter, we explored the different ways Looker content can be interacted with outside the Looker instance itself. Developers learned how Looker can be used to automate function with the Looker API/SDK.

Additionally, the chapter covered how external sharing can be accomplished with the embedded URLs. With this knowledge, we hope that Looker's use can be expanded far past manual and internal use to become a platform that developers can use both as a tool for internal users and a product for external users.

CHAPTER 10

Looker Project Walkthrough

Introduction

In the preceding chapters, we have explored the intricate components, features, and functionalities that comprise Looker, gaining a comprehensive understanding of its capabilities. Now, armed with the knowledge of Looker's potential, it is time to move forward on a practical journey that translates theory into action. In this chapter, we will traverse the field of complete project creation within Looker, guiding you through each step with a hands-on example scenario.

We will begin by immersing ourselves in a sample scenario, where we will gather requirements and outline objectives. With a clear understanding of what needs to be achieved, we will navigate through the process of creating a tangible solution using Looker's robust toolkit. Throughout this chapter, we will uphold the principles of best practices, ensuring that our code is not only functional but also maintainable, scalable, and efficient.

The example scenario we will explore serves as a practical foundation for applying Looker's capabilities in real-world scenarios. From data visualization to analytics and beyond, how Looker can be leveraged to unlock insights, drive decision-making, and empower users with actionable intelligence will also be covered.

Structure

In this chapter, we will go through the following topics:

- Looker requirement gathering
- Create the placeholders
- Creating LookML
- Creating a dashboard
- Setup security

Objectives

As we continue with this journey, our goal is not just to showcase technical proficiency, but also to instill a mindset of innovation and problem-solving. We will encourage experimentation, iteration, and creative thinking, fostering an environment where the boundaries of what is possible with Looker are continually pushed.

Throughout the chapters, you will find a blend of theoretical discussions, practical examples, and hands-on exercises designed to reinforce your understanding and proficiency in using Looker for project creation. Whether you are a seasoned data analyst looking to enhance your skills or a newcomer eager to explore the possibilities, this chapter offers valuable insights and guidance to help you navigate the exciting world of Looker development.

Looker requirement gathering

The first step of any project is to gather the requirements. Here is the scenario: an e-commerce company has been selling merchandise (clothing and accessories) and has been storing the data in a database for a few years. Now, they want to create a dashboard that shows the overview of sales. This will be a dashboard for executives and analysts to see the overall sales and the data will be in **BigQuery**.

Note: We are using a public dataset: `thelook_ecommerce` for this exercise. The organization chose to use GitHub as the version control tool.

The business users and analysts provided some requirements for the dashboard. It should have the following measures or KPIs:

- Sales overview
- Total sales:
    - Total # of items sold
    - Total gross margin

     o   Total # of returns

     o   Total # of users (/ Customers)

- Total Sales and Total Returns by Category
- Returns by brand with Order and Return details and percentage
- Top ten high gross margin products
- YoY sales
- Monthly orders % by traffic source
- Users by state

The additional requirements include:

- Users should be able to slice and dice the data using the filters: date, country, state, and traffic source.
- The currency should be in USD, and all dates should be in the Pacific Time Zone.
- The users are internal. Two groups of users use the dashboards:

     o   Executives need read-only access.

     o   Analysts need to edit the dashboard and should be able to create additional visualizations and dashboards.

Create the placeholders

The steps to create a new LookML project are as follows:

1. Login to Looker and turn on the developer mode.
2. Select **Project** under the develop menu. The Project window will open.
3. Select **Create New Project**. This can be seen in *Figure 10.1:*

ở Looker

LookML Projects   Configure New Model   New LookML Project

Figure 10.1: *Create a New LookML Project*

4. Create a new project by entering the details like name. In this case, the name is **ecommerce_sample**. Select a blank project option and click on **Create Project**. The option is demonstrated in the following figure:

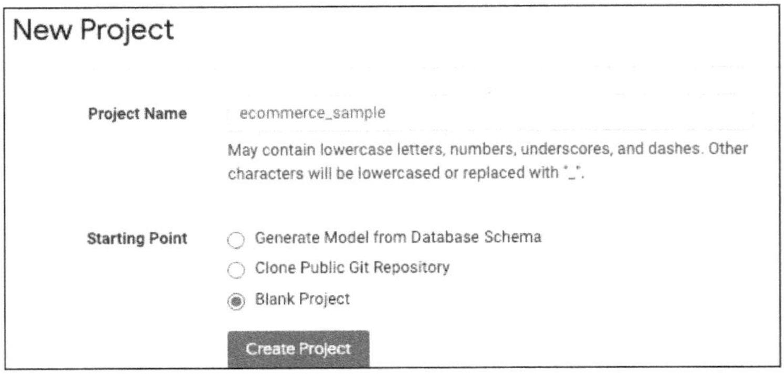

Figure 10.2: Creating a Project

5. A new blank project will be created, taking you to the project folder in LookML interface.

6. On the top right side, you will see a blue button showing **Configure Git**. Click on the **Configure** button.

7. We are using GitHub as the Git provider for this project. Create a repository in GitHub and get its URL.

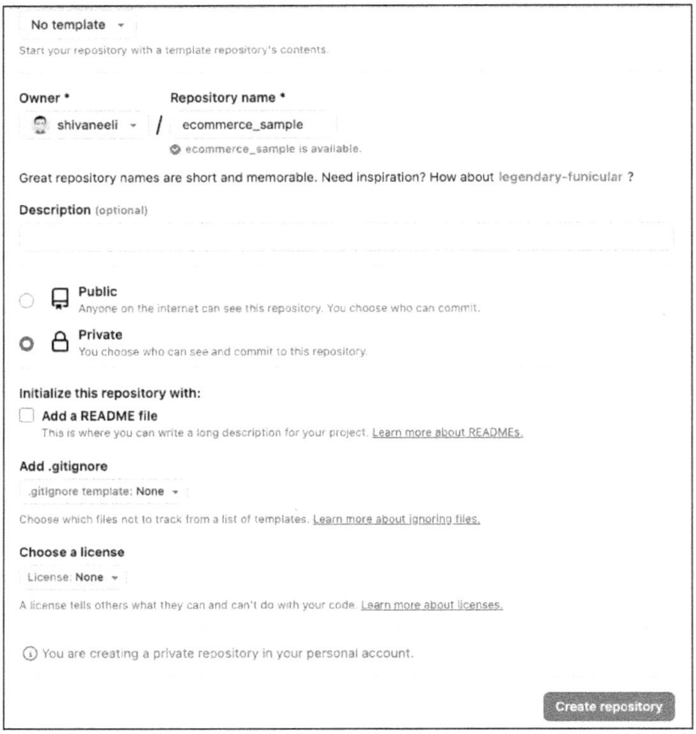

Figure 10.3: GitHub Repo creation

8. Paste the GitH ub SSH URL (for example: **git@github.com:shivaneeli/ecommerce_ sample.git** or **https://github.com/shivaneeli/ecommerce_sample.git**) in **Configure Git** window and click **Continue**, as demonstrated in the following figure:

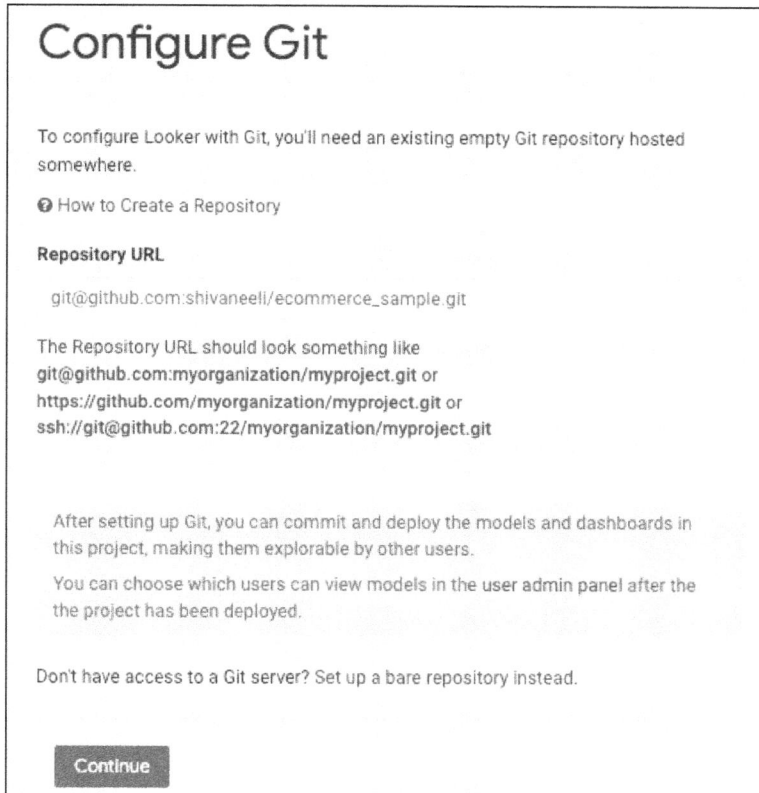

Configure Git

To configure Looker with Git, you'll need an existing empty Git repository hosted somewhere.

❷ How to Create a Repository

Repository URL

git@github.com:shivaneeli/ecommerce_sample.git

The Repository URL should look something like
git@github.com:myorganization/myproject.git or
https://github.com/myorganization/myproject.git or
ssh://git@github.com:22/myorganization/myproject.git

After setting up Git, you can commit and deploy the models and dashboards in this project, making them explorable by other users.

You can choose which users can view models in the user admin panel after the the project has been deployed.

Don't have access to a Git server? Set up a bare repository instead.

Continue

Figure 10.4: GitHub Configuration for a Project

9. A new page opens up with a GitHub Deploy Key. Copy the key:

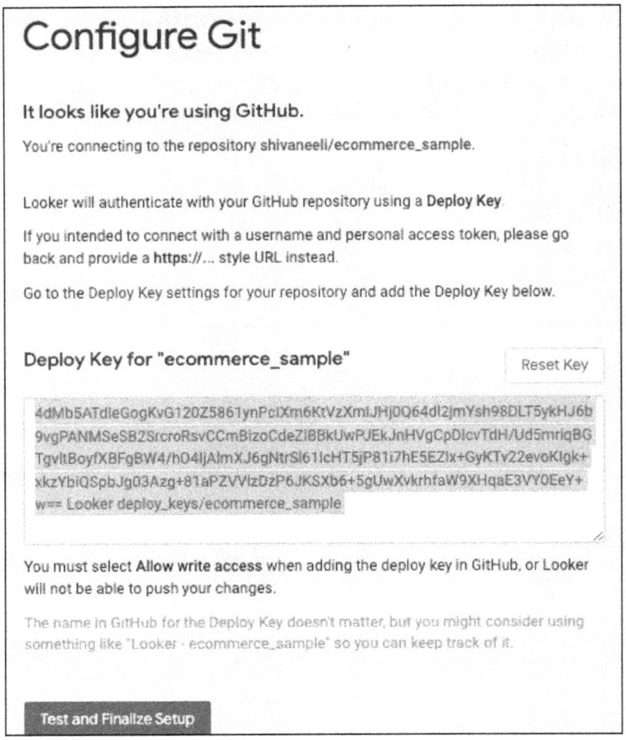

Configure Git

It looks like you're using GitHub.

You're connecting to the repository shivaneeli/ecommerce_sample.

Looker will authenticate with your GitHub repository using a **Deploy Key**.

If you intended to connect with a username and personal access token, please go back and provide a **https://**... style URL instead.

Go to the Deploy Key settings for your repository and add the Deploy Key below.

Deploy Key for "ecommerce_sample"   Reset Key

4dMb5ATdIeGogKvG120Z5861ynPcIXm6KtVzXmIJHj0Q64dl2jmYsh98DLT5ykHJ6b
9vgPANMSeSB2SrcroRsvCCmBizoCdeZlBBkUwPJEkJnHVgCpDIcvTdH/Ud5mriqBG
TgvItBoyfXBFgBW4/hO4IjAlmXJ6gNtrSI61IcHT5jP81i7hE5EZIx+GyKTv22evoKIgk+
xkzYbiQSpbJg03Azg+81aPZVVIzDzP6JKSXb6+5gUwXvkrhfaW9XHqaE3VY0EeY+
w== Looker deploy_keys/ecommerce_sample

You must select **Allow write access** when adding the deploy key in GitHub, or Looker will not be able to push your changes.

The name in GitHub for the Deploy Key doesn't matter, but you might consider using something like "Looker · ecommerce_sample" so you can keep track of it.

Test and Finalize Setup

Figure 10.5: Deploy Key for GitHub Repo

10. Go to the GitHub repo created in *Step 7*. Under **Settings**, select the deploy key option, add a deploy key, give it a name, and paste the key we copied from *Step 9*. Make sure the **Allow write access** is selected, then click on **Add Key**, as shown in the following figure:

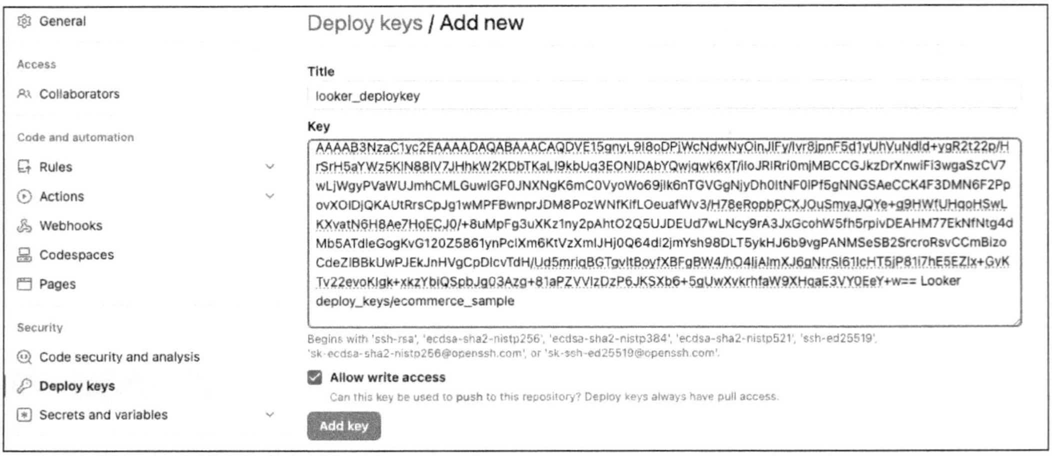

{% raw %}
General

Access
Collaborators

Code and automation
Rules
Actions
Webhooks
Codespaces
Pages

Security
Code security and analysis
Deploy keys
Secrets and variables
{% endraw %}

Deploy keys / **Add new**

Title

looker_deploykey

Key

AAAAB3NzaC1yc2EAAAADAQABAAACAQDVE15gnyL9I8oDPjWcNdwNyOinJIFy/Ivr8jpnF5d1yUhVuNdld+ygR2t22p/H
rSrH5aYWz5KlN88IV7JHhkW2KDbTKaLl9kbUq3EONIDAbYQwjqwk6xT/iloJRIRri0mjMBCCGJkzDrXnwiFi3wgaSzCV7
wLjWgyPVaWUJmhCMLGuwIGF0JNXNgK6mC0VyoWo69jIk6nTGVGgNjyDh0ltNF0lPf5gNNGSAeCCK4F3DMN6F2Pp
ovXOIDjQKAUtRrsCpJg1wMPFBwnprJDM8PozWNfKIfLOeuafWv3/H78eRopbPCXJQuSmyaJQYe+g9HWfUHqoHSwL
KXvatN6HBAe7HoECJ0/+8uMpFg3uXKz1ny2pAhtO2Q5UJDEUd7wLNcy9rA3JxGcohW5fh5rpivDEAHM77EkNfNtg4d
Mb5ATdIeGogKvG120Z5861ynPcIXm6KtVzXmIJHj0Q64dl2jmYsh98DLT5ykHJ6b9vgPANMSeSB2SrcroRsvCCmBizo
CdeZlBBkUwPJEkJnHVgCpDIcvTdH/Ud5mriqBGTgvItBoyfXBFgBW4/hO4IjAlmXJ6gNtrSI61IcHT5jP81i7hE5EZIx+GyK
Tv22evoKIgk+xkzYbiQSpbJg03Azg+81aPZVVIzDzP6JKSXb6+5gUwXvkrhfaW9XHqaE3VY0EeY+w== Looker
deploy_keys/ecommerce_sample

Begins with 'ssh-rsa', 'ecdsa-sha2-nistp256', 'ecdsa-sha2-nistp384', 'ecdsa-sha2-nistp521', 'ssh-ed25519',
'sk-ecdsa-sha2-nistp256@openssh.com', or 'sk-ssh-ed25519@openssh.com'.

☑ **Allow write access**
Can this key be used to push to this repository? Deploy keys always have pull access.

Add key

Figure 10.6: Add Deploy Key in GitHub

11. Once the deploy key is added, you can click on the **Test and Finalize** button in *Step 9*. If the connection is successful, you can see the configuration under **Project Configuration**: **Git Summary**:

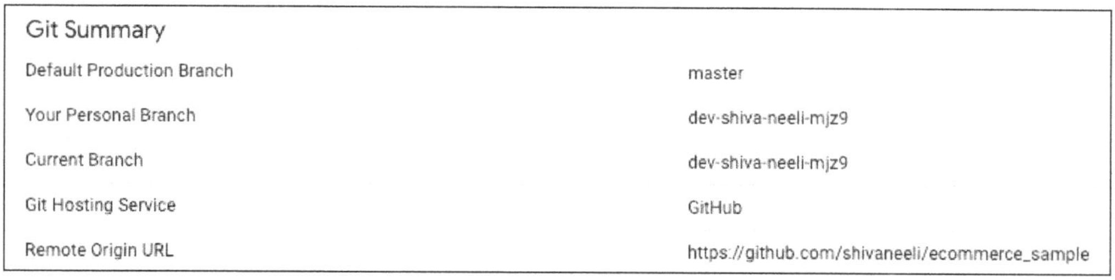

Git Summary	
Default Production Branch	master
Your Personal Branch	dev-shiva-neeli-mjz9
Current Branch	dev-shiva-neeli-mjz9
Git Hosting Service	GitHub
Remote Origin URL	https://github.com/shivaneeli/ecommerce_sample

Figure 10.7: Git Summary

12. Once done, push the branch to remote and deploy the project to Production.

In order to create a database connection, refer to the following the steps:

1. Under **Admin** | **Database** | **Connection**, create a connection to the database that hosts the data. We are using a public dataset in BigQuery.

2. Create a connection to the **thelook_ecommerce** dataset.

Edit your database connection

Fill out the connection details. The majority of these settings are common to most database dialects. Learn more

Name *
thelook_ecommerce_sample

Connection Scope *

All Projects   Selected Project

Dialect *
Google BigQuery Standard SQL

Billing Project ID *
bi-eng-internal

Dataset *
ecommerce_sample

Authentication *

Service Account   OAuth

Upload new Service Account file

Figure 10.8: Create a Connection

In order to configure the project to use the connection, refer to the following steps:

1. Go to **Manage Projects** and select the **Configure** button next to the newly created project to configure the model:

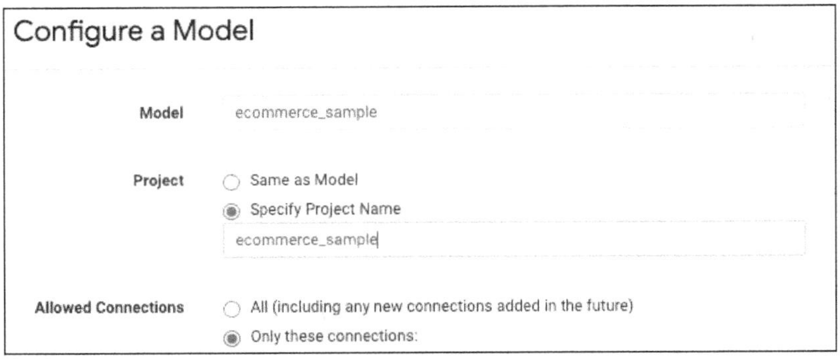

Figure 10.9: Configure a Model

2. Save the configuration, as shown in the following figure. This will allow the model to use the connection:

Figure 10.10: Connection selection under configure model

Creating LookML

Let us look at the steps for creating LookML:

1. Create folders for different types of files: views, models, and dashboards.

2. Import the tables by clicking the three dots menu on the views, then select the **Create View from Table** option:

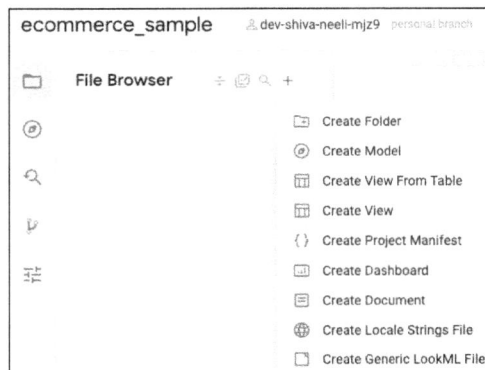

Figure 10.11: Create view from Table option

3. Select the tables from the database that need to be used, as shown in the following figure:

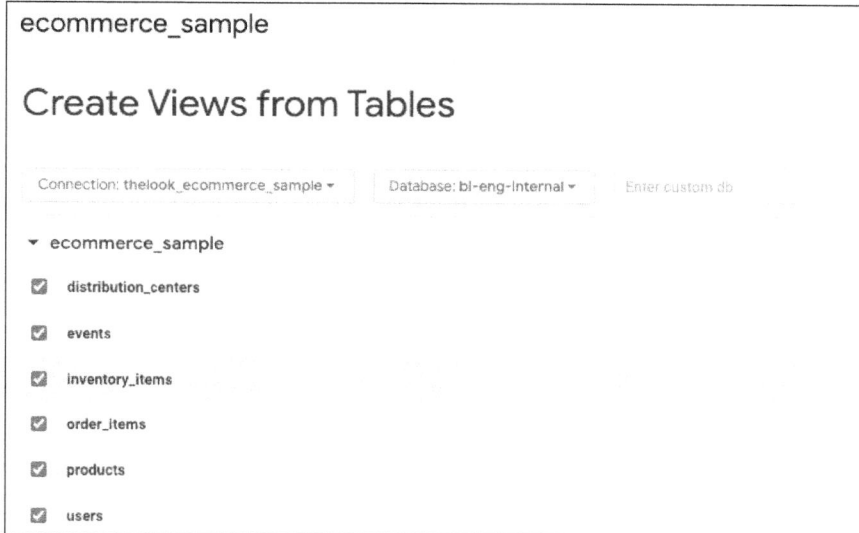

Figure 10.12: Creating Views from Table selection

4. Once the views are created from the table, LookML project will have the view files (one view per table):

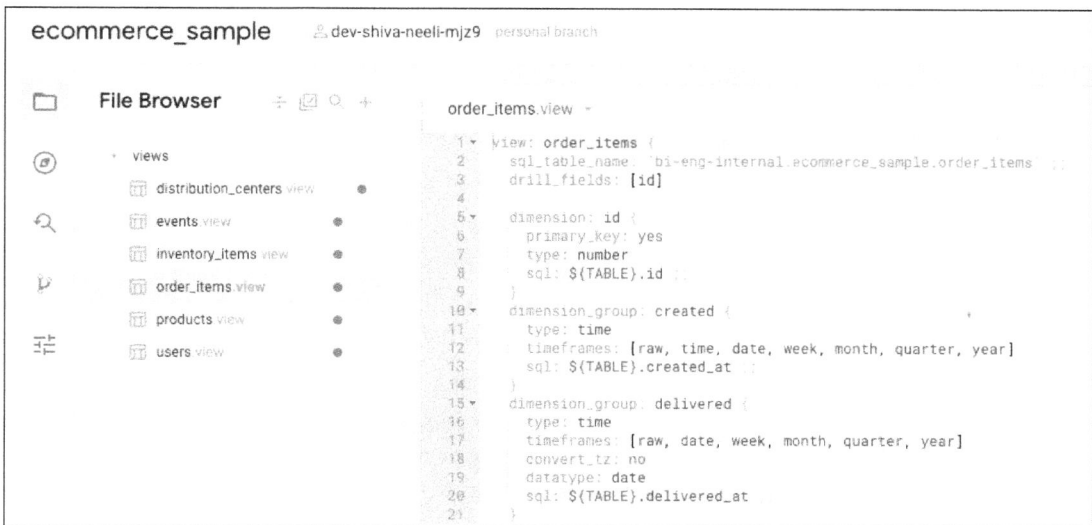

Figure 10.13: Imported Tables

5. In order to **Create a model file**, right-click on the three dots menu of the model and select **Create a model file**:

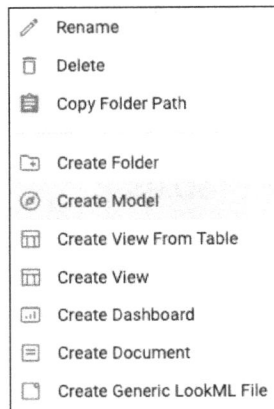

Figure 10.14: Create Model option in Menu

6. Give a name to the model:

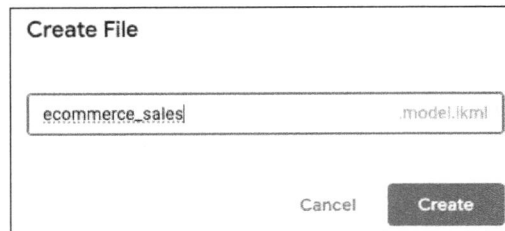

Figure 10.15: Create a Model

7. A file will be created with a connection name and also include a statement that includes all the views in the views folder.

```
connection: "the look_ecommerce_sample"
include: "/views/*.view.lkml"          # include all views in
the views/ folder in this project
```

When there are few files and all are in use, it is acceptable to include them all. However, as the number of files increases, ensure that only the necessary files for the model are included.

8. In order to create an explore, we need to identify the relationship between the tables. The relationships can be found from the data model (if it exists and is provided by the ETL/EDQ team) or by examining the tables and fields.

As we learned before, explore includes the relationships between the tables.

The code for explore is as follows:

```
explore: order_items {
  label: "Orders, Items and Users"
```

```
view_name: order_items
description: "This explore includes Orders, Items and Users"

join: inventory_items {
  view_label: "Inventory Items"
  type: full_outer
  relationship: one_to_one
  sql_on: ${inventory_items.id} = ${order_items.inventory_item_id}
;;
}
join: users {
  view_label: "Users"
  type: left_outer
  relationship: many_to_one
  sql_on: ${order_items.user_id} = ${users.id} ;;
}

join: products {
  view_label: "Products"
  type: left_outer
  relationship: many_to_one
  sql_on: ${products.id} = ${inventory_items.product_id} ;;
}

join: distribution_centers {
  view_label: "Distribution Center"
  type: left_outer
  sql_on: ${distribution_centers.id} = ${inventory_items.product_
distribution_center_id} ;;
  relationship: many_to_one
}
```

9. Now for the KPIs that we need to create, identify the fields needed and the formulas for calculations.

In the following LookML code snippet, we will be creating dimensions and measures based on these requirements:

KPI	Fields used	Tables/view	Formula
Total Sales Price	sale_price	order_items	sum(sales_price)
Gross Margin	sale_price , inventory_items_cost	order_items	sale_price - inventory_items_cost
Total Gross Margin		order_items	sum(gross_margin)
ruturned_count	is_returned, id	order_items	count_distinct(id) where is_returned = 'true'
total_customer_count	user_id	users	count (distinct user_id)
Order Items Count	id	order_items	count(id)

Table 10.1: Identify the fields needed and the formulas for calculations

The LookML code that can be added to the **order_items** table is as follows:

```
dimension: gross_margin {
  label: "Gross Margin"
  type: number
  value_format_name: usd
  sql: ${sale_price} - ${inventory_items.cost};;
}
measure: total_sale_price {
  label: "Total Sale Price"
  type: sum
  value_format_name: usd
  sql: ${sale_price} ;;
  html:@{short_currency_value_format} ;;
}
measure: total_gross_margin {
  label: "Total Gross Margin"
  type: sum
  value_format_name: usd
  sql: ${gross_margin} ;;
  drill_fields: [user_id,  total_gross_margin]
  html:@{short_currency_value_format} ;;
}
dimension: is_returned {
  label: "Is Returned"
  type: yesno
  sql: ${returned_raw} IS NOT NULL ;;
}
```

```
    measure: returned_count {
      label: "Returned Count"
      type: count_distinct
      sql: ${id} ;;
      filters: {
        field: is_returned
        value: "yes"
      }
      drill_fields: [detail*]
  #   html:@{short_number_value_format} ;;
    }
    measure: returned_total_sale_price {
      label: "Returned Total Sale Price"
      type: sum
      value_format_name: usd
      sql: ${sale_price} ;;
      filters: {
        field: is_returned
        value: "yes"
      }
      html: @{short_currency_value_format} ;;
    }
    measure: total_customer_count {
      label: "Customer Count"
      type: count_distinct
      sql: ${user_id} ;;
      drill_fields: [detail*]
  #   html:@{short_number_value_format} ;;
    }
    measure: count {
      label: "Order Items Count"
      type: count
      drill_fields: [detail*]
    }
```

10. Additionally, we need to make a few changes to the existing dimensions:

    a. Add the month name to the list of timeframes for the created dimension group:

    ```
    dimension_group: created {
        type: time
    ```

```
        timeframes: [raw, time, date, week, month, month_name,
    month_num, quarter, year]
        sql: ${TABLE}.created_at ;;
    }
```

    b. Add the map layer name to the state dimension. This will allow us to create a geographical heat map later on:

```
dimension: state {
    map_layer_name: us_states
    sql: ${TABLE}.state ;;
}
```

11. KPIs in other views are automatically added when we import the table.

12. Validate the code and make sure there are no errors.

13. The formatting option is added here using the **manifest.lkml** file. The code for formatting the values/KPIs is mentioned as follows:

```
project_name: "ecommerce_sample"

constant: num_format{
  value:"
  {% if value >= 1000000000 %}
  {{ prefix }}{{ value | times: 1.0 | divided_by: 1000000000 | round:
1 }}B{{ suffix }}
  {% elsif value >= 1000000 %}
  {{ prefix }}{{ value | times: 1.0 | divided_by: 1000000 | round: 1
}}M{{ suffix }}
  {% elsif value >= 1000 %}
  {{ prefix }}{{ value | times: 1.0 | divided_by: 1000 | round: 1 }}
K{{ suffix }}
  {% else %}
  {{ prefix }}{{ value | round: 1 }}{{ suffix }}
  {% endif %}
  "
}
constant: short_number_value_format {
  value: "
  {% assign prefix = '' %}
  {% assign suffix = '' %}
  {% if value < 0 %}
  {% assign value = value | times: -1 %}
  {% assign prefix = '(' %}
```

```
      {% assign suffix = ')' %}
      {% endif %}@{num_format}
      "
  }
  constant: short_percent_value_format {
    value: "
    {% assign prefix = '' %}
    {% assign suffix = '%' %}
    {% if value < 0 %}
    {% assign value = value | times: -1 %}
    {% assign prefix = '(' %}
    {% assign suffix = ')%' %}
    {% endif %}@{num_format}
    "
  }
  constant: short_currency_value_format {
    value: "
    {% assign prefix = '$' %}
    {% assign suffix = '' %}
    {% if value < 0 %}
    {% assign value = value | times: -1 %}
    {% assign prefix = '$(' %}
    {% assign suffix = ')' %}
    {% endif %}@{num_format}
    "
  }
```

This has been used with html parameters in the KPIs in the preceding code.

Creating a dashboard

In order to create a dashboard, refer to the following steps:

1. Under **Shared folders**, create a new folder for the dashboard. Enter the Folder Name: **eCommerce Sales**:

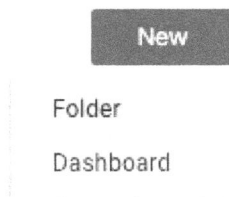

Figure 10.16: Create new folder option

Selecting *Folder* will lead to the following pop-up, where users can name the folder. Folders can be renamed after creation:

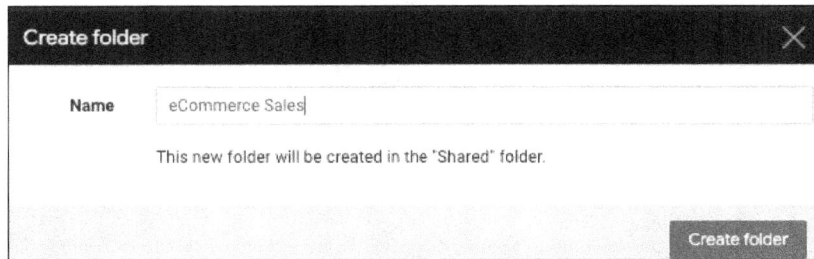

Create folder   ✕

Name   eCommerce Sales

This new folder will be created in the "Shared" folder.

                                                          Create folder

Figure 10.17: Creating a new folder

By clicking on **New** and selecting **Dashboard**, a window will open up:

New

Folder

Dashboard

Figure 10.18: Create new dashboard option

Enter a name for the dashboard: **eCommerce Sales Overview**, as shown in the following figure:

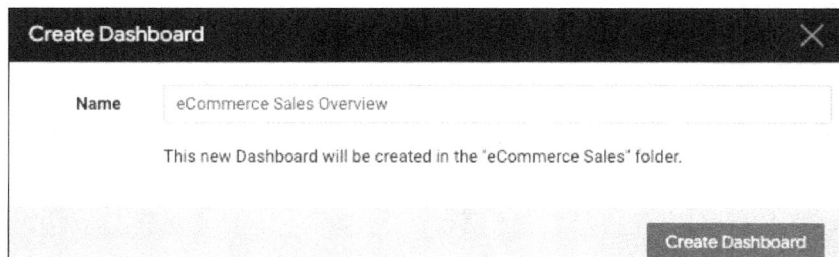

Create Dashboard   ✕

Name   eCommerce Sales Overview

This new Dashboard will be created in the "eCommerce Sales" folder.

                                                        Create Dashboard

Figure 10.19: Create new dashboard

2. Click on the new dashboard that was created in the previous step. The empty dashboard will open. Click on the **Edit Dashboard** button.

3. Click on the **Add** button and select **Visualization**.

4. In the explores, select the **order**, **items**, and **users** from the eCommerce Sales model we created.

5. Explore window opens with the views and fields on the left and filters, visualization, and data on the right.

6. For the first visualization, we will create high level KPIs. In this visualization, we will show the total sales price, order item count, total gross margin, return count, and user count for the current year:

   a. Select the fields Total Sales Price, Order Items Count, Total Gross Margin, Returned Count, and User Count from users explore.

   b. Under Filters, add Created Date and select *is this Year*.

   c. Under Visualizations, select Multiple Value.

   > Note: **Multiple Value Visualization is available in the Marketplace. If not installed already, go to the marketplace and add this visualization to your instance.**

   d. Click on the **Run** button and the visualization shows up.

   e. Name the visualization as Sales Overview—Top Level KPIS and click on the **Save** button on the right.

7. In order to Create the Sales and Returns by Month Trend, click on **Add Visualization** and select the same explore as previously. From the explore, perform the following on the dashboard:

   a. Select the fields Created Month, Order Items Count, and Returned Count.

   b. Under Filters, add Created Date and select *is this Year*.

   c. Under Visualizations, select **Column** and **Edit** the options.

   d. Under Series, do the following:

      i. Keep Order Items Count as Type Column.

      ii. Select Line type for Returned Count:

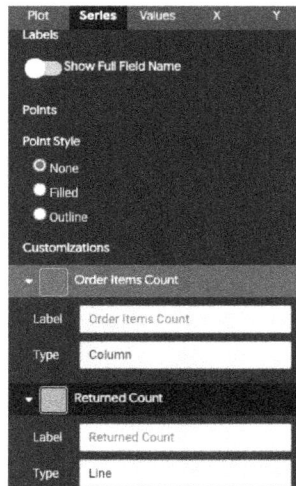

Figure 10.20: Line and Bar Chart Combo

e. Under Y:

i. Keep Order Items Count under Left 1.

ii. Move the Returned Count under Right 1.

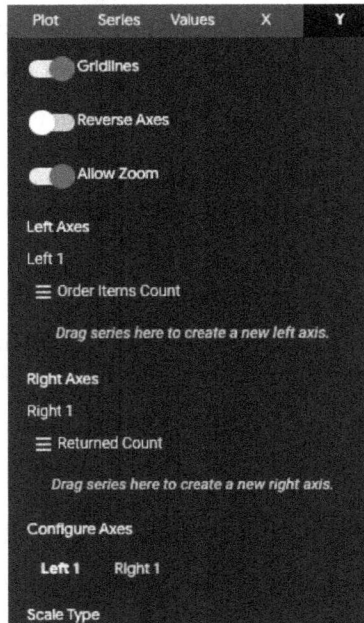

Figure 10.21: 2 axes on 2 sides

a. Click on **Run** and **Save** with a name—Sales and Returns by Month Trend.

b. The visualization shows up, as depicted in the following figure:

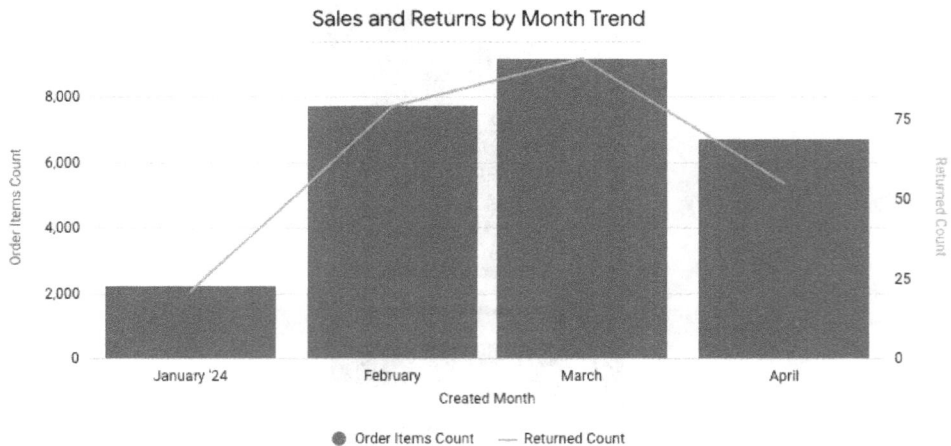

Figure 10.22: Sales and Returns by Month trend

8. In order to create the Sales by Category for Top 10 Categories, click on **Add Visualization on the dashboard** and select the same explore and do the following:

    a. Select the fields-Category and Total Sale Price.

    b. Under Filters, add Created Date and select *Is this Year*.

    c. Sort the Total Sale Price in descending order and Enter 10 under Row Limit.

    d. Under Visualizations, select the Pie Chart option.

    e. Edit the visualization and enter 60 for the inner radius.

    f. Click on **Run** and **Save** with the name Sales by Category.

    g. The output will be the same as shown in the following figure:

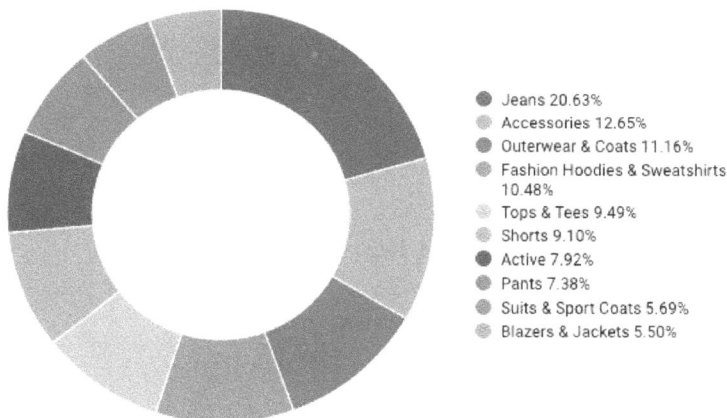

Figure 10.23: Sales by Category

9. In order to create the returns by brand, click on the **Add Visualization** and select the same explore and do the following:

    a. Select the fields-Brand, Order Items Count, Returned Count, Total Sale Price, and Returned Total Sale price.

    b. Under Filters, add Created Date and select *is this Year*.

    c. Add a new Table Calculation and enter the formula for Returns %:

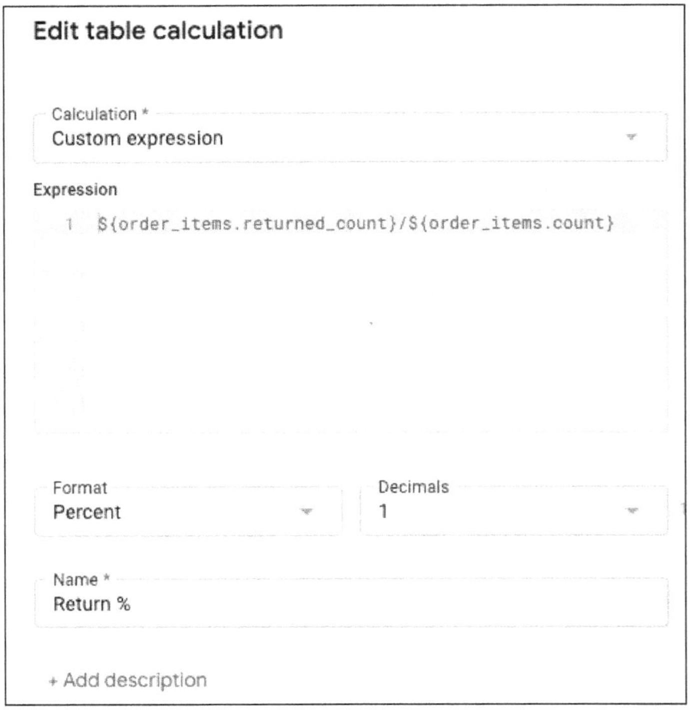

Edit table calculation

Calculation *
Custom expression

Expression

1    ${order_items.returned_count}/${order_items.count}

Format
Percent

Decimals
1

Name *
Return %

+ Add description

Figure 10.24: Returns % Calculation

d. Sort the Returns % in descending order.

e. Under Visualizations, select the Table option.

f. Edit the visualization and under the series tab, remove cell visualization for all columns and add/keep it for Returns % column.

g. Click on **Run** and **Save** with the name-**Returns by Brand**.

h. The output will be as follows:

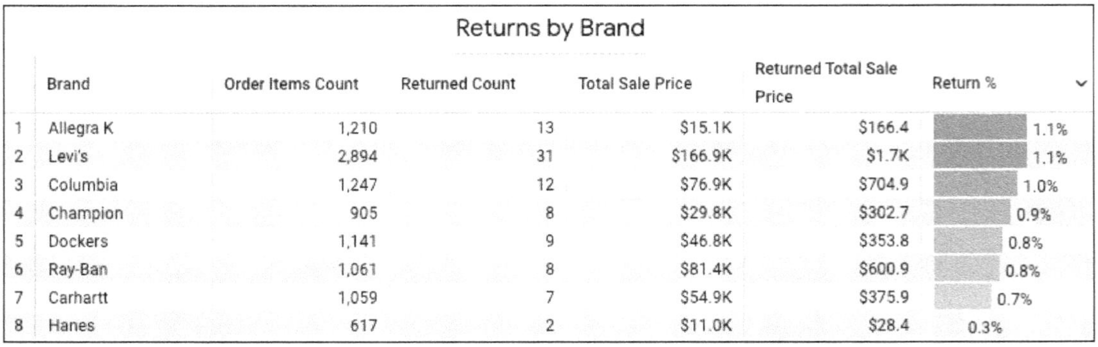

	Brand	Order Items Count	Returned Count	Total Sale Price	Returned Total Sale Price	Return %
1	Allegra K	1,210	13	$15.1K	$166.4	1.1%
2	Levi's	2,894	31	$166.9K	$1.7K	1.1%
3	Columbia	1,247	12	$76.9K	$704.9	1.0%
4	Champion	905	8	$29.8K	$302.7	0.9%
5	Dockers	1,141	9	$46.8K	$353.8	0.8%
6	Ray-Ban	1,061	8	$81.4K	$600.9	0.8%
7	Carhartt	1,059	7	$54.9K	$375.9	0.7%
8	Hanes	617	2	$11.0K	$28.4	0.3%

Figure 10.25: Returns by Brand

10. In order to create the Top 10 High Gross Margin Products, click on **Add Visualization** and select the same explore as preceding and do the following:

   a. Select the fields-Name and Total Gross Margin.

   b. Under Filters, add Created Date and select *Is this Year*.

   c. Sort the Total Gross Margin in descending order and enter the Row Limit as ten.

   d. Under Visualizations, select the Bar option.

   e. Click on **Run** and **Save** with the name, Top 10 High Gross Margin Products.

   h. The output will be as follows:

Figure 10.26: Top 10 High Gross Margin Products

11. In order to create the YoY Sales (for the last three years), click on **Add Visualization** and select the same explore as preceding and perform the following steps:

   a. Select the fields-Created Month Name, Created Year, and Total Sale Price.

   b. Under Filters:

      i. Add Created Date and select-is before (relative) 0 months ago.

      ii. Add Created Year and select-is in the last 4 Years.

   c. Sort the Created Month Name in Ascending Order.

   d. Pivot the column Created Year.

   e. Under Visualizations, select the line option.

   f. Click on **Run** and **Save** with the name-Returns by Brand

g. The output will be as follows:

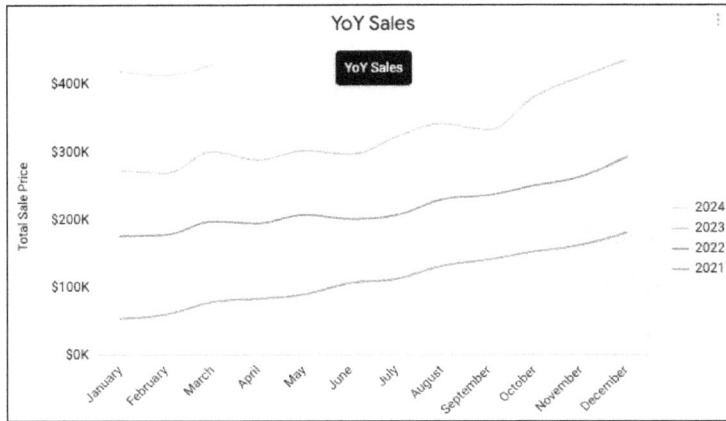

Figure 10.27: *YoY Sales*

12. In order to create the Orders by Traffic Source, click on **Add Visualization** and select the same explore as preceding and do the following:

   a. Select the fields-Created Month Name, Traffic Source, and Total Sale Price.

   b. Under Filters, add Created Date and select *Is this Year*.

   c. Sort the Created Month Name in Ascending Order.

   d. Pivot the column Traffic Source.

   e. Under Visualizations, select the Line option.

   f. Click on **Run** and **Save** with the name-Orders by Traffic Source.

   g. The output will be as follows:

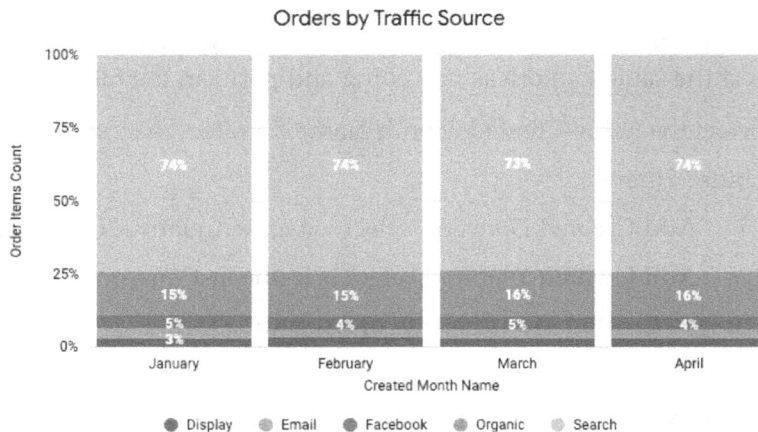

Figure 10.28: *Orders by Traffic Source*

13. In order to Create the Users by State, click on **Add Visualization** and select the same explore as preceding, and do the following:

    a. Select the fields-State and User Count from Users.

    b. Under Filters, add Created Date and select *Is this Year*.

    c. Under Visualizations, select the Google Maps option.

    d. Click on **Run**, and **Save** with the name-Users by State.

    e. The output will be the same as shown in the following figure:

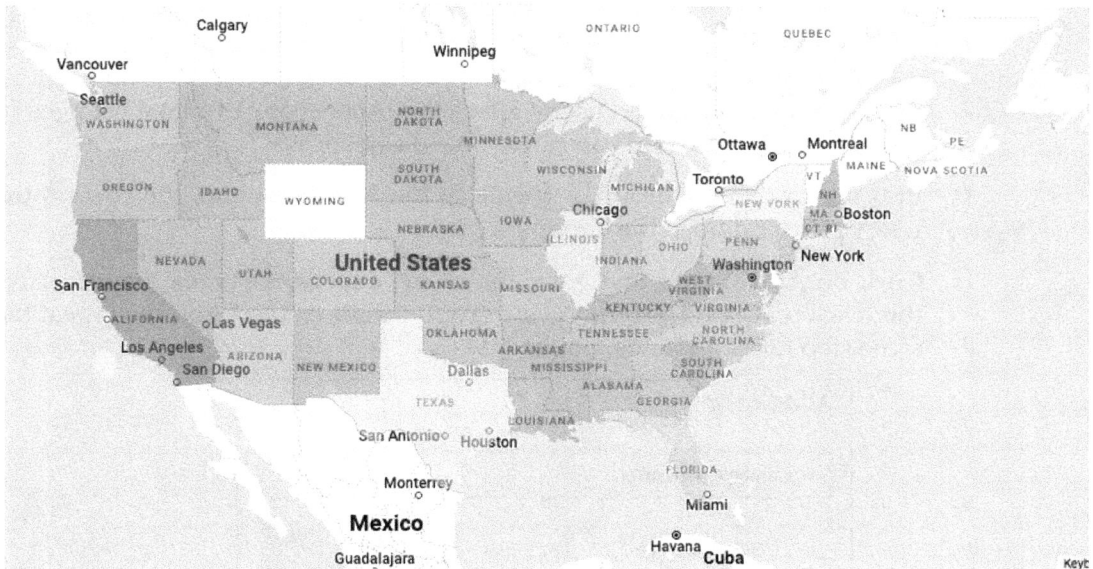

Figure 10.29: Users by State

14. Add the Dashboard filter by editing the dashboard and selecting Add Filter for the following fields:

    a. Under Created Date, select *Year to Date*

    b. Under Country, select US as the default value

    c. For state select tag list form the control section

    d. Traffic Source select tag list form the control section

    e. For the Created Date under the *Tiles to Update* option, choose *Do not Filter* for **Year-over-Year** (**YoY**) Sales. The dashboard filters are shown in *Figure 10.30*:

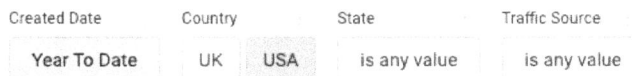

Figure 10.30: Dashboard Filters

Setup security

As per requirements, we have two sets of users, Viewers and Dashboard creators. We have one model, one dashboard, and one folder for which we need to provide proper access to these users. Follow the steps given to set up access for data, features, and content:

1. **Create groups**:

    a. All access to the dashboards and the explore will be controlled using groups. We will create the following two groups:

        i. **ecommerce_view_users**: Here, the users that can only view the content.

        ii. **ecommerce_power_users**: Here, the users that can make changes to the dashboard and can create new dashboards.

    b. In order to create a group, navigate to the Admin section, then access the Users page and open the Groups section.

    c. Click on **Add Group** and enter the name: **ecommerce_view_users**. After this, click on **Create Group**. A new group will be created. You can repeat the same step for **ecommerce_power_users**:

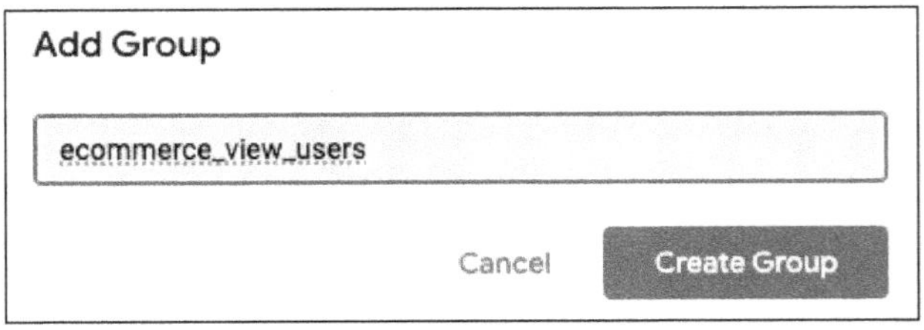

Figure 10.31: *New Group Creation*

2. **Role:**

    a. This is a combination of the permission set (controls the features) and the model set (controls the data).

3. **Model set:**

    a. We have one model called **ecommerce_sample** and we can create one model set. In order to create a model set, go to the **Admin**, users section, and open the Roles Page.

    b. Click on **New Model** set, enter a name, select **ecommerce_sample** model, and click on New Model set. A new model set will be created under the Model Sets section:

ecommerce_sample_only   ecommerce_sample

Figure 10.32: Model Set Creation

4. **Permission set:**

   a. Looker already has some permission sets predefined. We can use those for our usecase.

   b. We will use the Permission Sets Viewer and User as they are sufficient for us.

5. **Create roles:** We will create two roles and assign appropriate models and permission sets to this role:

   a. In order to create a role, click on **New Role** and give the name, `ecommerce_view_users_role`. Then, select the permission set viewer, model set `ecommerce_sample`, and group `ecommerce_view_users`. Select the users that need to be part of this group and click on the new Role.

   b. Create another role and name it: `ecommerce_power_users`. Select the User permission set, Model set `ecommerce_sample`, and group `ecommerce_power` users. Then, select the users who need to be part of this group and click on the New Role button:

| ecommerce_power_user_role | User | ecommerce_sample_only |
| ecommerce_view_only_role | Viewer | ecommerce_sample_only |

Figure 10.33: New Roles creation

6. **Content access**: All content access is controlled by the folder. We can give access to the folder we created for the dashboard:

   a. In order to give access to the content we created, go to the **Admin Users** section and open the **Content Access** page.

   b. Select the folder we created, eCommerce Sales, and click on **Manage Access**.

   c. Select a Custom list of Users and remove all other groups/users except for Admins by clicking on the x.

   d. Select the group `ecommerce_view_users`, then select **View** under **Manage Access, Edit,** and click on **Add**.

   e. Select the group `ecommerce_power_users`, then select **Manage Access** and **Edit** under Manage Access. Edit and click on **Add** and **Save**:

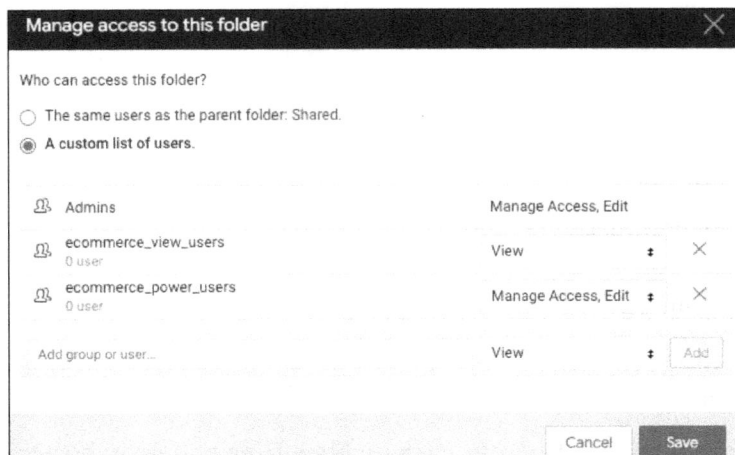

Figure 10.34: Manage Access

Conclusion

Throughout the preceding chapters, we delved into individual concepts of Looker. However, by embarking on the creation of a sample project and dashboard, we explored various facets of Looker in practical detail. This encompassed Project creation, GitHub setup, LookML Creation featuring a model and an explore with multiple views comprising diverse measures and dimensions, Dashboard Creation incorporating various visualization types, and the establishment of security measures. In striving to adhere to best practices, this exercise mirrored a real-world scenario, serving as a comprehensive walk-through of the process.

While your specific use case may entail more intricate calculations and nuances, the fundamental procedures largely remain consistent. We trust that you can adapt and apply a similar methodology to craft Looker models and dashboards tailored to your unique requirements. Our aim is for this experience to ignite your journey with Looker, empowering your organization to glean invaluable insights from data.

Join our book's Discord space

Join the book's Discord Workspace for Latest updates, Offers, Tech happenings around the world, New Release and Sessions with the Authors:

https://discord.bpbonline.com

Index

www.ingramcontent.com/pod-product-compliance
Lightning Source LLC
Chambersburg PA
CBHW061803210326
41599CB00034B/6867